A Wayward Angel

A Wayward Angel

by
George Wethern
and
Vincent Colnett

Richard Marek Publishers, New York

We gratefully acknowledge
permission to quote and
paraphrase articles from
the following:
The SanFrancisco Chronicle:
Copyright Chronicle Publishing
Co.

The Associated Press: Copyright
The Associated Press

Second Impression

Library of Congress Cataloging in Publication Data

Wethern, George.
    A Wayward Angel.

    Includes bibliographical references.
    1. Hell's   Angels.   2. Wethern,   George.   I. Colnett,
Vincent, joint author.   II. Title
HV6489.C2W47   364.1'57'0924   [B]   78-1989
ISBN 0-399-90006-3

Printed in the United States of America

Acknowledgments

The authors wish to extend their sincerest thanks to former U.S. Marshal Arthur Van Court, whose unwavering cooperation and encouragement helped make this book possible, to Deputy U.S. Marshal Warren Bearup, who provided valuable assistance, and to others in the Marshals Service. Our gratitude also goes to California Department of Justice special agent Jack Nehr and former U.S. Attorney James L. Browning, Jr., for their cooperation. And to those numerous sources who cannot be identified, we convey our appreciation.

Note

In violation of the Hell's Angels' incredibly strong code of silence, George and Helen Wethern have taken the risk of writing about their fourteen-year association with the motorcycle club. Besides hoping book proceeds would help their family reestablish itself in a faraway place, they wanted to set the record straight about this most misunderstood and romanticized group. And, perhaps most of all, they desired to deter others from pursuing such a destructive lifestyle. This was best expressed in a jailhouse letter from Wethern to his wife:

"Maybe we can help other people from getting involved in drugs, so they won't have to go through hells too. I know quite a bit about drugs through my own stupidity, but I think I can turn it around to help other people. If some of the damn drugs can be stopped through my efforts, maybe some of the killings will stop. If what I'm going to tell saves one life, it'll be worth it. . . ."

They wanted the book to be an honest and unrestrained portrait of their family and the royalty of outlaw motorcycling. And, thanks to new identities provided by the U.S. Marshals Service, they could use their true names and tell their story relatively free of threats of retribution. They took advantage of their unique situation by relating in intimate detail the secrets, motives and personalities behind the most infamous bunch of bikers in history. They wrote about the good as well as the bad because they knew good times and bad ones, friends as well as enemies. Now what they have written—and what they have told authorities—will keep them many miles from family and friends for the rest of their lives.

VINCENT COLNETT

PREFACE

Road's End

UKIAH, California, October 30, 1972. By 6 A.M., about three dozen law enforcement officers had taken up positions around a single story redwood house nestled at the base of a wooded hillside. Crouched behind cars and flattened against tree trunks, they drew beads with pistols, rifles and shotguns. But there was no movement from the house other than the wisps of smoke curling from the chimney. They waited and listened.

Then, at the sound of scrambling feet inside, one officer raised his bullhorn:

"COME OUT WITH YOUR HANDS HIGH!"

The first response was a paper bag sailing out the door. Then a 280-pound bearded man lumbered onto the porch with his hands up. "Don't shoot," he yelled. "This is my family in there."

George Wethern walked forward with a ponderous sway.

In a moment, his wife, Helen, a tiny woman with an elfin face and close-cropped blond hair, was standing in his shadow along with their chubby nine-year-old son and thirteen-year-old daughter. Raiders from state, federal and local jurisdictions swarmed around them with guns drawn.

They handcuffed the parents, then state narcotics agent Jack Nehr read from a search warrant that referred to narcotics, firearms, explosives and "human skeletal remains."

With his family under guard and a dozen investigators fanning over his 153-acre ranch, Wethern took bomb squad experts and some other officers on a tour of the house and a children's dormitory. A pair of stolen .30-06 rifles and seven legal guns were seized along with the paper bag's contents —an ounce or two of methamphetamines, a pound of marijuana, some Seconal and other pills.

Later, Wethern was driven a few miles to the Mendocino County jail and interrogated by Nehr, Bruce True and other agents. He admitted being a former Hell's Angels motorcycle club member, but he remained faithful to the club code of silence and dodged questions with word games and roundabout answers.

The questions, however, indicated someone in the club had betrayed him, and possibly was trying to set him up. He gaped when Nehr said matter-of-factly, "Ya know, Tiny's dead . . . He took his last boat ride. Was cut to pieces by nine-millimeter slugs. He squealed like a pig."

"Tiny" was Michael Walter, a close friend and the Oakland Angels No. 2 man. He had vanished the previous month, leaving behind his motorcycle and all personal belongings. The agent was stating hearsay as fact, but Wethern didn't know that. He was certain authorities were putting a murder on his doorstep, although his only crime had been providing two empty pits to Angels leader Ralph "Sonny" Barger as a favor. He didn't even know the names of the dead buried on his own ranch.

10

"I don't know anything about it," he said.

When the agent asked him whether there were any well holes on his ranch, it became obvious that authorities had been told about the burials. Wethern's family and his own life were at stake. So he put aside the possible consequences of breaking silence, then let out fragments of information. Finally, he took a long breath and said, "I'll show you the wells."

When they returned to the ranch, backhoes and other machinery were already scooping dirt at the front of the property where an informant had directed them. Wethern pointed out a spot twenty-five feet from that excavation, then, after some hemming and hawing, guided authorities to a flower garden less than fifty feet from the house.

Later that day, the stench of decayed flesh rose from two yawning excavations at those spots. The skeletons of two men were lifted from a twenty-two-foot-deep, dirt-filled well shaft. The partially mummified body of a red-haired woman was exhumed from the second hole. An informant had reported that Tom Shull and Charlie Baker—a pair of Georgia cyclists missing for more than a year—were buried on the ranch, and the two male corpses matched their descriptions. Yet the unidentified female corpse was a total surprise to the raiders.

The news rolled across the country. "Hell's Angels' burying ground" was the phrase thrown out by the state Attorney General's office and fielded by news media. Helicopters flew over the ranch for aerial photos. And a herd of journalists soon was at the bootheels of Sheriff Reno Bartolomie, a paunchy, silver-haired lawman who looked like a cattle rancher.

In the same twenty-four-hour period, two other widely reported events also gave the Hell's Angels winged skull emblem a new, more sinister meaning:

—In Sacramento, the California Attorney General's 1972

Crime Report branded the Angels a major narcotics distributor. It credited the hitherto loosely organized clan with trafficking $31 million in illegal drugs from the West Coast to the East in one three-year period alone. Club members, it said, were hitting the big time, getting credentials as large-scale organized crime operators who actively purchase land, invest in legitimate businesses and deal with major crime figures in the state. The report said the Angels availed themselves of sophisticated electronic devices to intercept police communications, thus enhancing their extreme mobility. And it said the Angels, Chinese youth gangs and other organized groups accounted for more than 100 California gang slayings in the previous few years.

—In Oakland, home of the club's controlling chapter, Angels President Ralph "Sonny" Barger and three other members were going on trial, charged with executing a Texas drug dealer over an estimated $80,000 in cocaine. They were accused (and later acquitted) of shooting the man as he slept, throwing the body in a bathtub, then setting the home afire. Authorities said the murder weapon was the same silencer-equipped pistol used to kill one of three men found murdered in a nearby house the same day.

The Wetherns were held on bail of $100,000 each while their children remained in protective custody at the home of a deputy sheriff. From past experience, Wethern knew the Angels drew no lines at retaliation—torture, kidnaping and murder were possible. His violation of the club code made it a good bet they would try to silence him temporarily by getting to his family or permanently by getting him. He realized it was only a matter of time before Barger would be connected to the burials—and implicating the club chieftain almost certainly would be a capital offense.

Still, he and club leaders maintained a semblance of loyalty that first day. He tried to warn those drug dealers whom he might incriminate, and Angels acting president "Big Don" Hollingsworth offered him legal aid and any other club assistance, presumably hoping to keep a lid on things. The club's offers were transmitted through J.B., Wethern's closest friend and a retired Angel, during a jail visit.

Later, Wethern was reunited with his wife in a special cell on the women's side of the jail—a compact room within a room, like a gas chamber with bars, four bunks, a metal table, toilet and stall shower. Agents with mud-caked boots had come to her cell earlier and told her about the grisly find. And the television news had said the same thing. Once they were alone, Wethern told her what he had done. And she wept, knowing he was a dead man whether he went to prison or not.

The next day, after an Angels attorney excused himself from the case because of potential conflict of interest, the Wetherns met with a Mendocino County public defender named Richard Petersen. The attorney convinced the family that an immunity deal was the best long-term answer, if they could be provided with protection against the club. Immunity also was attractive because Wethern felt an acute psychological need to flush all the dark secrets from his mind.

Two days after the raid—with several Angels in custody and several more fugitives in the case—a formal immunity deal was proposed by county District Attorney Duncan James. During the Superior Court session, the Wetherns were chained together in their jail blues. The couple were puzzled by the legal jargon and alarmed by the seemingly rushed procedural matters, a commotion in the bulging press section and the last-minute substitution of another public defender. And all too suddenly Judge Timothy O'Brien was asking them whether they were willing to reveal everything about the Hell's Angels.

13

"Your honor," Wethern declared, "I don't fully understand this and won't agree to anything unless I do." He also thought the proposed deal was too narrow. He wanted immunity binding on both federal and state courts, plus protection for his entire family. He demanded all or nothing.

By day's end, the Wethern children had been placed in a foster home. And the parents found themselves back in their cell, without their children, immunity or means of making bail. The vise of Angels' law and society's law clearly was tightening on Wethern.

But his patience and bravado paid off by that weekend. Under the deal, he and his wife agreed to plead guilty to misdemeanor charges stemming from the confiscated guns and drugs, but they were granted immunity for all other crimes except any capital offenses in which they may have been principals. Authorities knew of no such offenses.

The government agreed to relocate the family in the U.S. locale of their choice, with new names, government-issued identification, all necessary appearance changes, guarantees of housing and subsistence payments until they could reestablish.

In return, federal and state investigators would draw upon their memories of a fourteen-year association with the Angels, including Wethern's two stints of active membership:

After joining the club in 1958, he became a vice-president around 1960, just as the club began to actively recruit the roughneck kids who hardened into the world's most elite corps of outlaw motorcycle riders, the Oakland Hell's Angels. In the mid-1960s, he turned his close leadership ties into big money as the Angels slid into drugs, guns and explosives. He became the club's top psychedelics distributor and kept several other Angels in his stable of peddlers. As a drug businessman, he dealt with the royalty of that realm, particularly the infamous underground chemist and "LSD

14

King" Augustus Owsley Stanley III, and he was there when the Angels played acid games with author Ken Kesey and his Merry Pranksters. He joined other Angels in exploiting San Francisco's Haight-Ashbury flower children and their petal-thin revolution. In the late 1960s, he made between $100,000 and $200,000 a year, adopted a free-spending life-style and witnessed the first known Angels execution of a club member. And in 1969, after shooting his partner during a drug-triggered violence fit, Wethern turned from narcotics and retired from the club. Still, his friendship with club leaders endured, and he continued to traffic guns and drugs with the club right up to his arrest.

As word of immunity leaked to the press, District Attorney Duncan James proclaimed triumphantly on November 4: "This may not shut the Angels down right away, but most law enforcement officials think it would be the beginning of the end.

"A Hell's Angel doesn't tell on a Hell's Angel," he explained to reporters. "At least that's the way it's been. If they get arrested, they do their time in county jail and don't talk.

"But now there's a person who has had a friendship with Sonny Barger, the Angels maximum leader, and he's turning state's evidence. Now that their code has been broken, other Angels can be expected to come out and do the same thing just to save themselves. . . . After all investigations have been concluded, and arrests made, the Angels will probably be no more than a fragmented group of motorcyclists."

This heralded a parade of law officials. From all regions of the state and every level of government, they descended upon the former Angels leader day and night, with questions about the club and its people, hundreds of questions. Even when the long debriefing sessions were over for the moment, the questions hounded Wethern. Normal memory lapses frustrated him. It became increasingly difficult for him to distinguish between things forgotten and things never known. Tranquilizers temporarily released tensions, but drug dependency further irritated him, so he quit them.

On the morning of November 8, after a night of pacing, Wethern ventured a few thoughtful steps each way across the cell. He had been trying to figure out possible identities for the dead woman. He awakened his wife to pick her brain.

"Go to sleep," she urged. "You need some rest."

He apologized for waking her, resumed pacing for a minute, then told her, "I gotta get you outa here."

"Whatta ya mean?" She cleared her eyes and her head.

Stolidly, he sat and pondered, as though listening to someone.

"Whatta ya mean?" she pressed, rolling from under the sheets.

"Shush. God's talking to me." He shut his eyes.

"What's he say?" She held his face in her hands, but he remained mute. His eyes popped open and glazed over. "George," she whispered urgently, "you gotta talk to somebody."

When Deputy Jim Tuso arrived, Wethern was hanging on the cell bars, reaching desperately for the deputy's gun. "Kill me, Jim," he screamed. "Do it. Do it."

Embracing the big man and stroking his forehead, his wife explained to the deputy, "He's feeling bad. He's upset. He won't take his tranks."

After a few minutes of more reasoned talking, Wethern canceled his death wish. "Never mind, Jim," he said. "Forget it. I'm okay now." When he rose from his knees, dropped into a chair and seemed to calm himself, the deputy departed.

Suddenly, Wethern was up again. "Lemme talk to Peter-sen. Dammit, lemme talk to him."

"Okay. Okay," she said. "He's already on his way."

"Can you handle it?" he added. "Can you get yourself out of here?"

"Whatta ya mean?" It was unclear to her whether he meant out of jail or out of the entire mire.

"Can you do it?" he replied with great emphasis.

"We can talk to Mr. Petersen," she said, terrified that she had lost his thoughts.

"Well, if you can't do it, I've got to," he said.

The attorney showed up, but, try as he might, he couldn't communicate with the former Angel.

"Don't give up," Helen entreated her husband. "Talk to Mr. Petersen. He's here to help you."

Wethern remained tense, frighteningly intense, obstinate yet incoherent. "No. It ain't workin'. No good."

After the attorney left, Wethern pounded and pounded the metal bed frame with his fist, telegraphing a crude message to himself.

"Come on, George," a jail matron called from the corridor doorway. "Calm down. Come on."

He smiled sheepishly and asked her to close the door so he could use the toilet in privacy. She hesitated until Helen assured her it was all right. Once the door latched and the matron's footsteps pattered off, he sprang to his feet, then fiercely pulled his wife to her knees. "Let's pray," he murmured. Then another thought struck him. He picked up a pencil, wanting to write a letter, so Helen joined him at the metal table.

With deliberation, he formed the letters of his first name. GEORGE. He stopped. Almost involuntarily, his head bobbed, rhythmic yet ponderous, a tousle of hair and whiskers. Images filled his mind: feelings intensified the images. Guilt for the life his wife and children would inherit. Fear for their future hells. Regret for abandoning old and loved comrades.

"Gimme another pencil," he said.

He seemed to be writing two-handed, right to left and left to right; then he turned the pencils point-up in his fists. He flicked away one lead with his thumb. His muscles bunched. His wide forearms wrenched upward. The pencils sank deep into his eyes, past the whites and toward the target. The brain, the source of his pain, had to be pierced, killed. His thick hands strained, but Helen threw herself across the table, with all her might prying them away, screaming for his life. To get the lances deeper, he tried to ram them on the table. Yet, as his head plunged forward, the woman gripped the bloody pencils and swiftly yanked them out.

Blinded by blood and pain, he clutched her throat, tearing her rosary and driving her back to the shower floor. "He's going to kill himself and take me with him ," she told herself. She held her breath at first. Then, when she desperately needed air, she found her throat passages closed. Panicking, she mustered all her strength to try to push him away. But her legs were hopelessly pinned under his huge body and her arms were too weak.

As she started to lose consciousness, deputies dragged George away and pinned him to the bed. After they held him for a while, he went placidly to a holding area.

A few minutes later, Helen watched from the corridor as he was led toward an ambulance. Her throat was bruised and her knees were quaking. "George," she called.

"Honey. I'm sorry. I'm sorry," he cried back.

"It's all right. I'm okay," she assured him. "Don't worry."

"Gimme a kiss, Sugar," he said—and they were allowed a brief embrace.

Speeding toward the hospital, he enjoyed a queer, peaceful joy in his blindness. The darkness relieved him of his real world concerns, but they rushed back on the hospital operating table, when one eye picked up the outline of the overhead light. "Oh, no," he told himself. "You didn't do it good enough."

Back at the jail, he was manacled so he couldn't touch his eyes. He cursed the chains, he cursed the deputies, he cursed the world, he cursed himself. He growled and snarled and shook the bars of his cell. When the doctor came, he demanded, "Gimme a shot. Gimme a shot." The first shot made him cry for more, reverting into a complete Hell's Angel.

He created such a disturbance that deputies finally wrestled him to an old storage room. His feet shackled and his hands chained to a belt, he stretched across the floor. He yawned, pretending to be sedated. He bummed a cigarette from one guard. As he smoked, he worked slack in his chains. Then, rolling over as though to snuff his smoke, he jammed the entire butt into his eye. Cursing their own stupidity, the deputies were immediately upon him, but the damage had been done.

With his chains cinched tighter, he was returned to his cell. Alone in the darkness and the eery, echoing jailhouse, he wanted in a desperate way to talk to his wife to make sure she was unharmed. He clamored until several deputies were standing in the doorway of his cell.

"I'm comin' out," he roared. "I wanna see my wife."

"No, you're not," one of the deputies said, but George exploded through the human barrier. Like a runaway elephant, he charged down the hallway with deputies clinging to his dangling chains. He reached the guardroom before a gang tackle brought him down just short of the women's side of the jail. "I'm goin' to her, and that's it! God help me!" He screamed it until a guard literally choked off the words.

19

The commotion carried to Helen's cell. Hunched at the edge of her bunk, she fingered her broken rosary. She ached to go to him but was helpless. She reconstructed the rosary, bead by bead. The matron left for a couple of minutes. "He had another sedative," she returned to say. "He's sleeping, finally."

At that, Helen surrendered to her own sedatives and slept too.

I—A Breeding Place for Angels

My home town was Oakland. It was a raw place, but it wasn't as bad as San Franciscans said it was. Like any other industrial city, it had its ugly face—waterfront warehouses, smoking factories, freighters and endless railyards. But those homely places put bread on the tables of families living in the pleasant working-class neighborhoods that sloped up the green hills to the east.

In 1955 my family lived in one of those neighborhoods of comfortable houses. My father was owner and chief bartender at Clarence's in Oakland, a down-to-earth, no-frills saloon that catered to officials from the nearby Alameda County courthouse, businessmen, blue-collar workers and local winos. He and my mother, a Pacific Telephone Company employee, worked long hours to keep me, my two brothers and my sister well clothed, well fed and well educated in Catholic schools. And they gave us all the luxuries they could afford. You might even say they spoiled us a little bit. On my sixteenth birthday, in fact, they surprised me with the fulfillment of every California high school student's dream—a 1950 baby blue Ford sedan with fender skirts.

Once I customized it by heating the springs, dropping the frame and yanking the skirts, it was my entrée to a car club called the Quads and to some pretty good times in the back seat with my steady girl, Judy. And there were a few other girls too—thanks to my wheels and the fact that I fit the stereotype of the day. I was about 5-10, 200 pounds, with a Tony Curtis curl, and I was uniformed in a white teeshirt, a woolen Pendleton shirt, a windbreaker jacket and Levi's, the stiffer the better.

Even in those days, I was the family black sheep. At Bishop O'Dowd High School, I managed only Cs, although teachers told me I finished third out of 500 students in an IQ test. Reading books was like doing penance. I hung out with other burly guys for the sake of status and enjoyed a reputation as a tough guy, even though I did far more bluffing than fighting. During my sophomore year final examinations, I swiped my father's revolver and ran away to the Sierra Nevada for a few days with a buddy, until our money ran out.

Naturally, females were my downfall. I was smitten with Judy, a willowy but full-chested blond I dated since junior high. At O'Dowd, my sister and other puritanical girls regarded her as fast because she was popular and seemed to know about things like monkey bites on the belly.

When we were sixteen, we got caught coupling on a backyard swing during a party and word got back to my mother. Our parents huddled, then sent Judy to a doctor. Tests showed everything was copacetic, but my mother decreed an end to the romance.

My mother was having enough trouble with my father's drinking binges, so she farmed me out to an all boys school in nearby Alameda. She gave the school administrators free rein to reform me, but they couldn't keep Judy out of my life. Soon we were bumping into each other at parties, hamburger joints and in the back seat of my Ford.

I started getting better grades, doing less—but my academic career was cut short. Judy was pregnant. We wanted to get married, but my mother withheld consent in characteristic fashion: "George, I'll nail the lid on your coffin before you marry her." She regarded Judy as a slut. Before the school year ended, she hustled me to the Air Force recruiting office.

For some reason, they trained me as a personnel specialist, someone who shuffled papers and kept track of leave records. It was funny to be breaking the very rules I was supposed to be learning as part of my specialty training. If I wasn't AWOL, I was clashing with my superiors. When they called me on the carpet, I used my thwarted romance as an excuse. Finally, some sympathetic officers transferred me from Lackland, Texas, to Mountain Home, Idaho—a Strategic Air Command base in a state that permitted eighteen-year-olds to marry without parental consent. When I went home on leave, Judy was giving up the baby for adoption. She told me she never wanted to see me again, and I never saw the baby.

Back in Boise, fifty miles across the sage from Mountain Home, I vented my emotions by prowling for local girls. They seemed to be indoctrinated by idyllic movies that pictured Californians with Cadillacs in their carports, blue water in their swimming pools and wads of greenbacks in their jeans. My buddies and I heisted beer trucks to supply our all night parties with these willing girls. After a few run-ins with the resident cowboys, I took to toting a .45 automatic pistol, and had to use it once to avoid a stomping. Then I unintentionally got engaged to a grocery clerk there, using my "ring hustle" to get a little sex in return for a gold band. Fortunately, I wormed out of the engagement and hocked the ring.

My military career was as mercurial as my romancing.

For being in a successful program, I won a medal. For being myself, I earned two summary courts-martial convictions and some AR-15 disciplinary citations, for things like smuggling girls into the barracks and almost running down a sergeant. Finally, I went AWOL all the way back to Oakland, to visit my sick mother and to party with old friends. I surrendered to the MPs after a few days of cat and mouse.

My special court-martial convened May 16, 1958, with military judges and two charges: being AWOL for six days and misappropriation of government property, namely two hunting knives found in my locker. It went on like a capital case with six days of witnesses, arguments and evidence that boiled down to twenty-one pages of summarized testimony. After being sentenced to three months' hard labor, I gave my guards so much trouble that a major came to the stockade personally to offer me an undesirable discharge. "Where do I sign?" I bubbled.

The glorious day I was marched from the stockade, I walked a few paces off base and saluted my favorite guards with my middle finger. Then I blew all my military pay partying in Boise with a bunch of other discharged troublemakers. I had to phone my father for money to get home.

II—Making of a Hero

In the summer of 1958, I hauled my party-racked body back to Oakland, still without a decent military record or education. My aimlessness worried my parents, but I was in no rush to enter the workaday world. I just wanted to take it easy and regain the year and a half and forty pounds stolen by Uncle Sam.

I suppose I was trying to recapture my high school years. Hanging out at East Oakland drive-ins soon made me a regular with a younger crowd from the Havenscourt District. Acting with the aplomb of a worldly stockade veteran, I impressed the girls and, at least, got the guys' attention.

The Foster's Freeze hamburger stand hadn't changed much since my own school days. There still were plenty of girls, flitting around the jukebox, waiting to be rescued from boredom or corrupted. They were looking for action 1950s style—smoking rubber, flashing chrome reversed rims, rumbling glasspacks, Butch Wax and sweaty pants-down love in the back seat. And few things did more for a guy's ego than having his tuck and roll warmed by pony-tailed, erect-breasted girls bebopping, twittering at his every word, reeking of Woolworth's perfume, Clearasil and cigarette smoke, packed in tight as a good bag of fries.

The drive-in was a place to pick up girls for cruising. After my mother's station wagon filled, I'd peel away from the parking lot's crisscrosses of burnt rubber. I'd turn up the radio rhythm and blues and spend more time watching the rearview mirror than the road. The mirror was indispensable; it saved me speeding tickets and it let me keep track of any interesting sweeties in my back seat. One particular girl always seemed to meet my eyes in the mirror. She looked like the younger sister of one of my girls. She was flat-chested and about ninety-nine pounds.

"You shouldn't look at me that way, little girl," I teased her. "You're too young for them bedroom eyes."

She blushed and indignantly denied the whole thing. I was shocked to learn this little thing in white bucks, Levi's and her big brother's dress shirt was fifteen, not eleven or twelve. I was even more surprised that she had a boyfriend who was two-timing her.

Her name was Helen. She thought I was too brassy and aggressive. But I eventually convinced her that dating me would make her boyfriend jealous. On our first date, I discovered she had a perky personality that was hidden in group situations. Pretty soon I had her cutting classes, and we'd go over to someone's house to play cards and neck. She thought I was all hands and glands at first, but later she lost her fear of me and accepted my St. Christopher's medal.

Going steady meant drive-in movies and lovers' lanes along Skyline Boulevard. When I was low on gas money, we would forgo the sparkling panoramas and would just pull into a dark lumberyard a few blocks from her house. Lots of times I'd follow my back seat routine with another girl the same night. Yet I didn't tolerate any unfaithfulness on Helen's part.

One day I spotted her riding in a car with a couple of boys and a few girlfriends. She tried to duck out of sight, but it was too late. I U-turned and tailed the car, hugging its bumper through a few evasive fishtailing turns. Like a maniac, I was blasting my horn and gunning my engine until the driver pulled over. One guy ran, but I caught the other, threw him across the hood and bent his nose with a pistol. "What're ya doin' with my girl?" I yelled. He stammered an apology, so I booted his butt, then turned to Helen. "Get outa the car."

"I ain't goin' alone." She would come out only after she convinced a couple of girlfriends to come along. I guess she was afraid of me.

Not everyone thought I was overaggressive. In fact, some of my friends found the trait desirable. Two of them, Jerry Jordan and Junior, were riding with the Hell's Angels, a fledgling motorcycle club with a local reputation. As I outgrew the high school scene, the club's kamikaze style and camaraderie fascinated me. I found myself wanting to join, but I didn't have a motorcycle, a rare conveyance in those days.

Thanks to my parents' pull with a union official, I got an apprentice job with a construction company and saved $125. That bought me a used Harley-Davidson 45, a half-red, half-green bike with white sidewall tires, the luxury of chromed handlebars and a beer can muffler. After Jerry and Junior helped tune it sweet and wire down the loose parts, I lapped the block a few times, then we headed for 23rd Avenue.

The crusty little shopping area there was like a small town toe-to-toe with a city. Store rooflines were cut low and irregular, the telephone poles high and irregular. The gutters always were cluttered with beer bottles, cigarette stubs and motorcycles. The favorite hangouts were the Doggie Diner drive-in, the raunchy Star Cafe and Poole's Locker Club, owned by an old motorcycle buff who kept the sailors in line and didn't mind young bikers leaning on his jukebox.

Under the feeble streetlights, the three of us parked at the end of a string of motorcycles, then headed for a loose huddle of guys against one building. They wore sleeveless Levi's jackets called "cutaways" with winged skull emblems. A skinny, dirty-blond, fight-scarred kid left the group and sidled toward us. His grease-black, steel-reinforced boots must have accounted for about a tenth of his 130 pounds, but he telegraphed heavier vibrations as he ambled along, his head cocked a little to one side, his puffy eyes leveled and his strong lower lip poised.

His name was Ralph Hubert Barger Jr., but his friends called him Sonny. He was born in Modesto, and when he was six months old his mother left him to be raised by his father. He never saw his mother again. Like me, he was an Oakland high school dropout who enlisted in the military. He used to tell people he quit school in 1955 as a tenth-grader, spent a year in the Army, then was discharged when authorities found him underaged. After an apprenticeship with the Angels' Nomad chapter, he organized the Oakland chapter and became president in 1957.

Sonny was unsmiling but not unfriendly. We shook hands and shot the breeze about motorcycles and the club. When the other Angels joined us, I did more listening and observing than talking. But Sonny—though he was only twenty—clearly guided the conversation.

Without seeming juvenile, he spoke of motorcycling as a lifestyle, not a hobby. "But why talk about it when you can do it?" He moved toward his mount, then with a casual roll of his head, added, "Come on, George. Ya wanna go?"

28

"Yeah, sure," I replied, and I was on my first "run," with maybe a total of twenty minutes' experience on a motorcycle. The pack took off down the boulevard, rip-roaring from stoplight to stoplight. I fell way back, especially in the straight stretches, because the bike would choke and die every time I tried to wind it out. I'd lift my leg and it would take off again. Then it would die a minute later. I was going crazy trying to keep up. Finally, we pulled into Top's Cafe, one of the regular coffee stops, after I'd stalled seven or eight times. After poking around, Sonny discovered that my problem was a pants leg that was keeping air from the carburetor.

With some minor repairs by Sonny and some riding time, I was gunning my Harley through traffic with the amazing grace of the rest, just loving the rumble of those big pistons. I even mastered the rear-mounted jockey shifts that were the rage. They demanded precise movements—one hand steered while the other swung back, shifting gears.

Our routine was: ride until your ass is sore, stop for coffee, then ride some more. We'd ride crazy-like, roaring into bars or along sidewalks. Pulling wheelstands. Just looking good. Feeling good. Class was riding four or five abreast along the street, taking up both lanes. And nobody passed; we piled up cars whenever we wanted. Just riding along, everything purring and everybody together.

About three weeks after my first run, I was waiting anxiously on the porch of a house across the railroad tracks from 23rd Avenue. Inside, the fifteen or so members were discussing their new "prospect"—my personality, my riding ability and, most of all, my desire to join. Two nay votes could have blackballed me, but everyone figured "the more the merrier."

When I was called inside, everyone congratulated me with handshakes and rough slaps on the back. I shelled out twenty-five cents for weekly dues and a few bucks for the club patch, but I didn't own a cutaway jacket. "Don't worry," Sonny said. He tossed me his old colors, the death's head patch stained with blood from a jaw-breaking spill. Surging with pride, I pulled on the snug jacket. The feeling of instant brotherhood, backing and status electrified me. I no longer was just a dropout and an Air Force reject. I was a Hell's Angel.

Coming home was a downer. Hatred was a mild word to describe my mother's feelings toward the club. The antigod name itself mocked the faith she celebrated with daily Mass. She saw us as arrogant punks in our late teens and early twenties, many living with parents or dependent upon them. And whenever members dropped by the house, she needled them about their greased back hair and grimy clothes, calling them a bunch of bums. Once she swatted a couple of guys with a broom.

Another night she tried to beat her view into my head with a No. 9 frying pan. My father was scuffling with me and my mother was screaming, "Call the police. Lock that kid up," so I broke away before matters got out of hand. I kicked over my Harley and blasted, soothed by the song of the beer can muffler. Free again!

Later that night, I was with Sonny and Waldo at the Doggie Diner when the pay phone rang. It was some girl asking for somebody in the club. She and her roommate wanted some company. "Let's go," I said to the other guys.

Her place was an old time duplex on 18th Street. And she turned out to be the wildest Avon lady I'd ever met. We got tangled up that night, and she clawed my back something terrible. In the morning, I had to go to court for traffic tickets, but she was saying how amazed she was at my prowess in the sack. I still had to leave, so I told her, "Compliments of the Hell's Angels," and rode off.

I dabbled in the club's regular "mamas" too. You might say they were sexual fringe benefits of membership. There was "Big Jan," a handsome, Amazonian blonde; she was strong enough to carry me in her arms like a baby. There was Sue, whose sexual capacity was legend; she and her roommate once banged me into submission, and I sneaked from their flat with boots in hand while they slept. There was Spider, whose moniker suited her dark hairy looks and sexual style. One of the most notorious was "Garbage Head," a San Bernardino reject who hustled quarters at bars by clamping her legs together and begging for Kotex money. We auctioned her body one night, but fourteen cents was the highest bid. Plenty of women viewed us as the James Gang reincarnated and went for our leather-denim-motorcycle erotica. The ones who lasted either could take lots of abuse or had no place to go.

At first, I shielded Helen from the club, partly in deference to her innocence, partly to keep my sexual options open. But gradually she was drawn into our wind-on-the-face world. Before her first ride, I said, "Get on and hang on. Lean when I lean." Our morbid trappings scared her, but she soon found that being an Angel's girlfriend gave her special status at school. Her girlfriends would say, "Gee, your old man's in the club. What's it like?" Her first Angels party, around a bonfire in the hills, provided the answer.

"It was wild," she told her friends. "I felt like a kid with all these big people. They were drunk and carrying on, having a good time. Lots were loaded on pills or something. I was having a good time watching them and pretending to sip my beer. 'Lookit that one,' I'd tell George. 'Lookit how weird he looks.' And all the girls were decked out seductive in tight sweaters, short skirts, leather. The women were downright hard and acted like the guys, big and bad. They had knives, and some looked like they shoulda been ridin' 'sted of the guys.

"George was mainly a watcher, except when he got up on a table and danced. He was usually off talking to people. He

31

sat me down and told me to stay, but I didn't like it. Whenever a guy came over to ask me to dance, George would come and stand over him.

"He was real protective. He came right out and told the Angels, 'That's mine,' meaning me. He said, 'I don't want nobody messin' with it. Stay away.' I really didn't provoke anything anyway. The Angels wanted some voluptuous thing to mess around with, not me."

Helen's parents weren't aware of that. They considered the club dangerous to her moral well-being, my bike dangerous to her physical well-being. Their fondness for me was wiped out by my wheelstands in front of their house. They declared motorcycles off limits, so I had to pick Helen up with a car, then switch to a two-wheeler.

The Bagleys had left their humble, moonshining Oklahoma home and come to California when Helen was a year old. Her father, Charley, was a feisty little man maimed by bar fights and an auto wreck that left one leg shorter than the other. He limped noticeably and spent lots of time and money at good old bars like the Silver Saddle. But his mallet-hard hands spliced shipping cable and supported three children. His wife did seasonal work at Del Monte cannery and secondhand stores to help ends meet.

Only recently could the family afford to leave the flat, predominantly black West Oakland ghetto for higher and "whiter" ground with better schools. Neither parent nor Helen's older brothers had completed high school, so she was groomed as the first graduate.

More than anything, she loved to draw and draft, but art school was impractical. She set her sights on beauticians' school, but $500 a year tuition was too expensive. She settled for a high school secretarial curriculum, and hoped to share an apartment someday with other single girls.

Other plans soon were proposed for her. As part of my hustle, I asked her to marry me.

"I don't wanna get married right away," she told me. "I wanna finish school."

"Well, you're gonna get pregnant," I informed her. And the prediction came true within a few months.

Keeping the pregnancy secret bothered her more than morning sickness. We decided to someday live in the country and to educate our kids as Catholics even though her family was Baptist. We were trying to muster the money to start life together and the courage to tell her parents.

Meanwhile, Helen was established as my old lady among Angels. Her coming out was the club Halloween party in 1959. She and J.B.'s wife, Irma, were elated to be included. After lots of consultation, Helen outfitted herself in a pair of Levi's and a borrowed green mohair sweater.

The entire Oakland chapter piled into the back of my father's two-ton van for the trek to San Francisco. "You ride up front with me," I told Helen, even though she wanted to join the wacky group in back. They were loaded, swilling and spilling beer before we left Oakland.

We were a little behind schedule, so I pushed the van to seventy miles an hour. For the hell of it, I was swerving from side to side going down the freeway, bouncing my riders against the van walls. At the Bay Bridge toll plaza, my painted and goateed crew put on a show for the motorists, toasting one another and peeing out the grating across the back. "Help. Lemme outa here," the females screamed. The toll collector went back to investigate but got straightened out in a hurry.

I had talked the club into taking the van because traveling en masse was more fun and safer than a nighttime bike caravan. There was less danger of loaded members getting hurt, harassed or lost on unfamiliar city streets. In the past, partybound members sometimes were turned back by San Francisco police, but this night the van rolled unchecked to the original Fillmore Auditorium. It was a musty, footworn upstairs dance barn on a street corner in the black Filmore District.

Once inside, Helen retreated to a corner near the refreshments stand while I made my rounds, socializing, popping pills, drinking beer and raising hell. The place was filling with bikers from clubs like the Mofos, Presidents and Gypsy Jokers, but the Angels stood out. We usually were in rare form on Halloween. More outrageous than outlandish, we tripped around with painted faces, shaved heads, chain whips, flashing light bulbs, Mohican haircuts, earrings, nose rings, Nazi helmets, swastikas.

In the fierce competition for attention, Sonny sprayed himself orange, but Frisco president Frank Sadilek outdid him by spraying himself green and wiring his Bismarck helmet with a blinking light. Frisco's 300-pound Filthy Phil lurched around in knickers and a Lord Fauntleroy outfit.

When guys started roughhousing and hands-on-ass womanizing, Helen frantically searched the crowd for me. When I came back, I found a persistent biker trying to hit on her. I went chest to chest with him and sent him away with a jerk of the head.

"You'd better stay in my pocket," I told her. She stuck her hand in my back pocket and followed me around, sort of like a pilot fish on a shark. We pushed through the tightly packed people, pausing now and then for talk, beer or diet pills.

She tired of that and wanted to dance. "You go ahead by yourself," I told her. Some Angels stomped and wiggled in rough time to music, but I didn't consider dancing manly unless it was on an enemy's face.

The star performer at a club dance usually wasn't a band member. He was the Angel who went most recklessly about his entertainment, copulating on the dance floor, ramming his head through a bass drum or doing similar stunts. On stage this night was Scab, a prospective member and sailor nicknamed after breaking both legs in his cycle debut. His reputation was fixed in everyone's mind after he fell a second time while juggling a case of beer and crutches on the back of an Angel's bike.

Plastered and gauzed from his two accidents, Scab got roaring drunk and staggered into a fight. But he passed out before the contest was decided. A few members locked him in the back of the van so he could sleep it off.

At about 2 A.M., the club was drinking at Jerry and Betsy Jordan's apartment when we heard faint cries, "Skip. Help me. Heeelp!" It was Scab. He woke up, thinking he was in jail, and called for Skip Workman, a Navy buddy. Once inside, Scab showed plenty of party spirit but made the mistake of relieving himself on the kitchen floor. "All over my floor," Betsy howled in disbelief. "Jereee! Shit! Get that sonofabitch outa here."

It was back to jail for Scab, but the party went on nearly until dawn. Helen and I slept there and drove home at mid-morning. It was our first all-nighter.

A month later, with her family down on me, Helen told her mother casually, "George and me are going to Reno."

"What?" The woman was flabbergasted. "What for?"

"We're gonna get married," she said without mentioning her condition.

We wangled approval from our parents, although mine declined to participate in the non-church wedding. We planned to drive to Reno on a Friday night and get married on a Saturday morning.

The night of our scheduled departure, I sold my motorcycle, then led Jerry and some other members on a roving bachelor's party to several bars. In the meantime, Helen stayed home with Betsy wondering why it took so long to sell a motorcycle. As midnight passed, she moaned, "I know he's not coming home. He's left." Worrying her most was a recent letter from my former Idaho fiancée. But at 3

A.M., I bounced in, a little stuporous. I'd blown a chunk of my bike money and the $100 wedding loan from my boss. To make amends, I kissed her and gave her a motorcycle-riding Santa Claus doll bought at one bar.

She forgave me, and the four of us piled into Jerry's Renault for the five-hour drive. "Reno or bust," we yelled as the little car strained up the west side of the Sierra Nevada. As day broke, we sputtered through the arches of "the Biggest Little City in the World," then changed into dress clothes in a gas station bathroom.

Outside the Washoe County Courthouse, Helen's parents and her brother, Dean, were asleep in their jalopy. Their motel money had been stolen by one-armed bandits. Charley wobbled as they groped up the steps like something out of *The Grapes of Wrath.* I led the way to a cold, stark office where several other wedding parties awaited a turn with the magistrate.

Eventually, we were called into the wedding chamber. With a justice of the peace jabbering the vows, we repeated the words and were married, with Helen's family still unaware that three were joined together, not two. After the Jordans captured our courthouse exit on movie film, we all brunched at a nearby gambling house, played a few slot machines, then hit the westbound highway. Our bridal suite was a stale-smelling little apartment near Fremont High, our honeymoon my forty-nine-dollar-a-week apprentice job.

III—A Young Family

The metallic din of a Big Ben jarred me awake. Head dangling, I hunkered at the bed's edge for a moment, then pushed to my feet. After a few weeks, the apartment continued to remind me of a four-dollar motel room, the kind rented by the hour. But painful encounters had taught my shins to avoid the radiator and moth-bitten furnishings in the dark. I left the rollaway bed that never was rolled away, then passed an overstuffed couch, an armchair and a secondhand TV set. At the open windows, I let the cold crawl over my chest. The air did nothing for my Ripple hangover, and my tongue stuck to my palate. My skull was drumming as I dressed, so I popped a diet pill. "See ya later, Idiot," I called to Helen's sleeping form, then left.

Hours later, she sized up her belly in the mirror then slipped on a maternity smock for the first time. With a sense of purpose, she hiked the few blocks to her parents' basement apartment and let herself in through the unlocked door. She stopped in the bedroom doorway. "Morning, Mom."

Adjusting her bifocals, her mother smiled then snapped upright. "Whatta you got on?"

"What's it look like?" She waited for some sign of forgiveness or acceptance.

But her mother demanded, "Why didn't you tell me?"

"I thought it was the worst thing that could ever happen."

"Do you love him?" she asked closely. "You know you didn't have to marry him if you didn't love him. Why did you?"

"I had to. I was pregnant." The truth came through her tears.

"You can still get out of it if you want. I'll raise the child as mine."

"Mom. How could I do that?" The thought crushed her face. "I'd see the baby as it grows up. I'd be its sister. I couldn't go through that."

Her mother took her hand. "I just wanted you to know you can do that. You don't have to stay with him."

"I love him really," Helen replied more confidently.

Back at our $57.50-a-month honeymoon apartment, she blocked out the dismal surroundings with dreams of a baby crawling around a blissful home with loving parents. The way it was in the movies.

In reality, she was grateful the baby would have a name and hopeful it would enjoy security. Unfortunately, neither of us was ready for conjugal routines, but we muddled through. As provider, I took home most of my meager paycheck, picked up her grocery list, then did the week's shopping. She was responsible for cooking, cleaning our trailer-sized apartment and pressing my clothes according to my mother's meticulous standards.

Each evening, we sat in our kitchenette playing roles that belonged on TV. I recounted happenings on the job, and she passed a few remarks about her day, reporting changes in her body or the latest news from her parents' house. I wasn't a very attentive listener, but I was an efficient eater. And after every meal I complimented her, no matter how rotten the food was.

She wanted to be with me at night, even if it meant waiting in the car during a club meeting or playing pinball machines and drinking soda pop at seedy bars.

Early in the pregnancy, I just couldn't resist buying another motorcycle, and for a while we used it to make our social visits. But later we switched to a car rather than risk harm to the baby. Making the rounds was a club requirement, and family men weren't exempted.

Our favorite hangout was Sonny's house. He held court elbow deep in motorcycle parts in the garage. To the sound of revving engines, clanking wrenches and husky laughter, we rapped out minor problems, killed six-packs of beer and watched his mad tinkering. He kept his wrenches flashing despite the distractions. And he was such a perfectionist that a slight oil drip would drive him to dismantle the entire engine. He actually wore out bolt threads.

"Hey, dummy," I'd razz him. "Doncha ever get tired of tearing down that motorcycle? So it leaks oil. Big deal. Add some more."

Rather than quit, Sonny would give me a greasy finger, then get me to help him carry parts into the kitchen, where it was cleaner. Even though we were in the next room, very few guys would mingle much with the women except to order them out for food or drink.

Like an obstetrician's waiting room, the living room was filled with wives and girlfriends. They were usually bored or pissed off at their men. Time was killed chatting or thumbing movie magazines. Very few were friends, many were competitors. And their hostess, Sonny's old lady, Sharon H., cared little for their company and showed it.

Helen was one of the few people the blond loner seemed

to like. "Come on," she would say, inviting Helen into the bedroom where she small-talked about Sonny, her four-year-old son and her mother, whose liquor store helped support them all. Helen was taken aback by the older woman of twenty-five. Sharon seemed very worldly. *True Confession* magazines fanned across her nightstand, and she always had money for household items and Sonny's motorcycle modifications.

Helen had no inkling why Sharon singled her out for friendship and hand-me-down household gifts. But for some reason, Sharon showed great interest in Helen's mother's hardening of the arteries.

"What kind of pills she got?" she asked.

"I don't know. Yellow pills for pain."

Sharon brightened. "For pain, huh? Can you get me some?" She was certain the pills were percodans, a powerful narcotic and good tripping medicine requiring triplicate prescriptions.

Helen reluctantly filched a few yellows for her, but they apparently weren't enough. We discovered by accident a few weeks later that Sharon was impersonating Helen to get the drug from her doctor and my dentist.

Sharon had Angels running around filling phony prescriptions for her. And it became an embarrassment to Sonny that his old lady was the most advanced doper around the club, because he was dead set against drugs at the time. He punished her by making her watch him flush her cache down the toilet.

The episode taught me that Helen was too naive to take along on club outings. So I started dumping her at the Jordans' apartment with Betsy, also pregnant, and sometimes with Irma, a recent mother. Helen didn't have the gumption to stand up to me, but Betsy, a big blond crazy about bike riding, demanded vocally but unsuccessfully to come along. And Irma, a hot-tempered Latina, used a baby carriage to knock her husband J.B. off his motorcycle. J.B. stayed home a little more after that, but Jerry and I roared off.

Helen and Betsy were in a tug-of-war with the club, and steadily losing ground. "Those dirty bastards, taking off and leaving us," they'd commiserate. "It ain't fair." They cussed us up and down, but there was nothing they could do except play another hand of canasta, flip the TV to another soap opera, embroider more baby clothes and fantasize about the joys of motherhood.

Angels activities and apprentice classes took me away from home several nights a week. But, as the months passed, I also started stumbling to bed drunk at 2 A.M. or later. Helen never demanded an accounting of my time until she uncovered long hairs and lipstick-stained cigarette butts in my car. My explanations were so plausible that she grew unresponsive to my sexual advances.

Looking back, I suppose she felt unwanted, like someone who was originally hustled for sex and later married out of guilt, some of it carryover from a first unwanted pregnancy. Her depression made her petulant and cranky.

IV—Young Angels

"It was a motorcycle club more than anything in 1960. They hung around bars, picked fights and pissed on each other's bikes. A lot held jobs and did their hell-raising at night."—An Oakland cop who knew the club.

After a sweaty day of lugging building materials and briefly playing expectant father, I wanted to get out and about. The more irritable Helen became, the quicker I escaped. I showered, groomed my goatee, slicked back my dark hair, then, with Helen looking on in disgust, put on my never-washed cycling duds. With the care of a gunslinger, I yanked Levi's up to my gut, the denim a matte black from grease and polished in the seat. After buttoning a black short-sleeved shirt, I stooped to lace matching black boots high up my calves—Highway Patrol style—then I let my pants cuffs fall over them. My colors went on with a jerk of copper-riveted lapels. Finally, with a brass ring

42

through my nose and a leather Harley hat on my head, I charged out into the night.

Around the city, other Angels were waving off wives, girlfriends and kids, slipping from gin mills and coffee shops, cutting free from factories, construction sites and truck rigs. Colors were dug from closets and car trunks; Harley 74s rolled from garages and from beneath tarps, then were kicked to life. Soon twenty or more Angels were converging on the appointed staging area, charged by engine and road vibrations. The fever was rising.

At the drive-in parking lot, the early arrivals horsed around and fiddled with their bikes. Some joked and smoked, while others wolfed burgers and beer. Leaning against our machines, we basked in the outraged glares of passing straights. We howled propositions at foxy ladies who tried to slip by, yet our own leather-clad women with jacked-up tits, strato sunglasses and makeup masks clustered nearby. Most were only in their twenties, but their fierce, pinched faces warded off most competition. Once in a while, a newcomer could cut the intimidation or handle a gang bang. Then she would become one of us, squatting on a chopper rear fender, wind slapping her cheeks, her thighs twined around some wild one.

We made song with our throttles as we fell into rough formation:

—Ralph "Sonny" Barger, with scars and a hardass demeanor, looked bigger on a bike than on his feet. He worked at the General Motors assembly plant, then as a pipe company machine operator.

—I was about six feet tall and 220 pounds, more muscle than flab and still filling out.

—Jerry Jordan, a dark-haired, clean-cut six-footer, carried his 225 pounds like a football player. He worked at the Peter Paul candy company.

—Junior, a 300-pounder too monstrous to call fat, hung

over all but the front and rear wheels of his chopper. A hard-drinking expert at leisure, he lived with his parents.

—J.B., an average-sized man with rusty hair, handled a bike with rare precision. The truck driver was one of my boyhood friends.

—Waldo, happy-go-lucky until drunk, waited behind deceptive horn-rimmed glasses for a chance to show he was one of the mightiest Angels at 6-1 and 260. He worked as a painter at the Alameda Naval Shipyard.

—"Skip the Scotchman," a former Navy boxer who sometimes fantasized he was refighting World War II, could be as genial as he was unpredictable. He collected war memorabilia and guns, and he worked as an auto assembly line inspector.

—"Johnny Angel" or "Polliwog" Palamar, 5-7 and 207, had swarthy broad-nosed looks that reminded us of a tadpole. He was the sort who would, and later did, fire a bullet past a bartender who had committed the sacrilege of calling him "brother." Johnny was a welder by trade.

—Elliott S. "Cisco" Valderama, a 5-11, 140-pounder, was a cycle veteran who started with the Misfits in Santa Rosa.

—Tommy, a gutsy, 5-foot-9 biker, immersed himself in motorcycle mechanics like Sonny, and covered his natural reticence with bizarre behavior. He was a lather by trade.

—"Swede" rode smoothly and talked suavely. He had an eye on the vice-presidency.

—"Gypsy," a hillbilly sort with a wife and a pair of snotty-nosed kids, escaped the squalor of his home life by riding with the Angels.

—Elvis, a wiry 6-3 with a red goatee, was on the lam from Southern California. Like "Norton Bob," he was one of the few Angels who rode a "limey," or English bike (a BSA), instead of an American-made Harley.

—Three brothers were in the club. Ernie, a rugged-looking, one-punch KO artist, was a former vice-president.

Amaro was one of my former schoolmates. Danny was an old buddy from the Air Force. The oldest brother, George, had abandoned the club for drag racing.

In addition to old-timers like Pete and Ike, and quiet newcomers like Brad and Andy, we were occasionally joined by nonmembers in their thirties and forties. Among them were Richie, peg-legged "Peg Leg," and "Dumbo," who had a protective steel plate implanted in his head after a seagull knocked him off his motorcycle and fractured his skull. Like outlaws in the Old West, many of us preferred to be known only by our first names or nicknames.

The Oakland chapter normally rolled alone and close to home, although gasoline cost only about nineteen cents a gallon. On almost any night and every weekend, the pack ate up East 14th Street. Like denizens of hell, with flapping denim and lethal boots, we hugged our hot, smoking metal monsters. In possession of the pavement, we rumbled along, the whole greater than the sum of the parts. There was no way to tell whether the men were extensions of the machines or the machines extensions of the men. We were tight.

As long as there was gas in our tanks or a buck to divvy up, we cruised around. We'd go nonstop until thirst drove us to bars like Hazels on Bancroft or the Hilltop Club on MacArthur Boulevard. Other patrons were expected to overlook insults or arrogance, because a critical stare, an unsolicited comment or failure to project timidity were good for a thumping or a stomping. We cared as little about clear-cut motives as fight preliminaries.

Sometimes trouble found us, sometimes we found trouble. Groups of cowboys, sailors or blacks occasionally filled themselves with enough liquid courage and bad judgment to challenge us. But normally we invited the combat. We singled out visible and hated minorities, such as blacks, for special humiliation and challenges. The smart ones ignored the heckling and slinked away, if they could get away.

We didn't lose many fights. Since we often traveled with an assortment of goodies like chains, wrenches, razors and knives, the advantage was ours from an equipment standpoint. And the regimen of slugfests, all-night drinking and grueling riding hardened us and gave us an experience edge. Our psychological edge, the club patch, proved as effective as a cocked shotgun, threatening that every Angel within hailing distance would jump to the brother's assistance. Anybody who thought that he was fighting an Angel one-to-one or that Marquis of Queensberry rules were in effect quickly discovered that "win" was the only rule. If a member was losing, we applied the latter half of the motto: "One on all, all on one."

Less direct intervention usually was all we needed. For example, one night Sonny squared off with a much bigger guy at a tavern. "Wait a second," I yelled, stepping between them. I fogged the guy's glasses, danced back, then said, "Now." Sonny unloaded a flawless Sunday punch. Another square was put down, another message dispatched to the outside world: "An Angel's always right."

That was my kind of fight—quick, clean and victorious. There was no point in groveling around the floor and getting bloodied when a surprise punch with a dozen follow-ups could resolve the disagreement in your favor.

I always thought of myself as more of a lover than a fighter, but my temper was quick. If a man flipped me the bird for honking at a stoplight, he could count on being run off the road and roughed up before the next light. If a man was leering at Helen, he could expect to be pounced upon, whether it was in a bar or a pizza parlor. My temper prevented Helen from ever really relaxing in public places, but it enhanced my club reputation.

My style earned me a spot among the "heavyweights," the front line of offense comprised of the biggest, brawlingest brothers. The line's average weight was more than 230 pounds, the average height about six feet.

We used to get in a lot of bar brawls. My big bespectacled buddy Waldo in particular used to get a few beers in him and tear up places. Wipe the floors with people. The Tail End in San Leandro used to be a steady place for us to demolish, because the Paisano Boys motorcycle club hung out there. When we were through, there was nothing but broken furniture and bottles and bloody guys all over the place. We'd ride around, make noise, show it off. Cut it up. Always with one eye out for the local heat.

Another night we met Frisco, Vallejo and a few other chapters in Rodeo, along the bay. There must have been fifty of us or more, and we planned to hit a Vallejo hotel, where a car club called the Slicks was holding a dance. They had been hassling some of our Vallejo guys and had dared us to take them on.

We parked our motorcycles at a gas station a block away so no one would hear us coming. A couple of security guards intercepted us outside the hotel, but they didn't last long. We just passed them overhead, then poured into the lobby. Then it was "cowboys and Indians." Bam. Pow. Over went furniture and people. We just steamrolled through the ticket takers at the dance hall door. Then we were throwing guys over the balcony, popping people right and left, slam-banging. Some of our women were blasting these Slicks with heavy ashtrays. During five minutes of pandemonium, we chewed them up. (Plenty can happen in five minutes.) Then someone hollered, "Clear out! Let's go." And we ran. After all, there were at least 200 car clubbers in there, and the element of surprise was the main thing going for us.

Unfortunately some cops pulled up as we were making our exit. A number of members and some broads were handcuffed. But we were pulling the victims out of the squad cars as fast as the cops could put them in. All of a sudden Frank Sadilek, the Frisco president, and Frisco Pete came staggering out of the hotel in a bloody mess. "You dirty sacks of shit," they were yelling. "You left us inside with all them guys." Once we rescued most of our people, we retreated to the gas station, with some of our women still wearing handcuffs, and 300-pound Filthy Phil yoked with a stolen tire.

As we roared off, somebody did a wheelstand right into the side of the gas station. The local gendarmes were converging in greater numbers and getting their act together. In groups of twos and threes, we beat it out of town for a fast ride home. At the Carquinez Straits toll bridge, we tailed cars right up to the collector, then hit the gas. We were paying no tolls that night. Go! Cross that bridge!

On the other side the Highway Patrol cars were waiting, three patrolmen per car. They'd pull alongside or behind you, growling over the bullhorn, "Pull over." Some tried to knock our guys off the road. But we just cooked down the highway, looking for exits and places to hide. Some members were captured, but I got away. It made the papers the next day.

There was a "king of the hill" mentality among different bike clubs—and even among Angels chapters. Territorial disputes cropped up because we saw the streets as our drag strips, the bars our private clubs and the women our property. Chance encounters led to grudges or feuds. A few escalated until we unleashed our ultimate weapon: disbandment.

To disband a club, you first thrash a significant portion of its members, then as a coup de grace rip the colors from their backs. It was like taking scalps. And that's how we destroyed the Paisano Boys and the Hayward Angels. We had granted the Hayward Angels (formerly the Question Marks) a club charter, but they didn't show proper fealty.

Things were different, and sometimes rougher, when we

battled black bikers. Racial feelings varied from member to member, but in general the club stood for redneckism and white supremacy. Many members, like me, were reared in tough racially mixed neighborhoods or saw their home turf "blackened." We were offended further that groups of "the niggers" showed the audacity to ride Harleys and call themselves motorcycle clubs. But their style was different, so we ridiculed them openly for riding jazzy, full-dressed "garbage wagons" with handlebar fringes, raccoon tails, saddlebags and more reflectors than a tow truck. And sometimes we crashed their dances looking for fights and laughs.

After one Peacemakers' dance, some Angels touched off a small-scale riot, then Dumbo was killed nearby when a carload of blacks deliberately stopped short in front of his motorcycle. That really pissed guys off; Dumbo was one of those fifty-mile-an-hour, slow laners who minded his own business. Through their families, the club told those responsible, "Go to jail or die." The guilty went to jail, their families moved away.

The San Francisco-based Rattlers was one black club we tolerated. They came close to being a black Hell's Angels: they conked their hair, wore funky hats and chopped their motorcycles. Once they invited us to a dance at their Filmore Street clubhouse, and we accepted. Music and booze got everybody fraternizing. Some Angels went so far as to dance with black women—at least one got more intimate than that. One minute I was munching phenobarbs from a Frisco Angel, the next I was being tossed on a sea of black and white hands to the stage. The singer, a 250-pound mammy type, pulled me onto her lap and belted out another bluesy number. Everyone rocked out, higher and higher. A white elite and a black elite together.

Entering the 1960s, we had few tangibles to distinguish us from the exhaust cloud of gangs inspired by Marlon Brando's *The Wild One*. The Angels were scattered statewide, but, for the most part, each chapter operated autonomously. We set some trends in regalia and cycle modifications, but our style was typically biker. Man for man we were as roguish as most clubs, but what really set the Angels apart, especially the Oakland club, was a sense of brotherhood traced to a web of long-standing friendships. Recruits were friends or friends of friends. "Getting in isn't easy," Sonny once said. "We keep it small, so there will be esprit de corps."·

In 1959, the Oakland chapter met on Friday evenings in the basement of Junior's house. After an initial scramble for the most comfortable crates, we passed cigarettes and cooled our heels, relishing our image as rebellious misfits. Guys would grapple a little and laugh over something. But they stopped as Junior's father came downstairs to do some work on his boat. "Hi, Mr. G.," we said politely, and the muscular little man exchanged niceties with us.

Once he was gone, we went back to being bad guys, guys whose "crimes" mainly involved rowdyism, underaged women, hot motorcycle parts and prescription drugs on a nickel scale. Most were basically honest blue-collar or unskilled workers looking for excitement. Others were hustling to stay alive and camping on friendly floors. The meetings and follow-up parties brought us together.

We boasted about fights, women, broken dates with death; and we downed cocktails of booze and codeine cough remedies. Motorcycle trivia—such as engine specifications and carburetion—were bandied about. Parts and entire machines were traded and sold by committee. And in the cycle world, each of us acquired a reputation. I constantly bitched about my electrical system and faulty lights. Oil drips drove Sonny crazy. J.B.'s bike was in such disrepair that he held up the entire club while trying to kick start it. (Finally, some of us forced him to make repairs by dismantling his bike and presenting it to him in boxes.)

Meetings were conducted by Sonny under rough rules of parliamentary procedure. Minutes of the previous meeting were read first, then twenty-five cents weekly dues were collected. The treasurer put heat on nonpayers, but some logged debts as large as a buck because each week they were down to their last two bits of gas money. Whenever the treasury swelled to about fifty dollars, kegs of beer were ordered, a band was hired and a party was thrown.

Sonny's organizational skills dominated the decision-making process. He thought well on his feet, steered discussions, recognized speakers and summed up arguments. When he finally said, "Okay, we're gonna do this," everybody was ready to accept it. His ideas for runs, assaults or social activities worked often enough that no one seriously challenged his leadership.

However, during one meeting at the end of 1959, his judgment was questioned. He took the floor to open discussion for selection of his vice-president. He sounded confident, almost casual, because, as in national political conventions, the club president had strong say in choosing his second in command. With a terse, low-keyed endorsement, Sonny nominated me.

With the seconding, I already was tasting power, and I could almost see that "Vice-pres." patch on my colors. In my excitement, I dismissed Swede's nomination as pro forma. But, in the first—and probably last—club decision to go against Sonny, a majority voted for Swede.

That crushed me. It was a flat out rejection by a group heavy with half a dozen of my longest and closest friends. I swallowed it without bitterness, realizing that Swede's seniority and slick manner provided the edge. Then I rededicated myself to getting that No. 2 spot. If the club was riding, my bike would lead the pack. If the club was fighting, I would jump in first. If the club was partying, I would gobble up the good times. Participation was the name of the game.

51

I stayed tight with the club leadership. Not many people could penetrate Sonny's forbidding aura, but I developed a close rapport with him. It was a strange friendship, because we weren't much alike. You'd sometimes have to pry a smile out of Sonny, but I was happy-go-lucky. He was tough for his size but not blessed with the best physical equipment, while I was a heavyweight by anybody's standards. He played the strong silent type, while I constantly was mouthing off.

Sonny was a notorious sheet creature, but I loved to roust him out of bed to go riding. "Get up, dammit," I'd shout, smacking his feet with a broom. "You can't stay in bed all day. I'm up. Come on." If Sonny cussed or rolled back to sleep, I'd ram a broom handle under the covers and jack him onto the floor. Then I'd badger him until he got dressed.

Many a weekend we took to the pine-lined winding roads of the East Bay hills. Sometimes we just raced around, with Sonny fixing my bike when it broke down. Other times we took women into the woodsy parks for two-couple orgies. In fact, I remember that once I caught sight of Sonny—pants bunched around his boots, white butt exposed—hopping through the greenery after a nymph. He was "Sonny Bunny" to me after that.

My time soon arrived. Swede's participation ebbed, and he was ousted from office. The second time around, Sonny put pizzazz into my nomination, describing me as an upstanding, "gung ho for the corps" and exemplary Hell's Angel. The membership agreed and the rectangular red and white "Vice-Pres." patch was stitched onto my cutaway.

The officer's patch gave me more prestige. It was easier to get a willing woman on my rear fender, and when cops hauled me over for a ticket, they got excited and said, "Hey, we got an officer this time." One of the disadvantages was that it gave me a high spot on the police harassment list. They pulled me over twenty-two times on East 14th Street one day en route to nearby Hayward, and another time I was arrested for "speed exhibition," accelerating too fast, although I was doing an honest twenty-five miles an hour.

All the leaders, with the exception of Sonny, weighed well over 200 pounds, but leadership wasn't a matter of brute strength. It was based on the ability to bring people together by getting them to like you and by forcefully stating your case. All the top club offices were held by my closest friends: Sonny president; Jerry treasurer; Junior secretary; and Waldo sergeant at arms.

As No. 2 man, I was expected to lead by example, namely to be more active than the average member. I helped promote and arrange club dances, parties and other social functions. If Sonny were absent, I was supposed to conduct meetings. And I sometimes represented the club at biker confabs or went along as backup on official business.

In early 1960, Ralph and I putted across the Bay Bridge to the home of Frisco president Frank Sadilek.[1] The Hell's Angels statewide leadership, including representatives from Southern California, was sprawled around the room tilting gallon jugs of red wine. Interspersed were leaders of clubs like the Gypsy Jokers, Road Rats, Galloping Gooses, Satan's Slaves, a North Beach club called the Presidents and the Mofos, a funky outfit that looked more like winos than bikers. (The Mofos was a contraction for "motherfuckers.")

It was a historic gathering, sort of like the Yalta conference. Clubs that had traded stompings and chain whippings for years were parleying over a mutual problem—police harassment. Our style was cramped by roust-outs at favorite hangouts and by "routine stops" on the road. Lawmen seemed to be chasing down anyone on two wheels, citing them for minor offenses like driving without a mirror or having handlebars too high. I was a typical case, with more than $1,000 in traffic fines in the past year.

"We gotta stop fighting ourselves and start fighting these

cops," we'd say as the jug was passed. Everyone related instances of overzealous law enforcement and downright frameups. And we kicked around a hostile statement from the American Motorcycle Association, the Elks Club of biking. To draw a distinction between its members and us renegades, the AMA had characterized ninety-nine percent of the country's motorcyclists as clean-living folks enjoying pure sport. But it condemned the other one percent as antisocial barbarians who'd be scum riding horses or surfboards too.

The Angels and our friends, rather than being insulted, decided to exploit the glowing tribute. We voted to ally under a "one percenter" patch. As a supplement to regular colors, it would identify the wearer as a righteous outlaw. The patch also could help avoid counterproductive infighting, because an Angel, Mofo or any one percenter would be banded against a common enemy.

Everyone knew the patch was a deliberately provocative gesture, but we wanted to draw deep lines between ourselves and the pretenders and weekenders who only played with motorcycles.

Buoyed by the alliance and wobbly from wine, the outlaws dispersed to all corners of the state to inform their troops and to order patches. Sonny and I mounted our Harleys, zonked yet obsessed with outdoing the rest. A little patch may have been adequate for other one percenters, but not for us. A trans-bay ride took us to Rich's tattoo parlor in downtown Oakland. After a briefing, Rich's needle made biker history. Although I was too drunk to know it until the next morning, Sonny and I had the first of the famous one percenter tattoos—a symbol that likely will survive as long as outlaw gangs.

Soon our Oakland brothers were lining up for theirs. We were beginning to believe our own mystique. As we stacked a few rules and rituals on the simple foundation of motorcycle riding, we thought we were building a little army.

But, in fact, it was a rough blueprint of a secret society.

We decided we needed our own headquarters, a place to cavort freely without offending Junior's parents or running afoul of the law. We rented a rickety Victorian house on San Leandro Boulevard in a black ghetto. It was a condemnation candidate, but the rent was right. And nobody cared how much screaming and glass-breaking went on. We christened it "the Snake Pit."[2]

A few members, including Johnny Angel, regularly crashed there, but mainly it was a meeting and drinking place—a social hall where we partied with established old ladies and community property "mamas." Now and then a stray teenaged girl would be "turned out" there, stripped and plugged until guys tired of her.

Once a week, we settled down to a serious meeting among the biker graffiti and little pyramids of beer cans. The floor was so gross with cigarette butts and whatnot that we fought for the few chairs and a disemboweled couch. All the drinking, wrestling and razzing stopped when the meeting was called to order.

We talked mainly about activities like weekly runs or just cruising up and down the streets. Contests also were set up to generate more "streetativeness," or involvement. We even had a special plaque for the most active member, and five-year membership plaques for the wall at home.

We started laying a groundwork of rules, but not many. A guy didn't have much of a chance of breaking the rules unless he was alone. If you were nearby, you'd tell him what he was doing wrong. The rules were pretty much understood, and we lived according to a loose code. The only secret aspect of the club was gossip about failing members. And even then, we gave failing members a chance to redeem themselves by full participation. If they didn't take the invitation, they were kicked out. Most of the expulsions were for missing three meetings in a row.

We also initiated an honorary Hell's Angels. It was for

guys who couldn't regularly make it to meetings and parties—usually because they were in the service. Honorary
membership allowed them to wear the colors and ride with
us whenever they were home. Paul, a friend from high
school, was the first honorary Angel.

Admitting honorary members was no small concession,
since our colors carried faintly military, nationalistic and
spiritual connotations, like the German Iron Crosses some
members wore. For ten dollars, new initiates received a red
and white patch that was the classiest in all of California. It
profiled a human skull, its teeth and jawbone in a wide
mocking grin, an old leather flyer's helmet on a fleshless
brow, a powerful set of wings in place of ears.

The first patches measured just six inches across, but a
bolder version adopted around 1960 spanned your entire
back. The words "Hell's Angels" arched across the top of
the death's head, the appropriate chapter across the bottom,
forming a semicircle.

Cities with long names were abbreviated. For example,
San Francisco became Frisco, San Bernardino Berdoo and
San Diego Dago. (Later, to prevent the "heat" from easily
identifying chapter affiliations, we would fill the bottom
rocker with the state only.)

The smaller patches showed paramilitary ranking or individual touches. In addition to the officers' patches, swastikas or Nazi war medals were worn for shock value. But
what would outrage the squares more than a fascist symbol? A sexual symbol. The brothers started wearing "69"
patches and awarding little red and black wings. Public
cunnilingus on a menstruating white woman earned you
the reds, and going down on a black woman got you black
wings. Some guys were big on wings, but I never had any.

Like nicknames, our colors incorporated bits of personal
history. For instance, the front of my colors was emblazoned with the "Vice-Pres." patch on the left breast, and

56

red and blue script spelled out "Baby" on one side and "Huey" on the other. "Baby Huey" was the mighty diaper-wearing duck in the comics. The name was supposed to exaggerate my image as a happy-go-lucky guy with a nitroglycerin temper and the bulk to back it up.

Brotherhood and hard-won reputations were wrapped up in those colors, so we didn't tolerate any affronts to them, whether it was an untimely smirk in a bar or another biker flaunting his own club's patch. We effectively prohibited other clubs from using a red and white color scheme or other Angel insignias. (Some chapters later would ban any club from flying any colors without permission.)

As our notoriety spread, so did the number of jerks impersonating us. We never minded taking the credit for our own exploits, but we didn't like being wrongly accused of running down kids. "The truth's bad enough," Sonny used to say.

We nabbed a few impostors riding brazenly through the streets, playing the role. In fact, Jerry, Waldo and I were in the Renault one night when a pair of strange bikers flew by wearing Angels colors. We came alongside and yelled friendlylike, "Hey, pull over a sec." When they touched the curb, they were mobbed by 750 pounds of genuine Angels, roughed up, reprimanded, stripped of their colors and sent on their way.

Incidents like that underscored a need for a foolproof identification. One that couldn't be slipped off when counterfeited. It would have to be cut off—or inked out.

Our tattoo wasn't mandatory at first, but it eventually became that way. It gradually changed from the words, "Hell's Angels" on your arm to the death's head. Then the logo "Oakland Hell's Angels" was added to the death's head. Then it was expanded to "Oakland, Calif. Hell's Angels." Then we added more things.

* * *

Still, tattoos and patches were little more than accessories for our motorcycles. An Angel's bike could be many things—his power symbol, his equalizer, his sex object, his religious object, and often his sole possession. A good chopper evaded precise definition, but you knew when you had one.

In 1960, there were relatively few custom shops where dollars could be swapped for a sleek, chromed stallion. Grooming one yourself was the surest way to get a worthy mount.

In addition to about $3,000, you needed mechanical knowhow and energy to break down and refine a seventy-four-cubic-inch Harley-Davidson that rolled from the factory with doughnut tires, a bulbous gas tank, heavy fenders, vanity-sized mirrors and an uninspiring paint job. We called them "garbage wagons," but the 700-pound Harley stockers rolled like two-wheeled Cadillacs.

Behind the piggish profile was amazing power waiting to be freed with welding torches, wrenches and screwdrivers. With the cycle stripped to bare frame, the engine was torn down, bored out to eighty cubic inches, pumped up in horsepower. A bicycle-sized, twenty-one-inch wheel was fitted to extended front forks that raked back the cut-down frame, the effect multiplied by riser handlebars with silver-dollar-sized mirrors. The fenders were thrown away or "bobbed" to the legal minimum. The cushy banana seat was replaced with a lean saddle, the gas tank exchanged for a stinger with a twelve-coat mirror finish of lacquer. Finally, chromed pipes snorting, the beast stood ready to buck with a chomp of metal gears. Two hundred pounds lighter, untested increments faster and more temperamental, it challenged you to new limits:

There were no speedometers on most of our bikes. We just rode fast—sixty in the twenty-five m.p.h. zones, no limits on the highways. Once, though, I know I hit 120 racing a Pontiac from Richmond one night. My face was sore and my arms were aching from just holding on. My body was stretched back by the wind as I cooked past Berkeley and toward Oakland. It was too fast. Just a blur of lights.

But I always liked a bike geared for top end high speed so I could get on the highway and go. My thing was getting on it at sixty-five or seventy, kick it into third, take it to eighty-five or ninety, then get that sucker into fourth gear and just wind it up. Spit out the bees. Speed was where it was at.

One of the drawbacks was periodic repairs. Many members were adept mechanics who specialized in "cannibalizing" stolen and junked bikes to keep theirs chugging along. But my most mechanical endeavor was pouring oil and gasoline or choosing a color scheme to exploit the low, clean lines. There was no need to mess with the greasy end of biking, because Sonny always was willing to do my mechanical work. In fact, he built me several machines from the ground up. He got a little peeved that I turned around and sold one for a profit.

Replacement parts were a fringe benefit of membership. There was an unwritten rule that a member with extra parts would lend or sell them to a member in need. We also traded in volume at commercial shops and often got good prices. But some guys also ripped off bikes by rolling them into pickup trucks to strip them clean within a couple of hours. Some Angels had more parts stocked in their basements than Harley dealerships. Even I bought an entire garage full of hardware, including four engines stamped with the same serial numbers. This, of course, meant that at least three were hot. I even sold some parts to a San Francisco cop who didn't bother to ask questions.

The police unwittingly helped us make illegal bikes into legal ones in the following way: Some Angels would go to police auctions and pay cash for worn-out patrol Harleys. Then they would install serial-numbered parts from the police Harley "hog" in a stolen motorcycle of later vintage. The end product was a new motorcycle for the auction price. What could be better proof of ownership than a police bill of sale?[3]

It was even easier to register a stolen bike with the Department of Motor Vehicles, and plenty were registered. Back in the early days, we didn't even bother to take the serial numbers off very often, because police seldom checked them. You could do anything with the bike. The numbers could be ground off crudely, and you'd get away with it. Then you could just take this complete motorcycle—with a hot engine in it—to the DMV. "I just built this," you'd tell them, and they believed you. For the price of a ten-dollar registration fee, you were riding a new motorcycle.

Then they gradually changed the laws so you had to worry about the motors. Instead of grinding the numbers, some members drilling them out, filling the holes with weld, then stamping in new numbers. Then the DMV started confiscating bikes if they found the motor numbers had been drilled out.

The war of technology escalated, and they introduced laws saying the frame number had to jibe with the other numbers. If the bike had been tampered with in any way, they would confiscate it unless you had a bill of sale saying you bought the inconsistent part from a motorcycle shop. But we found ways around that too. You'd get a hot bike, break it up, then you'd take, for example, a broken engine case to the shop and buy a new one. The shop receipt was good enough for the DMV. We always stayed one step ahead.

On the infrequent occasions when our bikes vanished, the club launched search and destroy missions. The crime was comparable to horse theft in the Old West. One week, we raided every known hot bike outlet in Oakland looking for bikes stolen from Gypsy and Elvis. Finally, as we sifted through heaps of machinery at Willard G.'s garage, Gypsy spotted a muffler with a telltale scratch. A guy knows every inch of his bike, so there was no mistaking that the muffler came from an Angel machine. When Willard was confronted, he denied any stealing but offered immediate restitution. We put him out of business until he delivered two new bikes to the club.

Worse than a ripoff was that momentary loss of control at high speed that would send you grinding along the pavement. A lucky guy's skin would be peeled back; an unlucky one would end up in the hospital or the graveyard.

Surviving the destruction of your bike initiated you into an intraclub fraternity. No matter how many sweaty nightmares you wrestled with privately, your scars were badges of class, and you embellished the episode over beers with the brothers. But a decent Angel would be obsessed with getting his bike back together so he could screw on that throttle and punish speed itself for thinking it could destroy him.

Post-accident demeanor was pretty revealing, no matter how much was for show. Some guys were rip-snorting again before their bandages and casts were cut off. Picture Sonny popping through traffic with his head swathed and his broken jaw wired up. Or picture Skip after a crash-landing while mound hopping at Portuguese Flats on the bay shore:

The bike dragged him on his face for about a block and a half. He was twitching. The blood wasn't too bad, but the twitching got me. We could see he was trying to breathe, so Jerry scooped him up and dug mud out of his eyes and mouth. A couple of us ripped down a fence with our bare hands so the ambulance could get to him. Five hours later, Skip was hospitalized, hollering for his old fifty-cent Salvation Army Levi's, his boots and his motorcycle. He caused so much trouble that he was transferred to Oak Knoll Naval Hospital.

61

Even at Oak Knoll, I'd get the word, "Skip's doin' his thing with the Japs again." When I came to visit, he'd be crawling under beds commando style, thinking he was fighting the Japs. The hospital people didn't know what to make of this guy playing combat with his hospital gown and motorcycle boots on. I never questioned him about it at the time. I was afraid he might take me for Emperor Hirohito or somebody.

My worst wipeout was a fifty-mile-per-hour meeting with a truck on Foothill Boulevard. When I came to, half a block away, I was screaming about my twisted bike. "My fucking front wheel," I swore over and over as a crowd gathered and cops hefted me into the ambulance.

After several hours, doctors determined that my right side was absent of sensation—which I could have told them. "This is bullshit," I blustered. "I'm all right, and I'm going home." I grabbed my clothes, dressed and stormed out. I had a predawn breakfast with two girls and Tommy, who had just bought the bike I crashed. After chow, one of the girls drove me into the hills, helped me out of my pants, then did her best to help me forget my numb side.

V—Angels Wings or Baby Things?

The prospect of becoming a father confronted me with the contradictions between club and family. I put off making a choice although the time demands of the vice-presidency were hurting my wife. "The club is my business, not yours," I'd snap every time she asked me to quit. But she kept echoing my mother's admonitions that "the Hell's Angels is no place for a family man." The women couldn't understand that my self-esteem and my deepest friendships were bolted to my motorcycle. As a club leader, I never had to fantasize about being like James Dean or Marlon Brando. I was my own hell-raising, bike-riding hero.

Oddly enough, Helen wanted our firstborn to be a boy and I wanted a girl. She wanted our daughters to have an older protective brother like hers. "I determine the sex," I declared, recalling the chromosomes game from high school biology. "It takes more of a man to have a girl anyway. It takes more power to blow the nuts off." In fact, I bet club members over beers that my first nine would be Amazonian girls and the tenth would be a runty, bookwormy boy.

Early one morning, Helen scooted her belly against me, so I could feel the baby pummeling her ribs and share in the discomfort. Later, a contraction made her clutch her stomach. "I got pains seven minutes apart," she said shaking me awake.

A half hour later, I was ushered to her bedside in the labor room of tiny East Oakland Hospital. Each time pain tore a whimper from her, the nurses looked at me as if to say, "See what you caused? You dirty son of a bitch." My guilt was bothering me. I patted her frail and childish hand. She was sixteen and terrified.

"Tell me anything, tell me what you see out the window," she begged. "Talk to me." I described the sunrise as best I could, but her pain wrenched more cries out of her. She crushed my hand with superhuman power and bit my arm, like a wounded cowboy bites a bullet. That was too much for me, so I pried myself away.

In the hallway, I cornered the doctor and some nurses. "You give her something for that pain," I said. "Get in there and do something for her or I'll throw you motherfuckers out the window."

The doctor gave her a sedative called "twilight sleep." It left her in suspended animation, heaving violently now and then as though in a nightmare. She floated through three-hour sleeps, then reawakened in agony. I went after the doctor again: "Get in there and give her something. I ain't gonna take all this." More twilight sleep. More pain. More twilight sleep.

While she slept, I paced every inch of the hospital and warmed every waiting room seat at least once. Loitering with other prospective fathers depressed me—especially after one guy was presented a new son, worked a full day, then returned for an evening visit. I felt exhausted and lonely, although friends in the club—including J.B., Junior, Jerry and Betsy—shared the watch.

Then, just as I was thinking about working over that doctor, the baby made an appearance, nearly fifteen hours after we arrived at the hospital. It was a girl.

But before I could collect my bets, the doc took me aside. "There's a little problem," he whispered. "We understand you're Catholic, so you'd better get a priest." He explained that Helen's fifty-pound weight gain during pregnancy had cut her kidney efficiency and left the baby with toxemia poisoning. My daughter already was in an aquariumlike respirator.

I grabbed the bearer of bad tidings and rammed him into the wall. "If she's that bad off, what the hell're ya doin' out here?" I yelled. "Get back in there. Do something for her."

Firing up my swastika-covered 1949 Ford, I raced to nearby St. Elizabeth's Church and dragged a Franciscan friar out of bed. He must have felt like a kidnap victim. Dazed and half-dressed, he gripped the front seat as we skidded through corner after corner. "Don't worry, father," I shouted above the squealing wheels. "We'll get there." We did, and the priest administered an emergency baptism. And, after a week on the respirator, the baby pulled through.

With the baby, our family bond strengthened. I came home from work on time and lavished love on our daughter, though I avoided diapers and baby bottles. Helen was happy, thinking I'd finally settled down.

But a few weeks later, the baby's crying awakened her and she found me gone again. There she was, a teenager with her breasts full and tender, a sick baby in bed with her, and her old man out partying, probably with another woman.

After four nights, I came home and she balled me out. "No good, sucker. Who you been with?" she hissed when I came near her. I played innocent at first, then jokingly taunted her about her old rival, Judy. After that she rolled away whenever I attempted lovemaking.

My waywardness turned Helen's family against me again. She started visiting her mother every day and complaining, "George is never home anymore. I don't know what to do." One night her vengeful father waited for several hours outside our apartment, but I never showed. Another night he went berserk when I booted Helen in the backside, half-playfully, to hurry her home from a family dinner. "Nobody kicks my daughter," Charley screamed. He came at me like a windmill.

I contributed to the problem by calling Helen's relatives "dumb Okies" whenever they meddled in our affairs.

Our families first met during a party my mother threw to introduce our daughter, Donna. The party coincidentally would double as a farewell for my mother. She was dying of cancer.

As cake was cut and liquor flowed, I was actually worried about the impression my earthy in-laws would make on my family, but everybody mingled. Charley limped around, being sociable, and his wife hit it off with my mother. They had something in common—alcoholic husbands.

My mother had been given only months to live after unsuccessful stomach surgery for cancer. She refused hospitalization, believing the costs would ruin the family financially. She stayed home, cared for by my sister, as a University of California nursing student. My mother was brave. "Don't feel sorry for me," she used to tell us. "Just accept it like I have. I'm gonna die." The only time we saw her cry was at the thought of leaving my three-year-old brother. Two weeks after she selected her own coffin, she passed away.

The death sent the family into chaos but put my father on the wagon. The thought of supporting and raising three small boys, one a toddler, was sobering. He hired a black domestic, and later remarried.

The loss of my mother left me with regrets and altered my priorities. I cried at the funeral Mass and was depressed for weeks. The motorcycle club lost its magnetism. Repetitive meetings and runs lost their thrill. Bikes were going out of vogue and buttoned-down Ivy League collars were coming in. Club popularity was declining, and it seemed only a matter of time before membership would slack off.

Also, my forty-nine-dollar-a-week salary was stretched too thin by dues, booze, cycle repairs and gas, plus more than $1,000 a year in traffic fines. I stopped enjoying all-night card games where I raised rent money blown on club activities. And, after a day's work, I preferred to be home with Helen and the baby rather than hustling to the same dowdy bars and women night after night. A number of Angels, particularly Sonny and Jerry, tried to dissuade me—but I finally turned in my colors.

We moved into a one-bedroom triplex apartment two blocks away from our old home. My brother-in-law lived in an apartment just to the rear. I bought a $3,000 life insurance policy and furniture on time. We ate better and saved a few bucks.

Since I seemed to be behaving myself, we were invited to spend a weekend with Helen's Aunt Pearl and Uncle Adam. Restful as its overgrown St. Helena River banks, their ranch meandered across seventy acres of Northern California wine country. Just above the house was a hillside of bleached-out grass. Below it, thick oaks shaded the river and supported a cool tree house where everyone nursed cold bottles of home-brewed beer—or my Ripple wine. From there, Adam could get clear shots at deer and rabbits lured into the vegetable garden. Everyone got a little high and a little lazy watching the waters flow into the nearby trout ponds.

One weekend led to the next, and I learned to understand and appreciate my in-laws for their wide-open hearts and dammit-let's-have-fun style. Charley was nearly shot beating the brush for deer at the local dump. Adam created a local fire emergency when he tried to smoke the rattlesnakes out of the berry patch. Pearl chased me around the potbellied stove, tipsy and making advances, while Helen's mother was hot on her heels, trying to stop her.

Their craziness kept us laughing, and we started to love that peaceful feeling of "country." "Wouldn't it be neat to have something like this?" Helen would muse as we wandered over the hills. I'd nod, then we would imagine out loud how our house and land someday would be.

When the baby could toddle, Helen decided to contribute some income toward our dream. The Montgomery Ward mail order department hired her as an order filler. After two months of hating the job, she got a complaint about her speed and became convinced it was a quit-or-be-fired situation. She resigned, saying she was pregnant again. She felt guilty when co-workers threw her a going away party and showered her with gifts for the "baby."

Coincidentally, she did become pregnant a short time later and gave birth to our son in late 1962. To have more room, we moved to an old house on Taylor Street in a predominantly white, middle-class area near Knowland Park and Zoo. A fenced yard with a big pine convinced us it was worth $100 monthly rent. It would be perfect for the children.

Meanwhile, life soured for our friends Betsy and Jerry. After I dropped out of the club, Jerry started to pal around with unmarried bikers who partied constantly and slept where they dropped. His work record was as sporadic as his home life, so he was fired. He drifted around and mixed liquor with commercial cough syrups. Finally, Betsy got fed up and they separated.

On April 4, 1961—just after his daughter was born and he talked about reconciliation—Jerry raced a freight train to the 29th Avenue crossing, and lost. His bike hit the second car back. He was drunk when he died twenty minutes later of a crushed chest and trauma. He was twenty-one.[4]

The Angel who died on the skids wasn't the friend who had ridden and caroused with me, so I bypassed the funeral. But we did help Betsy get back on her feet after Jerry's death and the accidental poisoning of one of their daughters a few months later. We played Cupid, arranging dates with Paul, the honorary Angel who was in the Coast Guard.

Betsy, big-boned and flamboyant, and Paul, a burly but reticent mechanical wizard, were married and became our closest friends. Over the next few years, we went picnicking and canoeing at Clear Lake, tobogganing in the High Sierra. We periodically attended Angels dances together, but all of us were drifting from the club lifestyle.

Nonetheless, Paul and I kept tabs on the club through old friendships, chance encounters and our jobs. Paul worked at a candy company with a number of bikers. And I ran into bikers on construction jobs. Everything I heard convinced me the club had no future. The statewide membership, which had reached about 250 in 1960, was well on its way to a four-year decline that would reduce that number by two-thirds.[5]

VI—The Road Back

"To a biker, being an Angel is like God. Not being an Angel means you live in fear of God. "—A biker who never made the grade.

My work took me to every corner of the San Francisco Bay area—from slapped-up East Bay suburbs to San Francisco skyscrapers. The diverse work challenged me and provided a grounding in several construction trades, including carpentry.

One of the major attractions of the trades was crew companionship. It was a little like Angels camaraderie, although my co-workers would huddle around scrapwood bonfires on cold mornings and razz me about the club. I wore a flat-brimmed Churchill cowboy hat and a beard instead of a hardhat and Old Spice, but I got along with most guys because I could do the job. In fact, I could carry twice as much sheetrock as most of them. My main shortcoming was my 260 pounds: I snapped so many planks that nobody wanted to work on scaffolding with me.

After my four-year apprenticeship, the gnarled, fingers-missing old lathers treated me as an equal. And, as my position solidified, work became less important to me than construction site recreation and union politics. I agitated for longer coffee breaks and shorter hours. Sometimes I usurped the foreman's power and ended up running jobs myself.

Over the years, our crew refined various shortcuts so we could do a day's work in several hours. This freed the afternoon for loafing.

Some guys played war, shooting nails through blowguns of copper tubing and breaking a few windows by accident. The practical jokers nailed lunchboxes to the ceiling and toolboxes to the floor.

Our gamesmanship reached its zenith on a highrise overlooking the Golden Gate. We wagered on the ponies en route to the job, then slapped up walls for an hour or two before calling it quits. Then we'd straddle the girders for a while, using opera glasses to scan rooftops and windows for exposed females. "She ain't got a stitch on," you'd hear somebody yell, then there'd be a mad scramble to that part of the building. But most of my time was spent in a poker shack we built to protect ourselves from the wind.

For the first time, I started socializing with work buddies, particularly John J. We developed a hobby together , working with various crafts in his backyard. Ashtrays and book-ends were standard hobby shop fare, but we advanced the art a bit, using seashells, driftwood and rocks.

After about $1,000 worth of experimentation, we were putting our wildest fantasies and ideas into saleable products. A few creations were peddled to friends to make room for more. The breakthrough came when I built a round table with a red, black and white swastika, a sure sale to a club member. But it first caught the eye of one of John's neighbors. The guy kicked in $2,000, and within a month, John and I opened a store at 38th and Foothill Boulevard.

While we raised a family and dabbled in capitalism, the Angels' image was reawakened after a few dormant years. More than any other event, the Labor Day weekend run to Monterey on September 6, 1964, was responsible. About forty-six members were taken into custody after two teen-aged girls said they were gang raped in sand dunes there. Four were charged—Terry, Marvin, Mother Miles and Crazy Cross. Although all charges later were scratched for insufficient evidence, outraged legislators demanded and got a state investigation of the club.[6]

The incident resurrected the old question: "What are the Hell's Angels really like?" It also gave the guys unprecedented news media access, and they ate it up.

"We're just a bunch of guys who like to be together, like the Masons or any other group," Tiny, a 6-foot-6 bearded giant, told reporters. "We just like to ride motorcycles."

And Tommy told the media, "The Attorney General wants to ban our club, but they will not break us up. We might drop into a hole, but we'll be back."

The club did drop into a hole for nearly a year. Admitted law enforcement harassment forced the Sacramento chapter led by Mother Miles to dissolve in May, 1965, and statewide membership rolls sagged to about eighty-five. But the club came back along an entirely unexpected route. The Angels were adopted by Northern California bohemia as coarse allies against the Establishment. Mutual curiosity contributed to the alliance, but both groups shared a free-spirited approach to life and a taste for drugs. Maybe Hell's Angels-style tripping dropped them in less intellectual and more violent places, but the bikers and the beatniks thought they were on the same rainbow, unclouded by phoniness.

On the weekend of August 7, 1965, a few Angels invited

me on a coast run to meet their new "friends." Riding a
bike borrowed from a buddy in the Gypsy Jokers, I joined
about fifty guys for the hour cruise south on Highway 1. We
all looked our rankest best, meanness plastered on our
faces, long hair and colors billowing in the wind. I'd all but
forgotten the thrill of being part of that rolling thunder-
head.

The entourage turned inland, entered spires of redwoods
near La Honda, then slowed at a twelve-foot banner that
said, "The Merry Pranksters Welcome the Hell's Angels."
Our gleaming bikes muted by the trees, we bucked to a
halt, surrounded by friendly yet freaky folks. They were
raggy, sandaled or barefooted, some half-naked and smeared
with dayglo paint.

The welcome took us aback for a moment, because we
seldom were received so graciously and fearlessly by non-
bikers. We were introduced informally and got high. Sonny
and the proprietor, the writer Ken Kesey, found each other
and exchanged greetings.[7]

The Pranksters used face paint and nicknames in our best
Halloween tradition. Handles like June the Goon, Mountain Girl and Hermit gave us something to guffaw about
while they checked out Buzzard, Baby Huey, Terry the
Tramp and Tiny, trying to figure out how the name fit the
man. Everyone was in costume and assigned a role, even
their holy men—poet Allen Ginsberg and LSD guru Dr.
Richard Alpert.

Almost before my machine was shut down, I began to
wonder what I was doing there without colors, wedged with
only a half-identity between the Angels and the Kesey me-
nagerie. Veteran Angels knew me, but I treaded carefully
around the tyros. Under the club code, even recent initiates
ranked higher than retired vice-presidents. If push came to
shove, I might be allowed an ungraceful exit, but more likely I'd have to stand dangerous ground.

Wandering through the redwoods, I unlimbered my legs

and sucked a marijuana stogie. Weed hadn't done much for me when I smoked it with construction buddies, but this time I was agog. Eerie sounds slithered out of speakers mounted in trees and on a cliff. The Pranksters' so-called radio station KLSD broadcast music, local news and commentary from whoever grabbed the microphone. One voice—I think it was Tramp—goaded San Mateo County sheriff's deputies hiding in a brushy creek bordering the property: "Mr. Sheriff! Who's home creeping between your old lady's legs while you're creepin' 'round the creek?" Then raucous laughter. The Kesey place seemed impenetrable.

As Pranksters took some guys on cerebral tours to places called LSD and DMT, I tripped through the structures: the main cabin crammed with sound equipment, cameras and other tools of the Kesey media freaks; the tree houses; a tepee; and a cave owned by Hermit, a bare-chested, wild child reputed to chase down deer and kill them with his knife. The cave, dug out of a gullyside, had elaborate occupancy rules. If the pink and green golf ball was in the tin can outside, anyone could take the ball and enter, assured of privacy for sex or hallucinations. An empty can meant an occupied cave.

The rest of the place was wide open. Some members were blown away by it. Angels were tripping through the forest like kids, nibbling from a drug buffet, sampling spacey ideas that came from books and these aliens. "This is the goddamned most wonderful scene," one guy said, with rapture.

In turn, the members let the hipsters finger their bikerotica—passing around chains, swastika earrings, medallions and chromed Nazi helmets. "Far out," the Pranksters said. It was all down to earth, asses in the forest humus, backs against trees and buildings, heads in the clouds. Some Angels were nearly catatonic, but most accepted the attention of the Pranksters, who pranced and flitted around like court jesters, lightweights delighted with the company of heavyweights. The heavyweights were content to lie back and take what was offered. There was no pressure, nobody's cool to test, no hard barriers in that kind of anarchy. The Angels enjoyed and bantered, taking as much as they gave but not caring.

As the day waned, I fraternized with the nature freak faction. Hermit gave me some crayfish, and I handed some licorice to Ginsberg. "Tonight you will fly," he said, but I stayed clear of his flowing robes and exalted eyes. I never liked those guru types from the San Francisco-Berkeley coffeehouse scene. Mountain Girl was more my style. She was a barefoot nymph with a sunshiny smile. I wouldn't have minded a little romp with her, but she offered me LSD. I turned it down, because grass, uppers and alcohol already had me flying.

The scene went beyond weirdness. Former Angel or not, I was a relatively straight construction worker among strangers on strange drugs. It put me uptight. Their behavior was one thing, but their talk of love and peace, universal this and that, their verbalization of everything—that seemed about as profound as a warmed-over fart.

In the main building, a Bob Dylan recording whined "Baby Blue" but it sounded like "Baby Huey." And I felt an old surge of righteous indignation when some guy slighted the club with a snide comment. Along with John T. "Terry the Tramp" Tracey and a few other members, I helped stand the guilty party on a chair and tie him up with a hangman's noose snug around his neck. When the rope was strung over a beam, we skinned him with threats and took turns kicking at the chair. After he toppled once, we boosted him onto a table where he'd have a more sporting chance, yet a longer fall. Tramp, who wore blind man's sunglasses in a jungle of hair and whiskers, got so bored that he ate a spider off the floor. I couldn't handle it, so I went outside.

Nightfall's activities shifted to campfires. Uneven light

shimmered through branches hung with mobiles, hunks of junk and effigies. While a handful of members kept some broad humping, I sat with others, warming my hands and watching some couples dancing. Then the stench of burnt hair smacked my nostrils: Hermit had tossed the main course directly into the flames. The 'possum's eyes whited and bugged out, and hair singed back to its ratty tail. Unappetizing as it was, Angels and Pranksters—the non-vegetarians—tore off steaming flesh and wolfed it, watching each other, licking their fingers and grinning.

After turning down chow and acid, I settled into a rock. I opened my eyes to sunshine and the sight of Kesey's woman and a child padding naked toward the creek. Members were up and about, but not one made a move toward her. It amazed me. I felt as outdated as my old leather Harley hat.

The club and its new "friends" fell out temporarily over the Vietnam war. We equated antiwar sentiment with weakness, cowardice, effeminateness and un-Americanism. "Our oath is allegiance to the United States of America," Sonny once proclaimed. "If there should be trouble, we would jump to enlist and fight. More than ninety percent of our members are veterans. We don't want no slackers." As the antiwar movement spread, Sonny wrote President Johnson volunteering the club for "gorilla" (sic) duty in Vietnam. In other words, hipster drugs and women were cool, but hipster politics were not.

On October 5, 1965, less than three months after the Kesey bash, Sonny gathered the club as 1,700 antidraft protesters marched from the University of California in Berkeley toward the Army's Oakland Induction Center. The cops herded the Angels behind their own lines. "We oughta turn over their wagon and get that commie flag," Sonny said, then the guys bought some soda pop so they'd have some bottles as bludgeons. Shouting "chicken shit Communists," the Angels slipped through police lines with surpris-

ing ease.[8] They wrested a banner from leaders of the Vietnam Day Committee, then ran roughshod over the protesters, a sixteen-man juggernaut of bottles, chains and boots.
Hundreds of marchers were scattered and some were beaten
along Telegraph Avenue before the cops arrested six Angels
and drove the rest away. Charges against all but Tiny were
dropped almost immediately. Tiny, a collection agent by
trade, was accused of breaking a cop's leg with a pop bottle.
(He later would plead to a lesser charge of malicious mis-
chief and would be fined $56.)

The attack was motivated by the club's hardhat mentality and a sense of patriotism. It alienated beatnik friends
but proved the club's finest public relations move. Many
people considered it the first positive thing the club had
done since Frisco members started helping stranded motorists and leaving Lone Ranger-style business cards: "You
have been assisted by a member of the Hell's Angels." Conservative columnists praised the club for teaching the peace
creeps a lesson. And a local director of the Republicans for
Conservative Action, Fred Ullner of San Rafael, formed an
unsanctioned group called Friends of the Hell's Angels[9]. It
raised $4,400 bail for Tiny and reportedly pledged further
support for the club's patriotic activities.

Like most club associates and the general public, Helen
and I regarded protesters as pinko draft dodgers and "com-
mie-Jew-beatniks" like VDC leader Jerry Rubin. Not our
kind of people. We got a kick out of hearing Sonny, Tiny,
Jimmy Hewitt and other members recount the brawl and
wave around their newspaper clips.

The implications hit closer to home one day when two
men in business suits walked into the plastics shop. These
friendly guys with Southern twangs introduced themselves
as members of the American Taxpayers Union, a mysterious group with a storefront down the street.[10]

We talked over a drink at Zella and Augie's Townehouse,
a bar next door. They heaped praise on the club for dis-

patching the marchers in such classy fashion and suggested that other "patriotic actions" would be needed to protect national security. "Our organization believes, among other things, that every American should possess three guns," one whispered. "One at home and two concealed in the country." After a spiel about the dangers of an unarmed citizenry in the face of domestic subversion, they came to the point. "We're here to offer the Hell's Angels any money or legal assistance you might need, or any of this," the second guy drawled softly, spilling a handful of .45-caliber cartridges on the bar.

"Wait a minute," I balked. "You wanna talk to somebody else. I'll see if I can refer you to somebody." As a retiree, I was in no position to speak for the club—so I borrowed a dime and telephoned Sonny. I called one of the men to the phone. Sonny was interested enough to set up a meeting.

Word was that the offer never panned out. Yet Sonny later announced that the club would counterdemonstrate wherever antiwar forces gathered. He even addressed a high school class in suburban Marin County wearing a Birchers' "Support Your Local Police" button. "I don't claim to be a good example to the American public," he told an American government class. "But we're not as bad as the papers make us out to be.[11]

"Some of those people in Berkeley mean well," he added. "But most of them don't know why they're demonstrating."

In spite of Sonny's public stance, events preceding a big peace march scheduled for November 20, 1965, unmasked the club's strongest allegiance—to money. First, he repudiated the Friends of the Hell's Angels for allegedly welshing on promises of funds. Second, the club agreed to parley with march organizers.

In a session at San Jose State College, Ginsberg whined: "We have fears the Hell's Angels will attack us, and we wonder why. We wonder whether they are doing it for kicks, publicity or to take the heat off themselves, to win the goodwill of the Oakland police and press, or for right wing money." The club's immediate response hardly was encouraging. "I got my guts shot out in Okinawa and Korea," said Louie from Sacramento. "If Uncle Sam wants me again, I'm ready to go. I got a lot of respect for Uncle Sam and for my mother and my brothers and sisters and for my own two little kids. If I catch my two little kids marching, I'll break their heads in."[12]

A different tempo marked a follow-up meeting at Sonny's house. Club members, Ginsberg and Kesey dropped LSD. Backgrounded by lilting Joan Baez records, they chanted Buddhist prayers, of all things. Then, after reaffirming cosmic tranquility, they discussed politics and agreed somehow to avert a slaughter on earth.

News media already were geared up for riot coverage, but on the day prior to the demonstration, Sonny assembled reporters. "Although we have stated our intention to counterdemonstrate at this despicable un-American activity," he sneered, "we believe that in the interest of public safety and protection of the good name of Oakland, we should not justify the VDC by our presence."[13]

The reversal was greeted in various quarters with mirth, disappointment, relief—and always surprise. But it was obviously induced by the profit motive. People close to the club knew many members were genuinely prowar in principle, but fondness for drugs and money outweighed principles in this case. Many of the club's best drug culture and business contacts openly, or at least ideologically, opposed the war. Besides, who would want to do business with neo-facists who got their jollies cracking heads of peaceniks? Clearly, Sonny's retreat was the only sensible and profitable tactic, no matter how embarrassing.

VII—The Lure

For several years, I had popped prescription amphetamines, to check my weight, to get to work on time, to
flaunt my capacity for self-destruction—and more recently
to get pleasurably high. I graduated from benzedrine and
dexedrine to methamphetamimes. With "crank" or
"speed" my mind turned with the power of a full-steaming
locomotive.

Helen was alarmed by my drug use. She even associated
marijuana with *Reefer Madness*-type films from the 1950s.
"If you wanna use thatTMS* stuff, I don't want you to do it
around the kids at home," she railed. "Do it somewhere
else!"

I did exactly that. LSD—the little-known chemical I'd resisted at Kesey's place—went down smoothly at the pleasant Castro Valley home of my friend Kooie, a window
washer. Aided by his elaborate music system, I floated in
and out of the lush backyard and took long journeys to
Psychedelia—and explored some females along the way.

My trip guides were friends like Tramp, who knew the terrain.

Marijuana was lost smoke compared to the capsulated miracles of LSD. Every trip orbited me beyond known experience. The universe exploded from light on a wet leaf. Sex was concentric orgasms and runaway laughter, the merging of holiness and depravity, pleasure and pain. Thoughts cataracted like Niagara Falls. The speed and force defied my senses.

The trouble started when I left the house and was forced to deal with the real world. On a trip to the dentist, J. B. and I were acid-tripping and rear-ended a car. Then, when the dentist had trouble reaching a rotten tooth, I told him, "Pull out the one in front of it to make room." I even grabbed the pliers to help him yank out a perfectly good tooth.

Another day, a double dose of acid rocketed me to a totem pole outside an antique shop. I must have been there for hours studying the tortured figures, cracked paint and wood grain.

"Where are you going?" a voice thundered.

"I'm going home," I said, vaguely conscious of a deputy sheriff in gray.

Instead of driving me home, the deputy took me to the city limits and pointed me away. I ambled to the Ness Electric Company in nearby San Leandro and stopped again, totally absorbed by light shooting and bending among dozens of glass, crystal and metal fixtures. Then I was clutching a chain link fence watching a misty rain dapple a swimming pool.

"What are you doing?" boomed a sea god's voice.

"I'm watching rain hit the water," I said meekly, holding my gaze.

Two men in blue checked my identification then drove me home. When one told the other, "Better let him out," I realized the glass and iron mesh cage was locked. From the *outside!* Claustrophobia! Just as I brought my feet up to start kicking out the windows, the door swung open. "Go home," a cop said, pointing. "Stay off the streets."

My eyes felt like whirligigs when I finally groped through the front door. Helen turned from the TV. "My God! Whatsa matter with you, George?"

"I think I took some acid."

In a while, my eyes were pulsing to silver dollar size, and shards of images pierced my brain. I screamed, collapsed and cried in my fists. "You gotta get me help or I'm leaving."

It was 3 A.M. She telephoned Tiny. "You gotta help George. He's on a bummer trip. He took acid. I don't know what to do."

Within ten minutes, Tiny walked in, wiping sleep from his eyes and straightening his clothes. He rolled onto the couch and listened to Helen's account while I blubbered incoherently in a chair. After a few minutes, I recognized my rescuer. "Hi. Hiya, Tiny. Man, am I glad to see ya."

"Howdy, George." Tiny, one of the biggest, baddest, bushiest Angels, kicked away his shoes. "I been there before. Tell me about it, George. Whatsa matter?" Resting one elbow, he probed, steering me to the good parts of my trip. My boundless fear and isolation drained away.

When I told him about the police encounters, he brayed, and I joined in that overamped Angels laughter. "Haw, haw haaugh!" The worst was over.

Tiny then stuffed me with peanut butter and jelly sandwiches until the floor was littered with bread wrappers and empty jars. We were just about to start looking for an all-night store when Skip showed up offering help and candy Life Savers. "George, lemme throw ya a Life Saver," he said speaking literally and figuratively.

Friends from the club were a great comfort. The episode made a believer of Helen too. Angels really did treat one another as brothers. They cared enough to help their own twenty-four hours a day, not just during runs, fights and parties with status at stake. The motto "Angels forever, forever Angels" was not just talk.

Helen's attitude toward drugs gradually softened too. She always had allied herself mentally with respectable citizens, but she wanted my companionship more. Realizing that I was gallavanting with women who didn't share her antidrug scruples, she chirped one day, "Hey, George. How 'bout gettin' me some grass? I wanna try it."

Pleased by her turnabout, I scored a fresh ounce, then took her to Kooie's place for her maiden voyage. Some people from the club were there too. As the room swam with music, I instructed her: "Don't do it like a cigarette. Suck in the air along with the smoke. Take it down deep."

The sugar-cured grass burnt her throat. "Shit, George. I'm gonna choke to death."

"You gotta hold it. Get it down deep."

On the first two passes, she felt nothing. But after the third hit, she shut her eyes—and I could see she was opening her mind, floating on the sound streams. Before she drifted too far, she looked around to make sure the Beatles hadn't driven a sound truck through the door.

Our drug experience added a dimension to our marriage. We got stoned at home and in the hills, playing, tripping and freaking out on sex. To Helen, the only negative aspect of drugs was my drift toward the club. I regularly bought "lids" of weed from Sonny and broke them down into five-dollar match boxes, making a few bucks and keeping some smoke for myself. Motorcycles recaptured my fancy too. I bought a fast, stripped down Harley KR that Tommy, a compact gutsy Angel, rode to a track victory for me.

The bike also started Helen thinking about the excitement of riding stoned. "George, why don't you take me for a ride on that thing?"

"I'll never ride again without a patch," I said pointedly. "You need that patch to really be doin' it."

That set her off. "Well," she huffed. "If you ever put that patch on again, I'm leaving. I don't want you back in. That's no place for a married man with kids. It's for guys footloose and fancy free. It's club first and family second to the Angels, and you know it."

Not having a patch didn't stop me from riding, bar hopping and fighting alongside the Angels by 1965. The statewide membership had dwindled, and Sonny was calling on me with increasing frequency for advice and help in fighting blacks. The racial climate was so hot that I started toting a shotgun to work every day. And that summer, I helped the club stand guard on the roof of the El Adobe, a club hangout where the ultimate race war was scheduled. About the only action was an old black guy running down the street after he looked up and saw Tramp leveling a rifle.

We felt we'd intimidated the blacks. But, on the night of November 6, Sonny and I were jumped by a carload of them as we left the Auseon Club. I suppose they figured it was a golden opportunity to wail on a couple of isolated bikers. But after a couple of dozen punches, we were standing our ground, operating a two-man disassembly line. One by one, I bearhugged them while Sonny conked them with a heavy padlock and chain.

We did okay until blacks poured out of the buildings like cockroaches in a fire. Badly outnumbered, we yelled for Tiny, who was bent over barbecued ribs in a soul restaurant. After polishing off a few more bones, he and a couple of other members stormed out, with table legs and bar stools for insurance. We cleaned house until the neighborhood caved in on us. There must have been a hundred blacks. Sonny shouted, "Let's get outa here. Retreat." We escaped in good shape, leaving behind a busted up car in the middle of the street and a litter of dazed and bleeding blacks, one with Tiny's Phillips screwdriver sticking in him.

That screwdriver thing tickled the hell out of us, but we expected retaliation. Tramp's house at 1051 82nd Avenue, in a black area, was a likely target. So we set up sandbag barricades on the roof and waited confidently with shotguns, carbines and rifles. When we figured the coast was clear, we went back to the soul food. I guess they were waiting for us to leave, because Tramp's place was firebombed a few minutes later. The house was gutted to the tune of $7,500, and Colby, Tramp's German Shepherd, was killed.

My road back to the club was steamrolled by my old friendship with Sonny and my new business relationship with Tramp, a native of Michigan who transferred to Oakland from the disbanded Sacramento chapter. Tramp arrived flat broke, with only a couple of boxes of motorcycle parts and a rap sheet nearly as long as he was—over six feet.[14] I befriended him, providing transportation and capital to establish a drug business. The two of us cruised the Bay Area peddling premium South American and Asian marijuana and a little LSD scored through Tramp's social contacts in the hip community, particularly the rock music scene. That would be Tramp's major contribution to the club: he was more of a hippie than most. His main man was Augustus Owsley Stanley III, a cocky little LSD chemist the club ran into at Kesey's place and rock concerts.

At first, we were nickeling and diming, and our account books contained notations like, "L. R. owes 67 cents." But within a few months, as I turned on fellow construction workers and friends, business burgeoned from ounces to kilos of marijuana, and from dozens of hits of acid to thousands. Something was happening. We weren't sure what it was, but we were in at the ground floor.

Members urged me to rejoin the club to tighten the dealing circle. They evidently thought I was a valuable and experienced salesmen, with certain natural assets. From my standpoint, the patch could become a valuable lever in conducting business safely and a ticket to big bucks.

In early 1966, Tramp submitted my name for readmission during a meeting at Tommy's house. With few preliminaries and no debate, I was voted back in and dubbed "Fat George." As a courtesy, initiation was waived. A proven member was back in the fold. I was twenty-five, five years wiser and fifty pounds heavier. There was a solid chance to move up in the club ranks, and I knew it.

After the meeting, we rumbled to a club dance at Erwin-Taylor Memorial Hall on East 14th Street. Inside, hundreds of bikers and hangers-on—looking good, cooking and greasing their brains with beer and pills—were dancing and rapping. Shouldering through there, I knew I was on top again. As we used to say, "There are only Angels and people who wish they were Angels."

Helen was chatting with J. B. and Irma near the refreshment stand when we arrived. "Zorro" sidled up to her with a fistful of papers and exclaimed, "Hey, look at these!"

She unfolded and few and each carried the word, "Yes." "What's it mean?" she asked just as I joined them. Z. spun me around and laughed.

Practically slapped in the face with my new death's head, Helen stomped away. Until then, she had no inkling I was rejoining.

Embarrassed, I overtook her and pinned her against the wall. "What is this shit?" I growled.

"Let go of me," she sobbed. "I told you I didn't want you back in. Why did you do it?"

My hands crushed her shoulder blades as she tried to squirm away, and I commanded her through my teeth, "I told you the club was my business. Now, enough!"

VIII—Marketing the Death's Head

"When George was in the club, there was always something to do. When out, he was dissatisfied and bored. There was only going to apprentice school, coming home, watching TV, getting drunk on his Ripple. It wasn't very exciting to him"—Helen Wethern.

The Angels had a kind of class, an uncouth polish, no matter how disheveled we looked in our complete array of colors and garb. At the same time, we could be incredibly individualistic yet as tight as blood brothers.

Helen never saw those qualities, so matters would have been bad enough if we'd just remained a bunch of overagressive ruffians. But the club quickly became more than a hobby.

One day Sonny phoned her and asked her to tell me a Southern California Angel wanted to score $600 worth of LSD. She drove to my Berkeley job site and relayed the message. Without a second thought, I threw down my tool belt and called to my foreman, "I gotta go now. Something important came up."

The sale turned out to be a one-shot deal, but at least it was bigger than the $50 and $100 deals I'd been hustling. And, a few days later, three unlikely looking characters approached me at a 23rd Avenue gas station. Solely on the basis of my colors, they asked, "Can ya get us some acid?" The death's head meant a number of things: the man wearing it was not a cop, because the club never had been infiltrated; and the man wearing it could get drugs, because the club was known to have some of the best sources in the Bay Area. The only risk involved was failing to get paid-for goods.

Chuck, a modish, rusty-haired guy, said two Angels, Okie and Spesh, had burned them for $5,000 just a few days before. That made me suspicious, so I looked them over closely.

Chuck seemed to be the leader but he did a bad job of hiding a genteel East Coast background behind bebop talk. He was about twenty-seven with a well-scrubbed, pasty face of faded freckles. Despite an aloof air, the more he said, the more eager he seemed to get some drugs. The others stood by—Chuckles was a genuinely mellow longhair and Steve gawked with the wayward eyes of a maturing runaway. None was a heavy. They simply wanted to buy a piece of action from the outfit with the muscle to control it.

"I'll look into it," I said cautiously. "Gimme your phone number."

After querying Tramp, I told the trio to bring $5,000 to his vacant house. As we got stoned, I explained the transaction: I would take the money, then would return with several thousand hits of Owsley acid. They looked to each other and shook their heads. They wanted to make it COD, but I insisted on advance payment. Tramp and I didn't have the capital to make the buy.

For hours, I argued, cajoled and pleaded with those guys. I explained and reexplained that I was interested in building a business and wanted honest relationships with reliable dealers. "I'd be cutting my own throat if I burned you," I argued.

Finally, Chuck conceded, "Okay. We know we're vulnerable, but we'll take the chance. You can get the stuff, and we need it."

"Trust me," I said grabbing the bills. "Wait here until I get back."

With helpless and hopeful expressions, they watched me go out that door. They fully expected to be left waiting forever.

Of course, a hitch developed. The $5,000 was part of a larger deal involving several transactions—and Tramp was having a hell of a time collecting the balance.

"Ya think ya can get more from your guys?" he asked me.

"Oh, man," I groaned. "I just spent the better part of a day convincing these people they're not gonna get burnt—and now I gotta go back and ask for *more* money?"

My buyers weren't overjoyed but they passed me another $3,000 front money. And their faith was rewarded several hours later with about 8,000 hits of quality LSD that would retail for three to five dollars a tab. They didn't even object when I pocketed a few hundred hits for myself. There was plenty of profit for everybody. In fact, they likely would have paid $8,000 for half as much LSD—if it was Owsley's. Tears in their eyes, they wrung my hand while a chick with them smooched and hugged me. An honest connection!

Visions of rainbow rides and pots of greenbacks in their heads, they popped a sample then carted their chemical treasure across the bay to the Haight-Ashbury.

The Haight was rapidly becoming more than just another San Francisco neighborhood. In the 1960s, bohemians— driven from the Grant Avenue North Beach scene by police and tourists—had packed into Victorian houses at the eastern end of Golden Gate Park. By 1966, the middle-class Haight Street shopping area was transformed into a walking circus. People talked about being themselves, but their costume was an hotchpotch of Indian, cowboy and vintage Salvation Army. They strolled in granny dresses, bright blankets, sandals, boots, bare feet, headbands, Stetsons, beads, wide belts, fringe, braids and all manner of imported and improvised garments. They passed one another with smiles and nods like small-town folk, pausing at "head shops" where each week of the Awakening brought new and more exotic roach holders, hash pipes, hookas, posters, leathers, incenses and glass and plastic liquid-filled things that did nothing but bedazzle a stoner. To the music of cash registers, flutes, harmonicas, guitars and idling cars, enterprising doorway denizens sang the mantra, "Acid, grass, hash, acid grass hash." Money, wine jugs, pills, trinkets and funny finger-rolled cigarettes were changing hands everywhere. And along with the sweet and illegal smells was a magic that made people call strangers "brother" or "sister."

Not everybody believed in the magic, but thousands made pilgrimages to the Haight to see for themselves. High school students hopped Muni buses for the short ride across town. Collegians showed on weekends. Runaways, dropouts and drifters poured into the street, hoping that the songs about flowers, love and warm San Francisco nights were true. The most idealistic—the ones searching for a place where work and pleasure were indistinguishable, pain and victimization nonexistent and sex and love freely extended—largely were disappointed. The ones satisfied hustling food and floor space found they could survive.

The community's rough institutional framework consisted of entities such as the *Oracle* newspaper, the Haight-Ashbury Free Medical Clinic, the Haight Independent Proprietors (HIP) and the charitable Diggers, who provided crash pads and food such as garbage can stews and coffee can bread. And, like churchgoers, the community assembled in the Panhandle's cathedrals of eucalyptus or the park's grassy corridors for free concerts by the Jefferson Airplane, Grateful Dead and other local bands who played their music from flatbed trucks. There was a spirit of enlightenment, and the electricity went beyond the music.

The club's role in the flowers-forever, God-and-country-be-damned Haight was enigmatic. Why would the club—the reputed disciples of violence and swastika-flaunting attackers of peace marchers—cosponsor the "World's First Human Be-In" along with Ginsberg, LSD high priest Tim Leary, the Diggers and others dedicated to the communion of mankind?

The Angels who addressed that musical feast for 20,000 white middle-class flower revolutionaries portrayed themselves as victims of society's prejudices. But what would be the club's posture during the "Summer of Love" later that year when it was predicted that five times that many would migrate to the Haight?

While a few members, particularly the more hip Frisco bunch, genuinely would sympathize with the hippie movement, the majority of Angels simply would exploit it, just as Ken Kesey and the drug chemists would exploit us. The wishful thinkers assigned us a role as protectors of the flower people. We were supposed to be the counter-society's police force, a benevolent gestapo which would, by our heavy presence, discourage alley-seasoned thugs from preying on the gentle people. We were also seen as longtime foes of Mainstream America, loners who banded with other loners. Those people had no idea what we were about.

In truth, we had plied the hustlers' trade from the start. We went on treasure hunts to the Haight, plundering clothes, furniture, drugs and women. Usually guys used subtle muscle or crude finesse, the choice of tactic determined by the individual's personality and the circumstances. Zorro and Okie were two of the best.

Zorro, a slender 6-foot-1, was a pool hustler as a kid. His

home was broken by divorce when he was two, so he was raised in Catholic schools by his grandmother and mother. He was pretty much on his own at thirteen and got street-wise pretty fast. He was Brazilian, although he hung out at pool halls with a lot of blacks. His arrest record dated back to a 1957 auto theft, but he also was busted for a few minor offenses. His marriage ended in 1962 after two years and two children, and he drifted into the club. Never really a tough guy, he built his reputation as a con man. He bragged about making $23,000 in one year by putting his motorcy-cle up for sale, collecting deposits or actual sales money, then keeping the machine. The club was his sanctuary.

"Okie," 5-71/2 and 140 pounds, was another from an un-happy home. As a youngster, he was put aboard race horses in Tulsa, Oklahoma, and when he lost, his father would beat him. "My father was always down on me for some-thing," he once wrote a probation officer. "I didn't do much other than race and fight. My people don't want me around most of the time. I slept on the doorstep many nights when my father had company or things like that." He attended Oklahoma Reform School for car theft from 1957 to 1958, then did another year's time for stealing a box of tools. Af-ter eating his way out of a career as a jockey, he came to the Bay Area and worked in a motorcycle repair shop, a Berkeley leather shop and an appliance shop. In the Haight, he used his gift of gab to befriend hipsters and talk them out of their possessions.

Z., Okie and plenty of others were successful hustlers be-cause so many people deferred to the club. Hippies volun-teered hospitality, and outright cash, just to establish some vague association with the patch. They knew being seen with us afforded implicit protection and some status—and it became fashionable to have an Angel at your drug or cocktail party. When we used strong-arm techniques, it normally was overlooked for obvious reasons. And snitching on an Angel would incur both the wrath of the club and the Haight community, which was extremely sensitive to police action.[15]

With all these forces at play, a tremendous profit opportunity was being squandered. Burns were one-shot deals, but good business practices would keep bringing in revenue. If the trust of people in the Haight, Berkeley and other drug markets could be won, I could sell the club's organization and mystique, using the name "Hell's Angels" like a nationally advertised brand. Its hallmark would be safety and reliability—exactly what those three dealers were looking for at that Oakland gas station.

As an initial step, I needed to convince other members that honest delivery of goods would profit them in the long run. I first approached Zorro and gave him an object lesson. "Here's the twenty dollars you loaned me the other night," I said handing him a twenty. "And here's the interest on the money," I added, slapping down $500.

"What's all this for?" Z. asked, astonished.

"I'm gonna show you how to make some big money without picking people's pockets or hustlin' 'em outa their shirts. Treat people right and you'll get their attention and their business."

Z. listened, and he was incorporated into my dealing business. His unsmiling, shifty manner and dark, penetrating eyes were valuable assets. Like a coiled snake, he kept customers off balance and a little edgy while I negotiated prices and terms. In addition to playing the gunsel role, he was ordered to abstain from drugs during dickering so he could drag me out if I keeled over.

The two of us—one burly and aggressive, the other lean and crafty—established a tight, slightly pragmatic friendship. I even shacked up at his house in Alameda for one month with Okie's ex-lady, "Mickey." While there, I laid groundwork for what would become the largest psychedelics distributorship in the Haight—and probably all of Northern California in the late 1960s.

The demand for LSD and marijuana soared along with the popularity of hippie fashions, psychedelic music and posters. We attracted so many new buyers, both large and small, that I needed additional help. Several other Angels were handpicked to work as messengers, enforcers and couriers. Under my commission system, Z. and I got equal shares. Bobby "Durt" England pocketed half as much and "Fat Albert" Perryman would get a little less than Durt. Sometimes Charles J. "Mr. Magoo" Tinsley, a 6-2, 215-pound health nut, would work with us, as would Arnold Paul "Animal" Hibbits, a prematurely balding reds freak whose personal hygiene was such that the club once mandated monthly baths for him.

I ventured home periodically to get fresh clothes or to give Helen money to feed the kids, run the house and pay the Montgomery Ward charge account. But the $1,000 a week didn't compensate for my absences.

"Where ya going?" she'd cry as I'd head for the door.

"Out."

"When you gonna be back?"

"When ya see me."

When I missed our son's birthday, she piled the kids into the car and prowled East Oakland until she spotted my car in front of the Luau Club on East 14th Street. She parked and waited, watching the neon blink for a couple of hours. At midnight, she left a note on my windshield: "Today was your son's birthday, and you couldn't even find time to come home. You'd rather be with your friends. If you don't want to come home, you can just stay away."

Meanwhile, Mickey was flushed with the prospect of becoming my No. 1 old lady. She was a black-haired beauty and catered to me, but she put heavy demands on my time. Although I was unwilling to make any commitment, I was content to enjoy our sexual and semi-emotional liaison for the time being. Mickey—the best friend of Sonny's wife Elsie—was an asset around the club, because she was respected. She also was savvy and tough-minded enough to help my dealing business, by acting as hostess or sitting on drug shipments.

The situation was brought to a head by Z.'s old lady, a speedy blond named Linda. Apparently fed up with house guests, she called Helen one day. "You don't know me that well, and I hardly know you," she said. "But this thing with Mickey really isn't what George wants. He really wants you back. He wants to be home with you and the kids."

My wife cut her short. "I don't buy that. If he wanted to be home with me, he would be home. Nobody tells him what to do."

I rushed home a few days later after hearing that Helen had taken her first solo LSD trip. When I got there, she was standing over a set of stereo earphones on the floor, thinking she was hearing voices from outer space.

"You're takin' some reds," I said. "We gotta get you down."

In the morning, I found a letter she had planned to place on my car. It expressed outrage, sorrow and humiliation over my open affair. She posed an ultimatum: either come home and be a husband and father or cut them free to salvage their lives.

Shamed, I refolded the paper. "I didn't know you felt quite like that," I told her and went on to explain apologetically, and not entirely truthfully, that I stayed away to protect our family. "The man's watching me. It's too dangerous to bring it home. It could come down on you too."

"I don't care," she said. "Just come home. I'll do anything."

Soon she was stringing the living room ceiling with a giant cobweb of multicolored yarn. It was trippy but not trippy enough. So we switched to Trader Vic's-type South Seas decor, with a low false ceiling of bamboo, and bamboo walls hung with an Angels banner, guns, knives and pagan masks and psychedelic posters. We stocked hundreds of records for a stereo system with hidden speakers.

It was an entertainment environment designed to keep a visitor's mind soaring, a place where I could show off my automatic weapons while Helen kept buyers comfortable with drugs, good liquor and giant floor pillows. Before business was broached, we normally proceeded something like this:

Introductory joints of high quality marijuana. Then something more exotic such as cocaine, opium or exceptional hash. It always was the finest dope available, so visitors frequently would roll their eyes and say, "Where can I buy some of this?" And I would smile slightly in a braggadocio way and reply, "That was something special that my man laid on me. It was just for you to enjoy. It ain't for sale." The point was made: gourmet items were the fringe benefits of dealing with me.

Here's how Helen looked back on it:

My job was to get the stash, prepare it and administer it to guests, to show them how much to take and how to do it—or actually do it for them. George taught me all the refinements.

In the beginning, I thought I was being hospitable, but I really was a tool. I was a hustler as part of the business. What it amounted to was that George would have his old lady lookin' good for the guys who liked to have a little sexiness around too. It does a lot for a guy when you tell him, "Don't move, man. I'll take care of ya." If the guy didn't know how to get loaded on a certain thing, I'd teach him so he wouldn't feel clumsy.

It was sort of neat. It was impressing people with all you could get through drugs, the fun of them. I felt special just being George's old lady when he got to the top levels of dealing and the club. He easily could have been vice-president again if he wanted, but when the police started busting officers, he decided he didn't want to be one. Still, aside from Sonny, George controlled the club. Sonny listened to George when they argued.

George could even think when he got loaded, and a lot of guys couldn't. That's a thing in itself, to be smashed outa your cap, sitting there with people getting loaded, and being able to function and deal. And George didn't cheat like a lot of people who would take acid or reds we gave 'em and stuff it behind the couch cushions when nobody was looking. Even when loaded, he could tell people what something would cost, how much to sell it for and how to sell it. Getting into that realm meant you had to listen to two or three conversations at once and still know what each person was saying and respond to them. You had to control it. Dealing was hard work.

New clients constantly were recruited, but our steadiest customers remained the three hippies. After the first $8,000 deal, Chuck, Chuckles and Stevie came up with $20,000 a week later—and from that day forward, the volume made quantum jumps to the $50,000 and $70,000 level. Their cash came wrapped in animal hides that we spread on the living room floor while counting out $1,000 piles. Fanning greenbacks, Helen thought aloud sometimes about the land we could buy, but money always was capital for new ventures.

So much cash came through the house that it was taking hours to count it. "Boogey on these five- and ten-dollar bills," I finally declared. Then I got on the phone and ordered all my clients to restrict the cash flow to $50 and $100 notes.

The problem arose because small denominations were the rule in the Haight. Chuck, Chuckles and Stevie maintained neighborhood networks that could fill a skin in several hours with $25,000 in small bills. They had dozens of people going door to door to friends and trusted neighbors, taking hundreds of orders for a few hits each. It didn't take long to add up, because, from the two-bit peddlers down to the guy dropping an occasional tab of acid in his Stanyan Street apartment, they knew they were getting righteous Owsley acid.

The name Owsley was practically synonymous with LSD in 1967 when the "Summer of Love" was predicted. Street connoisseurs even rated his acid superior to pharmaceutical stuff from the Sandoz Chemical Corporation. It was obvious the underground chemist would be among those profiting most from a massive influx of flower children.

More importantly, since Owsley's acid was piped into the Haight almost exclusively through us, I occupied an enviable position as the club's top psychedelics distributor. "The Owl's" acid went from Tramp to me for wholesaling and retailing. And we enjoyed a near monopoly on acid sales.

The club's reputation for quick and thorough retribution discouraged snitches. However, my troops and I were kept busy protecting our dealers from territorial challenges. Vanishing fast were the days when peaceful space cadets could make their rounds with thousands of dollars in their jeans. Our dealers were rolled and roughed up by common thugs and other pushers. "If you've got any problems, let me know and we'll take care of it," I told them. Protection was part of our service.

Usually troublesome challengers could be set straight with a verbal warning, backed by a cold .45 barrel in their ear or mouth. It was amazing how few argued when jacked up against a wall with oblivion just a squeeze away. The disagreeable ones were persuaded by a shot or two pumped past their sideburns or a few whacks to the skull. There was no need to kill anybody, but it easily could have happened in that gangbusters climate.

For instance, I responded to one call for help from my dealers by shoving a clip in my machine-gun-like Eagle, then gathering my private army—Durt, Z. and Winston McConney. We piled into Winston's Cadillac limousine with our weapons and drove to a Victorian house just off Haight Street. As we readied shotguns, pistols and automatic weapons within sight of a bustling intersection, I stationed Z. and Winston at the back door, then Durt and I went up the front steps.

We rammed open the front door and immediately dived for cover. Two pistols were jutting through the landing railing above. "We're comin' up, motherfuckers," I shouted, swinging my Eagle. As we stormed the stairs, the competition retreated into an upper room. Our boots wasted the door. Without a shot, we disarmed a few men and a woman, spreadeagling them all while the other guys went through the house kicking in doors and looking for others.

"You're creating problems," I snarled, reaming the leader's ear with my gun. "You deal through us or not at all. Anytime you wanna make a buy or sale, we'll set it up. There will be no conflicts with our people or else. Consider yourselves incorporated."

In that atmosphere—the display of firepower, the muscle, the splintering doors, the whimpering woman, my troops roaring, "Blast the bastards"—my ultimatum must have sounded pretty reasonable. Our captives agreed to everything, even to reveal classified information about sources. Over the next few months, they got in touch with us before making any deals, then they vanished.

After several hasty policing missions like that, I took a few pistols to Chuck, Chuckles and Stevie. "I can't be handling all your hassles," I told them. "Enough of the birds and the bees and the flowers while everybody's picking your pockets. You take your LSD and go to the firing range and practice with these."

Amazingly, they became infatuated with automatic weapons and shoulder holsters. And they took some pride in being able to squelch upstart dealers who put the squeeze on them. They reacted to the changing Haight by borrowing club tools, tools to protect their property and themselves during the "Summer of Love" plagued by bum trips, rapes, drug burns, muggings, wanton beatings and murders.[16]

While the Haight got more savage, things softened for me. I delegated problem solving to my dealers or to club members. My life consisted of staying home for days at a time, entertaining new customers, developing a speed habit and enlarging my weapons collection. Visitors often brought me gifts of bizarre guns and drugs like DMT, a home brew psychedelic [17] more volatile than LSD. Traipsing to the Haight, or even to club meetings, seemed an unnecessary inconvenience, although I might put in an appearance at a meeting or a run.

Why? Because I could have more fun at home. It was comfortable. I had my color TV there, a king-sized bed, my exotic guns and drugs. The motorcycle was all right for show and go, but after a while, when I was making good money, I wanted to take things easy, sitting in a chair with a telephone like a businessman. When I wanted drugs or money picked up or delivered, I telephoned guys in the club. "Come on over." It was like Grand Central Station.

I invested in drugs like blue chip stocks. The phone replaced the motorcycle as my communications instrument, the gun became my power symbol. There was real prestige in ordering four or five members around and I made all the money decisions. I trusted guys with $50,000 and none betrayed me.

A variety of personal and "political" factors helped me attain and hold my position. First, I was tight with Sonny and

Tramp, the club's best conduit from drug manufacturers. Second, my timing was good. (In fact, I turned down the opportunity to deal heroin, telling Sonny, "Psychedelics are the up and coming thing." That was prophetic.)

In addition to my proven loyalty, I could use my brains and tongue, as well as fists and guns. The club traditionally had too few of the former and too many of the latter. They turned to me when they needed a salesman also capable of playing gunsel.

Switching roles was challenging and fun. I could be a beer-and-football construction worker, a genial salesman, an organizer or a silent heavy. I stressed logic and simplicity when persuading people to deal with me. But my voice might shift in the course of a single conversation from husky and jolly to menacing, then back again. I believed in keeping on the offensive one way or another. If necessary, I could overpower people with an avalanche of words, backed by my presence and the patch. With others, gifts of guns, drugs and furnishings kept them indebted. And if friendly tactics failed, I resorted to thinly veiled intimidation or a little .45 caliber persuasion.

Business was conducted in the Mafia-type family tradition—with goodwill to the cooperative and swift retribution to the others. My basic philosophy was: you never bite the hand that feeds. Those who did got chewed up.

IX—Angels Come of Age

"The Angels are too obvious for serious drug traffic. They don't even have enough capital to function as middle men, so they end up buying most of their stuff in small lots at high prices. . . ."—Hunter S. Thompson.[18]

Just as I delegated tasks to avoid passing up new opportunities, the Oakland Angels began issuing new charters and assisting new chapters in setting up their own drug operations. But we didn't believe in granting charters just for the sake of growth, nor to provide us with a place to stay when we were on vacation. The additions were designed to contribute to our image and business concerns, by providing a drug route link, manufacturing a drug, supplying chemicals or distributing drugs in an untapped area.

The club set down a series of prerequisites for new chapters. The hopefuls had to be an established motorcycle club with at least nine members and a solid reputation as outlaws. They usually needed proven narcotics sources and outlets, competence in use of automatic weapons and explosives, and knowledge of burglary and robbery techniques. During a six-month probation period, the prospective chapter was subject to inspection on any of these points and others by the charter-issuing chapter, usually Oakland. No matter how far away they were, at least their officers would come to visit us and we would send an entourage to check them out. If we liked them, they got their patches. A new chapter, however, was strictly prohibited from overlapping another club's dealing territory without its permission.

In the mid-1960s—when we were portrayed as bigger-than-life folk heroes—few people, even among law enforcement agencies, were aware of our new entrepreneurial approach. But the biker grapevine transmitted word that big money was to be made in the San Francisco Bay area, and we were deluged with applications from individuals and clubs alike.

By 1966, after the club took out state articles of incorporation[19] and was authorized to sell 500 shares of stock, there were ten California chapters, eight out-of-state chapters and three international chapters. The California chapters were Oakland with about forty-five actives, San Francisco with thirty, San Jose with fifteen to twenty, Daly City with eighteen, the twenty-member Nomad chapter, which covered a few Northern California counties and later became the Vallejo chapter, Richmond with fifteen members, the Sonoma chapter based in Novato, the Marin County chapter in San Rafael, and in the south state, the forty-four-member Berdoo outfit and a somewhat smaller group in San Diego. Other chapters were reported in Omaha; Minneapolis; Cleveland; Buffalo; Rochester; New York City; Salem and Lowell, Massachusetts. Across the Atlantic, the club established chapters in Switzerland, England

and West Germany. The total club membership climbed to more than 500 in the late 1960s, including 250 to 300 in California.

Our chapter was inundated by transfer requests from Angels wanting to work the Wall Street of outlaw biking. So, to guard against overpopulation of some chapters and rapid turnover in others, we adopted clubwide rules on transfers. An Angel was required to live in the new chapter area at least four days a week, have all his club bills paid, produce a transfer slip signed by his old chapter's president, sever all dealings with the old chapter, change patches and have a telephone installed in his new home. After a discussion of the proposed transfer, the club voted, with two nays sufficient for a rejection. The Oakland procedures differed in that Sonny screened the numerous candidates before final vote.

As outsiders were attracted and assimilated, our chapter became less and less a fraternity of pure Oakland stock. By necessity, rules were substituted for loose codes, planning for spontaneity. New criminal activities ushered in Mafia-like governance.

We retained few features of our infamous initiation ceremonies, although we made sure in other ways that we weren't being infiltrated. Because initiation was not uniform, I can't speak for other chapters. But in Oakland, it made no sense to us to humiliate a future brother by dumping buckets of shit and urine on his head or smearing his colors with it. There were, however, some remnants of the old rituals. Sometimes an initiate would show some class by winning his red wings with cunnilingus on a woman in front of the club and a few prospects provided a willing broad for the other guys, to cement some votes. But usually we made sure that a prospective member wasn't an undercover agent by subtly leading him to commit at least one criminal act during several months to several years of riding with us. We tested them thoroughly. To see if they could hold their mud, we often pitted them against prospects and full-fledged members of other clubs—and they were expected to win. We also made sure they could hold their liquor and their drugs, and sometimes we had them sell narcotics for us or run an errand. Some members wanted nothing to do with prospects while others, such as Okie and Z., treated them like slaves. Prospects were made to run to the store for beer, liquor or food; some members had them wash their bikes or even do some wrenching. The dumb prospects wound up with flunky jobs, the smart ones stayed out of the way of actives when there was a chore to be done. The dumb ones didn't have the sense to realize they were being hustled like an outsider, hustled out of food, money, clothes, jewelry, anything. "Hey, I sure like that watch," a member would say to one of those dummies. And pretty soon the prospect would be asking other people for the time.

Rules evolved as problems surfaced, and revisions were made, often after Sonny consulted with older members like me. Once the membership adopted a policy, it was recorded by the secretary then added to either the bylaws or rules.

These were the bylaws:

1. There will be a meeting once a week at a predetermined time and place.

2. There will be a $2 fine for missing a meeting without a valid reason.

3. Girls will not sit in on meetings unless it is a special occasion.

4. There will be a $15 initiation fee for all new members. Club will furnish patch which remains club property.

5. There will be no fighting among club members. A fine of $5 will result for each party involved.

6. New members must be voted in. Two no votes equal a rejection. One no vote must be explained.

7. All new members must have their own motorcycle.

8. Members with extra parts will lend them to members. They must be replaced or paid for.

9. There will be no stealing among members. Anyone caught will be kicked out of the club.

10. Members cannot belong to any other clubs.

11. New members must come to three meetings on their motorcycles. They will be voted on at a third meeting. Votes will be by paper ballot.

12. Any persons coming up for vote are subject to club rules.

13. To be eligible to come up for vote in the club, prospective members must be brought up for vote at the meeting by a member.

14. Anyone kicked out of the club cannot get back in.

15. When packing double, members can let girl wear patch.

16. Anyone who loses his patch, or if the patch is picked up by an officer or member, the member will pay a $15 fine before he gets the patch back.

These were the special California Rules:[20]

1. No dope burns.

2. On California runs, weapons will be shot only between 0600 and 1600. Penalty for violation: patch is pulled.

3. No spiking the club's booze with dope.

4. No throwing live ammunition into bonfires on runs.

5. No messing with another member's wife.

6. You can't pull the patch of another chapter's member.

7. No snuffing a member with his patch on. (You can only snuff a member of your own chapter.)

8. No using dope during a meeting.

9. At least two officers from each chapter must attend a California meeting every two months (presidents' meeting).

A plethora of chapter rules were added, some with stiff fines and penalties. There was a fifty-dollar fine for missing a run or failing to bring a motorcycle on one. There was a five-dollar fine for failing to ride a bike to a meeting, but that was frowned upon more than the penalty indicated. In fact, if a guy's motorcycle needed overhauling, the club allotted an arbitrary period for the work, usually a few weeks. To escape a fine for missing a meeting or a run or neglecting to bring a motorcycle, a member needed a written excuse from his doctor.

A member could be fined up to fifty dollars for being too outspoken at a meeting, fifty dollars for brandishing a gun at a meeting, or $100 for shooting a weapon at the clubhouse or another member's home. A five-dollar fine hardly discouraged fighting among members. For instance, one veteran slapped down five dollars at the beginning of each meeting for several weeks, then whaled on a new initiate until the battered rookie dropped out.

Such fraternal practices conflicted with our public image as ever-loyal brothers. But the truth was that the most troublesome rule was the most basic one: "An Angel's always right." Time and again it compelled members to back each other in public—even when one Angel was clearly out of line. The backup men often brought up the incidents at meetings, and members who showed poor judgment were chastised and fined.

For the sake of unity, we were prohibited from messing with another Angel's current woman. Rape also was banned, because rapes were bad p.r. and rape prosecutions had been an expensive and unnecessary inconvenience with so many obliging women around. Expulsion was the approved penalty, but in practice, it ranged from a twenty-five-dollar fine to the one-year suspension of one prominent Oakland member who had allegedly raped one of another member's women a short time before she killed herself.

Violation of property rights was dealt with more severely

than violation of women. Expulsion was the penalty for burning another member in a dope deal or stealing from a brother.

To guard against undependable brethren who might steal or snitch, we prohibited needle use. "You can't trust a hype" was the slogan. A guy caught with needle tracks or paraphernalia was given one chance to quit cold turkey— and sometimes that meant being locked in a closet for a couple of weeks. If he went back to smack, he was banished, coldly and irreversibly. We lost a few popular members to the needle, including "Junkie George" and Waldo. (I tried to lure Waldo from heroin by offering him $5,000 cash, free room and board, a motorcycle and a job if he quit. He turned me down on the spot, then vanished.)

Respect for club property, namely anything bearing the death's head or the club name, also was a rigid tenet. Defacing the club flag was a $50 to $100 fine. Losing the patch—whether that meant leaving it someplace or having it captured by police—increased rapidly to a $100 fine. Members went to great lengths to get their colors back, because not having a patch left you vulnerable to attack by enemies within the club. Both members and their women—the ones who wore pseudo colors saying "Property of the Hell's Angels"—were required to keep their patches clean, even if that meant bringing them to the French laundry.

No longer was cohesion strictly a matter of fraternal pride. It was an insurance policy protecting our livelihood and keeping us out of the slammer. In the early 1960s, most of us had jobs, but by the late 1960s, being a Hell's Angel had become a full-time job for many and at least an income supplement for most. Very few members viewed the club as a hobby, and those who did were drummed out quickly.

The club structure was easily adapted to drug trafficking. All essential jobs could be filled with club members—distributors, dealers, enforcers, transporters. Although investigators came to believe that we accomplished our criminal missions like any army, more informal mechanisms operated.

Members weren't assigned to drug operations, and not every member was a dealer. But anyone interested in drug action sought out whatever was currently available. The members with the best connections emerged as leaders while the rest scrambled for a piece of the action. Most guys recruited their closest friends or the best available talent, although a member with real clout could elbow his way into a dealing collective. By the same token, a dealer could bar anybody he "outranked." For example, I vetoed Winston for membership in my group because his style was incompatible. He had more experience in dealing with heroin addicts than psychedelics-popping space cadets. Still, so many opportunities arose that virtually every member was able to grab one, if he wanted.

We knew in general who was dealing with whom and approximately how much. But, like any secret society, we believed a man should know only what he needed to know, for the protection of everyone. Drug transactions were never discussed during chapter meetings, although guys might discreetly set something up afterward.

It was known that Tramp and I operated the psychedelics facet, and Winston scored big mescaline supplies, Sonny controlled heroin and cocaine, which were making inroads to the hip community. He also farmed out marijuana deals to at least several members, collecting maybe a ten-dollar commission on a $125 brick.

A number of other guys established short-term connections with basement factories making amphetamines and other drugs. Tiny had good "crank" connections. Vern was the best supplier of Mexican drugs and our premier marijuana shipper, trucking kilos north from Fresno in his specially geared high-speed Ford Ranchero.

Sonny kept tabs on much of the trafficking. He could veto

any deal in the interest of the club, although to the best of my knowledge, club capital was never used. His personal contacts and other club contacts helped us promote and coordinate communication or trade between Oakland and other chapters, including European ones. Examples: Angels from Massachusetts came west to score LSD and other drugs, and I mailed them narcotics in a hollowed out book. A London Angel named Harley enjoyed my hospitality and was shown how to conduct business American style. In turn, a pair of Frisco Angels later flew to London to help with recruiting (using an office provided by the Beatles).[21]

Drugs noticeably strengthened communications between Northern and Southern California. The Bay Area was the hub for distribution, but Southern California was the first stop for cocaine, heroin and marijuana coming up from the Southwest, Mexico and Latin America via boats, cars and private and commercial planes. (When the government started tightening up on legal U. S. amphetamines manufacturing in the late 1960s, "speed" and raw chemicals were imported with increasing frequency from Mexico. Two amphetamines factories were set up in the Los Angeles area by Oakland members, who got the chemicals from San Diego Angels, according to state intelligence reports.)

It was common knowledge among bike groups and law enforcement officers that our club was using women to smuggle drugs north by plane in false-bottomed luggage. But the Los Angeles-to-San Francisco air commute traffic made detection difficult at best. The same technique was used to ship heroin between the Bay Area and Buffalo and Omaha, and to transport the Richmond chapter's LSD back east.[22] Federal authorities estimated Angels trafficked cross-country an average of $10 million a year in the late 1960s.

In California, some chapters established no solid connections of their own, so they traded with larger, wealthier chapters like ours. And when a club's sources went dry, it would solicit drugs from another chapter, the way an individual would ask for motorcycle parts. Seldom would our chapter or San Jose—which had righteous Mexican connections—go begging. There always was at least a trickle and sometimes a flood.

Even when things seemed a little slow, you would stumble on indications that money was being made. One morning at 6 o'clock, I was speeding on "crystals" when I spotted a window light in Sonny's place which was patrolled by a pair of Dobermans behind a chain-link fence. Inside, I found Sonny and Mexican Ed, a reputed member of the Galloping Gooses motorcycle club in San Diego and a main supplier of the Berdoo Angels, cutting and packaging a salad bowl full of smack. It turned out that Ed was Sonny's main connection when he switched from grass and a smattering of pills to harder narcotics. As we chatted and snorted coke (Sonny's favorite drug), I helped them fill balloons. Sonny's dealers in the club arrived at evenly spaced intervals to pick up their loads—usually an ounce or two—then they made their dumps. Sonny was smart; he wasted no time in getting those drugs out of his house.

X—What Dope Hath Bought

"The Angels always seemed to have lots of money and no jobs. You tell me how a guy gets $3,000 or $4,000 in his pockets when he's unemployed."—An Oakland cop who knew the club.

When I jounced into the job site with a new fire engine-red pickup truck with magnesium wheels, tonneau cover and stereo, there were plenty of raised eyebrows and a few hoots from the scaffolds. It was a fancy conveyance for a guy who'd been on unpaid sabbatical for a year—and all too soon my co-workers began to suspect that I'd been self-employed.

After a few days I was dispensing uppers and downers, undermining serious work efforts and incidentally creating a few customers. As much as I tried to give away chemical treats, friends and co-workers always seemed interested in scoring larger quantities—so I obliged by helping some set up small-scale dealerships.

I tried to be discreet in my on-the-job dealings, but matters got out of hand. More and more workers came from other sites to score drugs, and club members rolled up on choppers or in long luxury sedans with braces of Dobermans. The Angels reported developments, received new orders or slipped me proceeds, so I was sure my co-workers guessed that the tax man, not the bill collector, had driven me back to construction. A W-2 form would show legitimate income, no matter how small, and would explain how I could purchase a truck and other expensive toys.

Yet my willpower was being whittled away by the glaring contrast between the gritty tedium of lathing and my high-rolling, gun-collecting, shiny-machinery, loose-lady existence. The clincher came one afternoon when Durt slipped me $25,000 cash and took off to close another deal. I ducked into an outhouse and tried to stuff the husky wad into my nail pouch. As the bills unraveled, I saw the absurdity of a big-time drug distributor posing as a blue-collar worker. I kicked open the door, jumped in my truck and drove off, leaving my tools behind again.

A year or so after closing my first substantial deal, I was well on my way to annual earnings of $100,000 to $200,000. Some weeks I averaged only $50 to $100 a day, but other days brought me as much as $500. One week netted about $30,000.

I took great pride in my ability to turn big bucks, but my money management wasn't the best. It just spilled through the pockets of my multicolored "methedrine trip" pants. There always was another $300 weapon, another $3,000 motorcycle, another $500 party, another $500 shopping spree. All I could sock away was about $30,000.

Not many Angels were earning as much, but if they had

paid taxes on their illegal income, many would have moved to a higher bracket. The new affluence wasn't reflected in Brooks Brothers suits, penthouses, swimming pools or other affordable trappings of respectability. But money permitted guys to act out some of their wildest fantasies, made their daily existence comfortable and allowed some investments in property and small businesses.

We kept our biker's regalia, although expensive leather pants and vests replaced denim to an extent. Members rented bigger or fancier homes and apartments, and a few purchased houses. Virtually every member stopped camping on floors, and even Richard Hans "Monk" Munyer, a mossy-toothed biker who bragged about eating cats and lived in a tree house, moved into a real dwelling. Many of us were concentrated in East Oakland, a "blackening" district about halfway up the economic ladder.

Wealth was used to impress other members for the first time, and our favorite game might have been called, "Buy it first." If a member admired a certain object, you would slap down the cash first. Then you'd either lay it on him or keep it, depending on whether you wanted gratitude or envy. The more expensive the item, the more impressive the victory. Usually, the items were novelties or Oriental rugs, lamps, hookas and handmade clothing. But sometimes the bidding went pretty high. For instance, I had my eye on a forty-foot Higgins cabin cruiser when Zorro beat me to the salesman. "Don't worry," he told me as he paid for it. "We got it. It's yours too." In turn, I bought a $1,800 Harley Sportster off the showroom floor, logged fifty-five miles on a Daly City trip, didn't like its handling, then gave the pink slip to Animal to replace his rattletrap.

Not everyone stopped heisting bikes, but most no longer needed to scratch for cash to get superannuated choppers running. Guys could afford new bikes, with quite a few keeping one for everyday riding and another for special occasions. We could afford expensive chroming and customizing work.

Members were buying luxury cars with sound systems too. For fun, a two-wheeler was fine but a four-wheeler was less conspicuous for dealing and more comfortable for a night on the town. I liked Chryslers, Sonny preferred Lincolns and Corvettes, Tramp Jaguars, Tiny Corvettes, Winston Cadillacs. Vern owned a fancy six-cylinder Ford Ranchero that we called "the goin' down the highway Ranchero" because it was geared for marijuana runs at sustained high speed. Though not all Okie's machines were operable, he owned nine motorcycles and four cars, including a restored 1948 Lincoln. Many cars and trucks changed hands within the club. And we always were on the market for new, more powerful and classier vehicles as status symbols and out of love for the internal combustion engine.

Some members acquired exotic and rare animals for entertainment and protection. Cisco raised a dope-smoking monkey that was a big hit on runs. Lots of guys owned big watchdogs; German Shepherds were popular, but Sonny started a Doberman fad when he bought a pair to patrol his house. Tramp and Tiny owned rattlesnakes that we watched eat white mice: the reptiles also wouldn't be bad instruments of persuasion when you shoved an uncooperative guy's hand into their cage.

The most impressive pets were the big felines that Z. and Winston chained outside their houses, to the chagrin of their neighbors. In fact, some of Winston's neighbors went before the Oakland City Council to complain about his 300-pound African lioness named "Kitty Kitty." I didn't blame them one bit, especially after that cat swiped a Coke bottle out of my hand and nearly took my arm with it. Winston fed the cat downers to keep it calm and gentle, but it managed to convince several members of the Unknowns motorcycle club to confess the theft of Sonny's bike and tell where it was dumped. The thieves had endured bullwhippings while hanging from the rafters, but the sight of "Kitty Kitty" was too much for them.[23]

The gun challenged the motorcycle as the club power symbol. At least a few weapons were displayed or stashed in virtually every member's home, and some chapters actually had rules saying that every member had to own or have access to a gun. Some members built extensive weapons collections. Since his boyhood, Skip had specialized in antiques, while others like me opted for more modern and powerful firearms. Sonny usually kept about a dozen guns in handy places around the house, including a few 9 mm. pistols. And by actively purchasing through stores and acquiring through business dealings, I assembled the club's largest collection of automatic weapons. Usually there were three dozen guns and more than 10,000 rounds of ammunition around my house. I carried one, sometimes two, .45-caliber automatic pistols. And I mounted a seven-foot antitank gun (a birthday present from Tramp) in the back of my camper truck and aimed it down the roadway, so business could be conducted without worrying about Highway Patrol pursuit.

My guns were a hobby and an occupational tool. At first, I was collecting any guns available, even hot ones. Then I peddled most of them, because I could afford to buy legal ones. The only illegal ones I kept were machine guns and weird things like that. I also made my legal guns untraceable. For instance, for my .45s, I had extra barrels, sliders, ejectors and all the other things that mark your slugs and casings. If I wanted to use the gun, I could just throw everything away and put the stock back on. It might be the same trigger, but police could check the gun and never prove anything.

As a connoisseur, I had barrels custom made, even for a

Sten gun Z. cut up when he got paranoid about having it. That beauty was my pride and joy. It had a 9 mm. clip out of the side, would almost fit into a lunch pail and would assemble in less than thirty seconds. It looked plenty mean. If you whipped it out and said, "Up against the wall," everybody went up against the wall. No questions.

Some of my legal guns looked exotic too, particularly the Eagle, a thirty-shot, .45-caliber semiautomatic that was a ringer for a Thompson. For appearance, the Eagle ranked almost as high as my grease guns like the AK-47 Russian machine guns and Red Chinese machine guns. If you got people loaded and were having trouble convincing them of something, you reached for one of those. They always worked.

Aesthetically, automatic weapons were where it was at, but for enforcement purposes my double-barreled shotgun with exposed hammers proved more intimidating. That "dago" gun was effective because it made lots of noise and could do damage. Sawed off and hung inside my coat on a leather thong, it was easy to carry and was a good show of firepower.

I never blew anybody away with a shotgun, but I fired lots of emphasis rounds with my .45. I kept the range short so I wouldn't hit a guy, but he wouldn't know that. One night a member from Fresno dropped in and made himself obnoxious. We didn't get along at all. So when he ran out of cigarettes, I offered him a pack and said, "Take 'em or else." He said they weren't his brand, so I put a slug next to his ear. Then he couldn't grab those smokes fast enough. After that night, I never saw him again.

Prosperity helped us realize an old dream. The Snake Pit and subsequent clubhouses had been deficient on at least one count—they weren't public. And there always was restraint even at bars like the Sidetrack, which we sometimes appropriated for club meetings by ordering nonmembers out, then locking the doors. The solution was renting a restaurant and bar at 1215 23rd Avenue at the beginning of 1967.

The Angels Inn, as we called it, was in prime club territory. Tramp and Tiny paid the $300 monthly rent, but I was made titular head because my criminal record was relatively clean and my father already was in the bar business. We thought I would have an easier time getting a license, but the state Alcoholic Beverage Control agency denied it on the ground that it would "aggravate existing police problems." We won the first round of a legal fight when a state hearing examiner ruled in March that "sufficient evidence has not been introduced to support the finding that the Hell's Angels are disreputable or obnoxious in their conduct." Laughing over that, we prepared to open with a sixty-day provisional license and got some local merchants to write quite willingly that their crime problems vanished when we established residency. I guess the punks moved out when we moved in.

I served as chief bartender, manager, bouncer and remodeling contractor, and drew my work force from the Bay Area Angels flocking to the new hangout. "Okay, you guys," I would bark, rousting a dozen or so. "We need a hole in this wall." After unlimbering, they got into it, taking running karate kicks until the wall crumbled. Once they ripped away the studs with bare hands, we framed a passage to the cafe next door, where a pool table, vending machines and booths were arranged.

Then Skip and I went wild with $100-worth of spray paint in the bathroom. We attacked each other and the walls with swirls of ghastly phosphorescent colors. Stumbling out for more dope or more paint, we spent an entire day in there—but the health inspector ordered a fresh white paint job.

The bar was decorated with felt pen scrawlings, generally biker poetry or epithets like the giant "Fuck You" above the bar. "Freewheeling Frank," a Frisco Angel who taught himself to paint while in prison, promised to draw me a six-foot-tall Alice in Wonderland rabbit, but in the meantime, others penned something to personalize the place—some profound slogan, name or drawing. Death's heads reflecting long practice on jail cell walls. Motorcycles. "Angels forever, forever Angels." "When guns are outlawed, only Angels will have guns. Yeah!" There was no censorship, but everybody was subject to club rules, member or not. My partners and I laid down the house rules: "No hassles in here. No drugs in here either. If you've got anything when we get raided, then you eat it. None of that dumping it on the floor when the cops come, because the club will be held responsible."

While drawing beer, I sometimes flashed on the fact that my father was downtown doing the same, in a vastly different environment. Angels Inn was unique. In any other bar, the presence of so many guys wearing reputations and aggressions on their backs would lead to brawls rather than delicious brotherhood. At our bar, no one dialed the police at first shove, no one kept a finger glued to a silent alarm, and no one walked out because Angels were present. Like anyone else, when we felt secure, we were at our best, our most genial, raucous, foot-stomping, horse-laughing best. The place was charged with fun and excitement, and even my wife felt at home dancing, punching quarters into the jukebox, helping me shove drinks across the bar and taking billiard lessons from Durt and other members.

The club, particularly me, got some press over our eventually unsuccessful business venture. But the public was about to get a large dose of us in bigger-than-life color. In March, 1967, dozens of us were hired for the filming of *Hell's Angels on Wheels*, the first film to get the club's official blessing. Earlier films also had capitalized on our roguish antihero popularity. But some neglected to pay for borrowing our image and others simply offended us. In fact, the club filed a $4 million invasion of privacy suit on behalf of twenty-two members, alleging they were portrayed as "vicious, lawless and thoroughly depraved" in *Wild Angels*.

Helen and I were among the "actors" for the first authentic minutes of *Hell's Angels on Wheels,* a U.S. Films movie produced by Joe Solomon of Los Angeles and starring Jack Nicholson. After conceiving the film, Solomon had obtained Sonny's phone number from the state Highway Patrol, then convinced him the film would depict the club accurately. The producer also agreed to pay each member fifty dollars a day, plus consultant's fees to Sonny which would, incidentally, help him cover illegal income.

On the first morning of shooting, the cast grouped at the Angels Inn, then followed camera-equipped vehicles and a catering truck into the Oakland hills. At first, we enjoyed parading and playing ourselves for the camera. Then the filmmakers directed us through the same curve several times because of camera and choreography failures. Turning in a confined space and jockeying into the correct formation was a hassle. "Boogey on it," I griped. "Let's get loaded."

Thanks in large part to the food catering truck, U.S. Films survived the first day without a walkout. We weren't overjoyed with our fifty-dollar salaries, but moviemaking was a novel trip, an ego trip. Most of us got a kick out of calling ourselves actors. (In fact, for years to come, acting would be listed as the last employment for a number of dead or arrested Angels.)

That night some of the real actors partied with the real Angels. We were surprised that so many movie people got stoned, and we were impressed by one petite actress who horsed around a Harley better than the actors.

120

The next day, we overslept the alarm. And to complicate matters, I had borrowed J.B.'s motorcycle, which, as usual, refused to start. Blaming Helen for oversleeping, I pointed up the hill and commanded, "Push. We'll start it on compression." She inched me uphill with much grunting. At the crest, I told her, "Okay. Get on. If you fall off, you're gonna stay there because I ain't got time to stop."

The machine fired and we blasted off at full throttle, cutting corners radically as she begged over the rapping pipes, "Slow down, George. Slow down."

After catching the zany procession of choppers and camera vehicles, we were filmed streaming across the Bay Bridge to San Francisco, then ripsnorting through the Broadway Tunnel in North Beach, around Coit Tower and past Fishermen's Wharf area tourists. We were decked out in our greasiest finery and our women were in full plumage. We dueled a little with our throttles as they turned their heads. Helen—in matching black jacket and boots, plus Levi's slit up both legs to the thigh and laced with rawhide—hugged my colors, basking in the condescending or mortified stares of prim women locked into marshmallow lives with marshmallow husbands.

When the film was released in mid-August, Sonny made some promotional appearances with Solomon and actors John Garwood and Adam Roarke. Sonny said, "It's as accurate as they could put on the screen. There's some things we don't tell nobody. Anyway, if I ever told anybody what was going on, they wouldn't wonder anymore."[24] In private, he kissed it off as another phony portrayal.

We attended a special premier at the Ball Theater in San Leandro. In the foyer, I recognized myself on an advertising poster, with only part of Helen's foot visible behind me. During the showing, we sprawled across balcony seats, stumbled down the aisles and passed joints. And when a familiar face crossed the screen, the star bowed while the others howled and hooted. In general, we dug the film because we came off like Robin Hood and his merry men, beating up sailors who beat up Jack Nicholson.

Afterward some members celebrated at a MacArthur Boulevard saloon where real-life trouble was encountered. Police arrested Skip, but Edward "Deacon" Proudfoot and another Angel were blocking their exit. Other guys barricaded the door, but it was broken down by police reinforcements who dodged beer bottles, pool cues and chains before restoring order. Ten cops went to the hospital with assorted cuts and bruises; thirteen Angels went to jail. Skip pleaded guilty to being drunk in a public place, Deacon pleaded guilty to resisting an officer and they each served a brief county jail term.

Probably our most memorable movie outing was "2001: A Space Odyssey," a Stanley Kubrick product frequently consumed with psychedelics in hip circles. We chartered two buses for the fifty-mile trek to a San Jose movie house. Happy to be Angels, we rolled along getting ripped on various chemicals, including one Winston and I dubbed Dust of Angels, or DOA. We didn't know then that it was an animal tranquilizer, but it was so heavy that few people could handle it. Joints containing the stuff were called peace weed, for the violence they often triggered; and we inked them with the skull and cross bones.

By the time the movie rolled, we were loaded several times over and had taken over the place by being our boisterous, unpredictable selves. When the ape man battled a territorial invader, some guys clapped and yelled approval while Hi Ho Steve swung his arms and clambered over the seats, aping the ape. Later, guys identified strongly with Hal the computer's power bid during an astronaut's trek to Jupiter and inner space.

On our own return voyage, we had our bus drivers racing down the freeway at seventy-five miles an hour. "This is yours if you win," I hollered, whipping our driver's head with a few hundred dollars. "Faster, man. Faster."

"I'll get a ticket," the driver protested.

"We know the judge. Get goin'."

Winning was a serious matter. We shouted at our driver when he lagged behind, and a few guys waved pistols around. Swaying along, the buses were neck and neck approaching Oakland, so Tramp and a couple of other pistol packers leaned out the window to blow out the tires of the other bus. Some of us had enough presence of mind to drag them back inside before they wiped out half the club. But the gunplay upset our driver so much that he took the wrong exit ramp. "Run the red light," I shouted. He did, but we lost anyway.

XI—Gang Bangs, Frying Pans and Hair Triggers

"Women were treated like dogs. In fact, even the Angels dogs, which were kicked around a lot, got better treatment. If you performed your duties well, you were a good old lady. Whether someone was a good old lady depended on how well trained she was, how well she was able to respond to the snap of a finger, or one word. In order to keep her man around, she had to be a mind reader, to anticipate his needs. You had to know whether he wanted a glass of water, what he wanted for dinner. If George had to tell me something once, it was too much. He'd take off if I didn't treat him right."—Helen Wethern.

The women established an informal hierarchy. At the bottom were the newest arrivals, and at the top were those who endured longest, not necessarily with one member. The men treated the low rankers best when they first entered the scene, although the established women hated them.

There always was an influx of "mamas"—juicy teenaged runaways, seasoned bike ladies, women on drug skids, just women wanting to hang out with the baddest bike outfit around. They showed up at parties and runs, sometimes uninvited but always welcome, or they were picked up at bars or dances. Once the partying was under way, and everybody got loose, one member usually gave her a test drive or two. Then he would invite his brothers into the cockpit. Word spread quickly. Guys gathered around a bedroom, a car, a van or a soft spot on the ground, looked the woman over, felt the pertinent parts, then decided on a rough order of mounting. The line sometimes was fine between rape and orgy as guys dropped their drawers and plugged the "new mama," spitefully initiating her, testing her endurance—or their own—for the hell of it. In fact, some orgies turned to rapes as the minutes of humping became hours, and an Angel or two became half a dozen or more. If the mama didn't drown in sperm, she was allowed to rise when the guys tired of her. Some guys, like me, weren't big on group gropes.

After a humping session, the new "mama" would stay close to the men, because the tenured old ladies would tear her apart if given a chance. If there was a clash, the guys would rush in to protect their fresh piece of ass. And the regulars like Helen would retreat to one side to throw some bad vibes.

"Hope that dirty cunt bleeds to death," they'd sneer. And if the new "mama" started rubbing up against a member, you'd hear one of the regulars snarl, "Hey bitch! Get offa my old man!"

The "mamas" underwent a filtration process, usually settling with low-level Angels after being passed over by ranking members or guys whose old ladies were particularly territorial and emphatic about it. Lower-echelon members, such as Monk the cat-eater and "Pops" Lindeman, a fortyish ex-Navy man with an eye for porn, often ended up with less than alluring "mamas." Good-lookers sometimes were snatched up by high-ranking members like Tramp, who once bragged about keeping a couple of women holed up for a few days in an orgy. Tiny, an unlikely looking Lothario, loved his ladies three at a time when he could get them. And "Big Al" Perryman complained one horny "mama" nearly screwed the testicles off his dog.

The turnover was high. A few durable ones hung around the club for six months, a year or more, living now and then with members, but otherwise servicing just about anybody who wanted them. They were turned off and on, shoved aside, slapped down and around like flesh-and-blood robots. The ones who could take it without moaning were "good mamas."

Most came to the club for the same reasons as the men— fun, status and open-ended thrills. More than a few were given risky dealing chores, such as flying coke and heroin on commercial airlines, because they were expendable. They realized that risk, like abuse, was the price of the fast, romantic life, and they learned, as a few had tattooed on their asses or emblazoned on their jackets, that they were "property of the Hell's Angels." They were subject to club punishment, which could be anything from beating to gang bang to worse.

When they got out of line by butting in on a conversation, contradicting a member or enticing the wrong guy, they learned about conditions of slavery. For instance, some guys dragged Jan, a well-circulated one with a habit of interrupting, into Monk's basement, stripped her, lashed her to a post, then peppered her body with BB's until she was impressed with the rule: women should be seen and not heard. It all was done with the consent of her old man, Sweet Terry.

"Napa Bob" Holmes, an old Frisco Angel, had an old lady who used to get to me with her opinionated interruptions. A couple of times I told him, "Tell your old lady to shut up.

If she doesn't, I'm coming to you." He was a big cat, but I finally busted him and left his blood all over the place. He should have kept his old lady in hand.

On the other hand, righteous old ladies like Helen were given respect, because they were recognized as a member's property, an extension of his personality and tastes. They neither were to be touched nor taken until their old man relinquished claim.

By the same token, it was taboo for an old lady to openly criticize other Angels. A member would invariably slap down his own woman before taking on another Angel. Club loyalty came first. Helen learned this, so she usually let things ride until she could complain in private. She did that when Tommy shot her ass with an automatic BB gun and claimed it was an accident. But she drew the line when she thought I was being manipulated.

During a Squaw Rock run on the Russian River, we both dropped some STP, a rough-edged psychedelic, then Tiny entered the camper rattling dice. "Hey George, how 'bout a game?"

We threw the bones for a while, then switched to poker. I was so loaded that Tiny hustled me through hand after hand. As Helen sat on a rear bunk watching me lose, she boiled at the thought of Tiny taking me for a ride. She thought, "Tiny, you dirty bastard!! You're really playing him even though you know he's loaded to the gills."

When Tiny glared back with his lethal lion's eyes, she realized she had spoken what she was thinking. "Yeah, I'm gonna play him," he said scooping up a pot. If looks were gunpowder, both of them would have been blown away.

Helen was infuriated because I didn't seem to mind losing $1,500. "How can you like that man after he took your money?" she said later.

"You don't understand," I told her. "Who better to take your money than another brother? It's no big deal anyway."

* * *

127

Losing and spending chunks of money without a blink showed class, as did the finding and keeping of sexy women. In our system of natural selection, the ideal woman might be equipped with a Mae West chest, B. Bardot buttocks and the face of an angel. Very few measured up to that, but members came up with surprisingly good-looking women sometimes. Women who saw character in scarred, wind-leathered and whiskery faces. Women who saw raw masculinity in tree-stump thick tattooed arms or sexuality in lean bodies strung out by irregular meals, late hours and drugs. Women who overlooked funky clothes and oily hair to see the power of the death's head and the men wearing it.

Sonny's love life was a case in point. He was a scrawny 5-foot-9 with jutting chin whiskers and a receding hairline that made his head appear to be permanently raked back by years of riding into the wind. Try as he might, he never could gorge himself above 140 or 150 pounds because he was hyperactive, going for days at a time without sleep. His eyelids were puffy, his mouth pinched arrogantly. He wore an earring through his left lobe. His feet were large for his size. His presence, however, transcended his appearance. His carriage was self-assured, his voice commanding and his smiles somehow charming. His macho was like something out of the movies or the way you imagined Jesse James—but it was so consistent with his behavior that everyone knew it was more than veneer. He seemed to get everything he wanted—respect of his brothers, and women. After losing his wife, Elsie, to postabortion complications in 1967, he met Sharon Gruhlke, the winner of the Maid of Livermore beauty contest that year. The green-eyed blond cowgirl was only nineteen or so, but she was adventuresome. She became Sonny's old lady and moved into his bungalow, the First Lady of Angeldom. Years later, she would become Mrs. Barger.

Not every woman was treated like a queen, but we did

outfit our own to the best advantage of their sexual attributes. Helen, filled out to a fetching size five by her
mid-twenties, constantly was being sent out for new
clothes. Sometimes I even pawed through clothing racks of
expensive shops, telling her what to try on. Price was no object. Forty dollars for a bathing suit was cheap if it wowed
the guys on a lakeside run. And I didn't care if a thirty-dol-
lar blouse was ruined by motorcycle oil or frying-pan spat-
terings after one wearing. Whether she was cooking, cleaning house or riding with me, I wanted her dressed alluring-
ly. There was no telling when or where a dealer or customer
might be encountered.

Here's how she looked at it:

He liked me to wear anything that fit tight and was revealing. For bathing suits, lowcut tops and hip-huggers, he always made me go to Fredericks of Hollywood. We used to
drop $300 to $400 in an afternoon. I looked at the pricetags,
but he never did.

Actually, I was only an ornament, something to be used.
George dressed me to fit the part, and if he didn't like what
he saw, he'd say, "Put your wig on. Go fix your face. Fix your
hair. Change that dress." I guess it worked, because lots of
times people would ask him, "How'd you get something like
her?" Anything for a distraction while he did business.

For the sake of practicality and her moll's image, I bought
her a .380 Llama semiautomatic pistol, a smaller replica of
my military .45. I upped its firepower with a fifteen-shot
clip that protruded from the grip; then we went to the
shooting range.

After some instruction, she learned to squeeze rather
than pull the trigger, but the target was too far away for her
to tell if she was scoring. For the hell of it, she took aim at
some small rocks—and sent several flying without a miss.
When the clip was empty, I looked at her skeptically then

said, "Okay, Annie Oakley. Put it away. Back in the trunk. You don't need any more practice than that."

"Whatta ya mean?" she objected, her voice rising. "I was just gettin' the hang of it. It's neat. I like it. C'mon, meany."

We went home, mission accomplished. She was competent enough to back me or protect herself. Her new skill was insurance for a house stocked usually with more than $10,000 in drugs and enough guns to outfit a military platoon. She was ordered to always keep her gun within reach with a bullet chambered. When she answered the front door, she hid a .357 Derringer behind her back, ready to be fired. (This greatly impressed other members and prompted several to arm their old ladies too.) And, when Helen left the house to go shopping, to pick up drugs or to drive the kids home from school, she tucked the Llama in her purse. Once, she stuck her equalizer in the face of a black guy bothering her outside the grocery store. She confessed later that she was terrified by how close she had come to blowing off his head.

When we relaxed at home, watching television or listening to music, she was posted on a big pillow behind the front door, and I sat across the room in my favorite chair, like a Buddha beneath my club banner. Together we could place any uninvited guest in a murderous crossfire. It wasn't just paranoia: the cops conceivably could storm in at any time.

One day, however, I noticed she was slacking off, leaving her gun on the ottoman while doing housework. "Big Al," fresh out of prison,[25] was visiting so I told him, "Watch this." When Helen wasn't looking, I unloaded the Llama, put it back down, then called her into the living room. "What're ya doin' leavin' this here?" I admonished, and she picked it up.

"Shoot Al," I commanded next.

"What?" she screeched as Al, a swarthy, heavyset guy, squirmed and fingered the conchos on his black hat.

"Shoot the sonofabitch, dammit. Don't ask. Just do it."
She aimed at Al's gut and squeezed. The hammer fell, but
only with a click.
"Now, what if I'd really needed you?" I reprimanded her.
"I'd be up shit creek." That was a lesson she never forgot.

Although Helen still appeared a lot like a naive, fresh-
faced teenager, she had matured into a drugwise, street-
wise, uncompromising woman who'd shoot in defense of
herself, her children—and her marriage. Her years around
the club taught her the art of intimidation. She no longer
stood by helplessly as groupies sat on my lap or fingered my
beard: she went chest-to-chest and told them, "Keep your
fuckin' hands offa my old man. Move, bitch." And they
moved.

One night I began to think I'd created a monster. She
heard I was at Okie's place partying with my old lover,
Mickey. Already loaded on reds, Helen stewed for a while
then planned to burst into the party, blazing away at the
two of us. Fortunately, as she was loading a 12-gauge aveng-
er, Durt and Z. dropped by and wrestled the gun away. Then
they stopped her from killing herself with reds.

When she seemed to pull herself together, they let her go
out the front door, figuring the worst she could do was dis-
rupt the party. Then, as she chugged toward the car, Durt
asked Z., "Hey man. Did ya check her purse?"

"No. I thought you did."

They intercepted her and found a Derringer in her purse.
Two shots were all she would need for Mickey and me. The
guys forced her back inside, without excessive manhan-
dling, then Z. volunteered to fetch me.

When I exploded through the front door, she was sitting
in my chair cradling my Eagle, and Durt was cowering behind the door. Rather than try to talk her finger away from
the touchy trigger, I slapped my .45 level and put a slug
through the club flag, inches above her head. As she froze, I
bounded forward, left-hooked her and knocked that wicked

thing out of her hands. "You dumb piece of shit. I outa kick your fuckin . . . Don't you ever . . ."

Durt exited discreetly while I pelted her with curses and flung her into the bedroom. As she turned turtle on the bed, I roared, "Now. Hear this!" I threw my .45 against her head, and with the barrel riding her ear, fired a round through the bed. The percussion nearly knocked her out. With the painful ringing in her head, she wasn't sure whether her brains were intact or splattered over the bedclothes. She cringed as I slapped her around the room and screamed, "Don't do anything like this ever again!"

My wife had embarrassed me in front of the club and ruined a perfectly good party. Although the club fined me $100 for shooting up the Angels flag, I felt justified in punishing her.

I thought I had taught her to look the other way when I messed around, but she was as stubborn as I was. She scared me again one night when Z. and I happened upon two unattended women at another member's house. Before dinner, we gave each $50 for new clothes and hair styling to make them more appetizing. After an evening on the town, we ended up on Z.'s boat, stoned and prancing around the cabin, naked under the black lights. As Z. reached outside to fit a pair of leopard print panties to the running light, a premonition crawled over me. "Z., we've gotta get outa here," I hollered above the stereo. "I don't know why. But I got a feelin' it would be a helluva idea to leave this dock." So, Zorro jagged to the controls and headed us for open bay waters, zigzagging from one side of the estuary to the other. Looking back, I saw a familiar white Chrysler prowling the docks. "Geez, that was close," I said.

XII—Angels Roost

"I always believed the kids came first and should be well taken care of, and the house should be taken care of. But when he started getting into drugs, when he started dealing and bringing people home and partying and stuff, the kids got shoved into the bedroom. They were only five or six."—Helen Wethern.

Our home belonged to the club, not my family. One bash seemed to flow into the next before last night's holdovers could haul themselves off the floor. Old Angels, young Angels, retired Angels, prospects, a smattering of buyers and dealers, women and just friends seemed to stream in all afternoon and evening.

Since hospitality went hand in hand with friendship, good business and my high roller's image, nothing was done on a small scale. The guys could swill Jack Daniels until their eyeballs melted. I broke out candy-bar-sized chunks of hash and opium, and spread $200 kilos of marijuana on the coffee table saying, "Take what ya want, everybody."

When everybody got loose, some kicked back and listened to the Jefferson Airplane and Grateful Dead pulsing through the bamboo screens. Others kicked into gear, dancing and laughing, tripping out on each other, their erotica, the guns and cutlery on the walls. And always at least one tried, and usually failed, to lift my 300-pound tractor wheel.

As soon as the party got ripping, Bobby and Donna were dispatched to their bedroom. They entertained themselves for entire evenings in front of their television, eating their dinner, keeping each other company, snacking.

We neglected them on party nights, and we seldom really talked to them, but we provided for them otherwise. We bought them solid religious and educational training in Catholic schools, good clothes, plenty of food and more toys than their playmates. And the Angels treated them like celebrities, because Bobby and Donna were about the only club children old enough to have well-developed personalities. They gave the kids gifts—five, ten and twenty dollar bills from Z., snare drums from Winston. Animal took them kite flying or played army with them. A number of guys took them for spins around the neighborhood on motorcycles, and that was the biggest thrill for Bobby.

Bobby was enthralled by the Angels, Donna was in fearful awe of most of them. But both were curious and fascinated by what they saw eavesdropping on us from the hallway:

They saw their mother in marijuana lethargy from being constantly high. They saw their father bouncing from speedy highs to comatose lows that put him on all fours. And they saw their parents' friends, desperadoes they read about in newspapers and heard about at school.

Dozens of scenes generated during those marathon orgies. Sonny kept a spellbound audience, including Sharon, as he bragged about beating another rap and spooned cocaine. Magoo, the top-hatted club medic, made his rounds, stroking his scraggly beard and peering over teatimer glasses while dispensing vitamins, penicillin and other pills from his battered doctor's satchel.

Meanwhile, Monk, the honorary club dietician, tried to convince some of us that cat meat tasted like chicken, but when he invited us for dinner, everyone begged off, joking about not liking "cat cacciatore." Monk was a crusty, funky smelling guy, but he and his equally smelly true love, Little Bonnie, mooned over each other like Clark Gable and Myrna Loy—and once rolled to the floor and balled in front of us all.

Across the room, some women were enrapt as "Boomer" Baker demonstrated his talent for munching crisp apples bare-gummed. In a corner, Tramp was working the drawers off some young thing freaking out on LSD. Durt was on the front steps with his old lady, Sherri, discussing mysteries of cosmos with a neighbor's four-year-old son. Mustachioed "Foo Manchu" Griffin came over to talk LSD business with me while his old lady, "Super Sharon," bullshitted with some guys about choppers, which she handled adroitly. She was one of the few women who commanded an audience because she was gutty enough to knock Tramp on his ass one day.

Big Al and Okie were sitting to one side, jive-assing each other, as they would say, like "a couple of niggers on East 14th Street." Another Oklahoman, Hi Ho Steve, shook his green Mohican-style topnotch, flourished a hatchet, then let out a whoop. "Green power's where it's at! Fuck black power!" Then he stopped to tell someone about his new loudspeakers on his twelve-foot-tall gasoline drum totem pole outside his house.

More serious matters were being discussed too. Winston and his cotton candy blond lady, Pat, were telling some people about their exotic felines. Zorro—by his own count the father of nine children by seven women—was hustling another one, keeping an eye on the front door for his current old lady, Linda. Raymond Dale "Stork" Keefauver, a raven-haired, tall bony man with satanic features, strutted around vowing he would never return to prison. And "Pops," who looked more like an aging North Beach beatnik than a Navy veteran, flashed a new deck of dirty pictures.

Close by were Tiny and Johnny Angel, inviting people over to try their new craps table. Gary Popkin, a 5-10, 225-pound cold-eyed blockhouse with a Ricky Nelson face, huddled with "Sir Gay" Walton, an airstream-haired delicate-looking guy who would become Sonny's sort of major-domo. There also were Tommy, an expert mechanic, who never could grasp the drug wheeler-dealer style and "Clean Cut," who looked more like a high school valedictorian than an Angel. And outside, Skip was crawling around the yard with a BB gun, playing army with Animal, plinking each other and toy tanks.

The gunplay shifted inside as I broke out automatic BB pistols for target practice. But that degenerated into a small war with BBs bouncing off bodies and pocking the walls—until I signaled a truce by firing a real .45 into the bamboo wall.

"Shit, I'm hungry," someone cried, then Helen went into action, frying chicken, broiling filet mignons by the dozen, whipping mashed potatoes by the bowlful. And when the food ran out, we sent for fast food. It wasn't uncommon to spend $300 or more for one of those near-nightly parties.

No matter how much fun people were having, there were violent undertones. No matter how much class a guy showed, he was unlikely to forget the unwritten dictum: never underestimate the power of fear. We all knew about the party games where sadistic minds shoved someone to-

ward the brink of terror or insanity. During a knockdown
drug bout, two members sometimes would do mental bat-
tle and a sideline man would join forces with the first guy
to seize the upper hand. Then they'd nip at the underdog
until he lost his composure.

I saw this happen again and again. And Tramp and I used
the technique to test Russell Beyea, a heavyweight who
came from Los Angeles' Satan's Slaves and later would be
convicted of both manslaughter and murder in separate
cases. We stuffed him with an arsenal of psychedelics, because he tried to show his machismo by shrugging off the
effects. But finally he was loaded beyond seeing and was
writhing in mental agony. Out of guilt, I fed him some tranquilizers and bedded him down with his girlfriend. "You
can't think, Russell, so just freak," I said. "Fuck and pass
the time."

When I got word that a drug shipment had arrived, joints
were snuffed and downers went down as I gathered my people and sent away the rest. The children slept as the payload
came home and our assembly line was activated. Reds and
whites were counted out, and the tabulated acid usually
was weighed, a chore that normally fell on Durt and me.
Preparations for the all-night packaging sessions were Hel-
en's responsibility. She purchased boxes of thousand-count
No. 1 or 00 capsules for secanol or methedrine capping, telling skeptical pharmacists: "My daughter's in the ballet and
us mothers use the capsules to divvy up dye so all their cos-
tumes are exactly the same color."

With raw grams of acid, I used Owsley's formula to calcu-
late how many hits could be made, how to buffer the drug
and how much would go to each customer. Generally we
made 3,000 to 4,000 doses from each gram and wholesaled
that for $3,000 to $3,500. Most deals ranged from five to ten
grams, but some were the equivalent of twenty-five grams,
which would wholesale for about $75,000 and retail for

137

$225,000 to $375,000, based on 1967 street prices of $3 to $5 a hit for Owsley acid. Our base prices varied according to customer and volume.

Delivery consumed a frantic twenty-four-hour day or two. Speed was essential, because sitting on a drug cache that could mean years in prison was sheer idiocy. I fueled myself with amphetamines and considered dozens of details and possible pitfalls before leaving the house with a small fortune in chemicals or sending my men out. While other members protected themselves by using walkie-talkies and monitoring police radio transmissions, I relied on my distribution techniques.

When I felt a customer couldn't be trusted completely, I dispatched one of my men to watch him so he wouldn't blow the whistle on us. Sometimes I stashed the drugs in a motel or some other safe place, then directed the customer to it. Usually, I sped around the Bay Area making drops myself. I got stoned over and over again as I bumped into well-connected dealers and bush league pushers while delivering to my customers. It was socializing for the sake of business, and in my loaded state of mind, it was tough to keep straight the various prices. Still, I always managed to follow the axiom: never let customers and sources meet. Familiarity between them might endanger my middle man's position.

XIII—The Acid King

Owsley's claim to the title "LSD King" was unchallenged, and his ascendency was nearly as rapid as the spread of acid use. Owsley was a somewhat independent spirit like his grandfather, the late Senator A. Owsley Stanley of Kentucky who declared in 1922, "You cannot milk a cow in America without an inspector at your heels." In June, 1956, young Owsley left home at the age of eighteen, then served a year and a half in the Air Force. Applying his military electronics skills, he got a series of engineering jobs in broadcasting, then drifted to the Bay Area in 1963.

After one semester at the University of California in Berkeley, he dropped out with low marks.[26] But his fortunes were destined to change because his girlfriend, Melissa, a twenty-four-year-old chemistry major, apparently had mastered the processes for manufacturing LSD and other marketable goodies.

On February 21, 1965, their bathroom lab in Berkeley was raided. Police were acting on reports that Owsley, a 5-7,

140-pounder who was as cleancut as a fraternity boy, was peddling speed to teenagers. Yet all the raiders found was a chemistry library, apparatus and nine bottles of a drug one step shy of being illegal. After his release, the brassy guy won a court order for return of his equipment, then the couple migrated to Los Angeles.

His first buys of lysergic acid, the main LSD component, came almost immediately, according to investigators. With $20,000 in $100 notes from an unknown source, he purchased 500 grams from the Cyclo Chemical Corporation, then another 300 grams from the National Chemical and Nuclear Corporation. To make the buys, he signed affidavits saying the chemicals were for research by the fictitious Baer Research Company.

In a way it *was* research. Police said Owsley manufactured and wholesaled LSD from his home overlooking California State College at Los Angeles and took mail orders at a Sunset Boulevard address. Narcotics agents estimated that the 800 grams of lysergic acid could have been turned into 1.5 million hits of LSD. So Owsley became known as the man who made $1 million before LSD became a controlled substance in April, 1966.

That year Owsley surfaced in the Bay Area, and Harvard psychologist Timothy Leary was preaching mind expansion for the masses. Thousands, and maybe millions, were turning on, if not tuning in or dropping out. LSD, once the chemical fare of controlled experiments, C.I.A. tests and avant-garde intellects, became a street drug.

To most people, Owsley was a mysterious Wizard of Odd who talked about turning on the whole world, hung out with the Grateful Dead and provided LSD to spike Kool-Aid at the famous "Trips Festival" in San Francisco. Newspapers portrayed him as a mad scientist or a playboy with a taste for beautiful women and fast cars. Many people had heard of him yet few even knew his full name then—Augustus Owsley Stanley III.

As the country's leading LSD chemist and the club's chief acid source, the Owl, as we called him, enjoyed celebrity status around some members. Guys overlooked his arrogance and made allowances for him, although Sonny would as soon have stomped on the quick-tongued wiseguy as rapped with him.

Public propaganda and Tramp's reverence put me in awe of Owsley at first. He was "the Man," someone to court to insure cordial financial dealings. Besides, his acid, namely "white lightning" and "Pink Owsley" was in such great demand and was so highly rated by street connoisseurs that I could almost name my price. Naturally, when I heard that Owsley was fond of his namesake bird, I put out word: "I want an owl within twenty-four hours. Price no object."

Duke, one of my suburban dealers, steered me to a bird collector who parted with an owl for $100. When Tramp saw the bird at my house, he volunteered for delivery duty, presumably to take credit for the gift.

"No way," I told him. "When the owl goes to 'the Man,' I give it to him."

After the presentation a few weeks later, Owsley showed his pleasure by treating me to some acid and other drugs as we drove to a few Berkeley area chemical companies picking up tanks of nitrous oxide, or "laughing gas," a currently popular party inhaler. We sampled it at Owsley's place in the flatlands.

Several months later, the chemist had moved to the upper-rent district surrounding Berkeley's Claremont Hotel, and he invited Tramp and me up one sunny afternoon. In the hills home with a peekaboo bay view, Owsley's confidence didn't seem so abrasive. He graciously set out a spread for us—including the caviar of psychedelics, DMT. In a careening euphoria, we listened to Owsley try in vain to verbalize the DMT trip, and we eyed Melissa, naked and glistening with oil, ambling back and forth from her towel to the swimming pool. It was an impressive showing.

141

In the fall of 1967, Owsley retreated deeper into the suburbs. He rented a home in Orinda, an area of young executives, scrub oaks and swimming pools. In this natural hideaway, Owsley set up a sophisticated drug factory and manufactured Pink Owsley in unprecedented volume in rooms meticulously taped off to prevent any escape of dust.

The LSD field had been dry in late 1967, so thousands of people were anticipating a new crop. Owsley kept us posted on production. And, in turn, we alerted our dealers and customers that something big was in the works. Orders and advance payment came to me day and night. It would undoubtedly be our largest deal ever.

As we geared up for a blockbuster distribution, there was a loud knock at Owsley's door on December 21, 1967. "Federal agents," came a louder voice. "Have search warrants for these premises. Open the door." Then authorities who had been watching Owsley for more than a year smashed their way inside with sledgehammers.

"How'd you find my lab?" Owsley asked as he was handcuffed. His ponytail hanging over a flowery shirt, he sat glumly on his couch while a dozen agents searched and seized. "You're uninvited guests," he complained. "Please take only the contraband."

In addition to the intricate, highly mobile lab, agents uncovered five three-foot-tall drums, several cases of assorted chemicals and quantities of LSD and STP. They arrested Owsley, Melissa and three other persons.

The next morning, I picked up the San Francisco *Chronicle* and read on the front page: "Augustus Owsley Stanley III, revered among hippies as the King of Acid, was arrested by federal drug control agents yesterday in a raid on a three-story house in suburban Orinda."

Reading on, I slammed down my fist. Agents called it the biggest LSD arrest in history and said 217 grams of acid—2 million hits, worth $10,850,000—and 161 grams of STP worth $130,000 were confiscated!

142

We got over our disappointment and did what we could to help Owsley. At Tramp's suggestion, I took a crew of four members and a rented van to the Orinda house. We found the front door open and the interior dusted with enough pink LSD to send an asthmatic breather on an endless trip. With one eye out for the cops, we cleaned up all possibly incriminating evidence, including dust and the butcher paper that covered the walls and windows. Flammable materials were destroyed in the fireplace. Everything else, along with Owsley's furniture, was carted to my house for storage.

When Owsley got out on bail, he dropped by to reclaim his furniture and to reestablish contact with Tramp and me. Forewarned, Helen straightened up the house, rolled a fistful of joints and displayed our finest drugs. Although she had the impression that Owsley was a charming ladies' man, the chemist in the flesh turned her off. She saw him as a smallish, rude, rodentlike guy who wore a buckskin jacket and raided her refrigerator without asking. While assembling a bologna sandwich, he grumbled, "Ya got any mustard?" Helen and I fumed while Tramp stood by as though nothing was wrong.

As we got stoned in the living room, Owsley made it even clearer that he believed Tramp was under his thumb and I was under his foot. His monologue about expanding ripples of consciousness, and Tramp's yes-man behavior, made me sick. Each word seared me. I stared him down, imagining how I would handle him if he weren't my supplier. I felt like a damn fool letting that little guy, with nothing except chemistry knowhow, come into my house and insult us. Finally, I gave him the heavy vibes that sometimes helped sell his acid. I raised myself in my chair a couple of times, glared, knit my eyebrows and whitened my knuckles. Then, Owsley took the hint and said out of the blue, "I gotta split."

While Tramp and I strained over his heavy furniture,

143

Owsley just stood to one side as though watching hired movers.

"Hey, goddammit," I snapped. "How 'bout giving us a hand?"

"Oh. Sure. Sure."

In spite of the friction between us, our paths continued to cross because Owsley didn't let his pending trial curtail his business. He had squirreled away large quantities of LSD in raw form. And rather than risk buffering and tabulating it, he sold us the stuff along with processing instructions.

We unloaded most of the acid on Chuck, Chuckles and Stevie and their dealing collective. After making a small fortune peddling among the flower children, they moved from the Haight-Ashbury to a curio store on College Avenue near the Oakland-Berkeley line. The location was convenient for me, and gave them easy access to both the Haight and Telegraph Avenue.

The first time I made my way through the displays of leather goods, candles and chintzy imports to the back room, it was obvious the store was pure front. It was as busy as the floor of the Pacific Stock Exchange back there. Runners were breezing in and out, pausing long enough to get stoned. Counters were counting drugs and money. One guy was paid to do nothing except take small bills to banks to trade them for $100 bills. He'd elbow his way through the room, snatch up a sack of cash, then gallop off like a Pony Express rider. The only ones not hustling were a forty-year-old hippie and a white-muzzled dog, both named Jack.

I visited the shop periodically, yet never made a delivery there. It was more proper and safer to have my dealers come to me. Each transaction was an opportunity to exercise control over the final product, and even their personal lives. Maintaining drug quality and imposing the club rule against needle use simply were means of protecting my livelihood. If my dealers developed heroin habits, they'd be unreliable. Or if the acid was cut so much that customers were dissatisfied or so little that they jumped out of windows, business would be hurt.

I instructed them in buffering techniques. But none of us were chemists, and no matter how hard we tried to follow Owsley's instructions, the procedures were imprecise and slipshod as often as not. The one thing I could control was the marketing. Under threat of cutting off their acid supply, I told my dealers how much of the drug to sell and how fast to do it without glutting the market.

Meanwhile, Owsley was searching for ways to wisely invest his profits. One of the most logical investments would be in rock music, because he had done music engineering work. He also was a close friend and associate of the Grateful Dead, a gutty and talented group that got some drug-bust press. In fact, he introduced Tramp and me to the Dead at a practice session at a rented hall in Novato—and we got stoned.

The next time Owsley brought us into his rock circles, business was in the offing. It was mid-1968. We threaded our way through dancers at the Carousel Ballroom, one of the half-dozen rock music palaces celebrating the "San Francisco Sound" and so-called "acid rock." We had gone backstage at other concerts—like the night Tramp spooned Otis Redding with cocaine to keep him singing—but this back office was the musical equivalent of the "smoke-filled room." In addition to Tramp, Owsley and me, there were several guys in the rock music business. Backgrounded by squealing guitars, they discussed a proposal to purchase the ballroom. They agreed it could be a good moneymaker and a solid competitor for impresario Bill Graham's original Fillmore Auditorium. All they would have to do was grab a bigger share of the top talent migrating to the San Francisco music scene. They sounded like hip baseball team owners.

"Think you'd like to invest?" Tramp asked me.

145

"Nope. Count me out." As I told Tramp later, further entanglement with Owsley was the last thing I wanted, and I didn't like the sound of the deal.

Once that was decided, I changed roles and played backup—bull-necked, mean-mouthed, bullet-eyed, hand quick to dip for my .45. The intimidation game was fun. Drifting behind the entrepreneurs, I cleared my throat or exhaled cigarette smoke to keep them off guard. Uneasy men were less likely to pull a shady business deal.

Finally, Tramp, Owsley and some others indicated their interest in giving the venture a try. I don't know if a final decision was reached later or not, but the Carousel soon changed hands. Officially, the ballroom, formerly known as El Patio, was taken over by a group that included Grateful Dead manager Ron Rakow; Brian Rohan, lawyer for many of the rock bands, and several "unnamed investors." The Dead and the Airplane each played for minimum scale to help build operating funds for the project, which was billed as a showcase for young bands. And for a while, Angels were admitted free to concerts there, and in turn, they unintentionally helped police the place. However, bad organization, police harassment and ego tripping punctured the dream project about three months later.[27]

Owsley apparently had plenty of money to invest or otherwise unload. He told Tramp he had socked away money in Swiss banks. Tramp said he accepted an invitation to stash some funds there too, but I declined outright. "Tramp, you gotta be kidding," I snorted at him privately. "I'm too busy giving money to my people. And, anyway, that's too far away to keep your money. If ya can't spend it at the corner store, then it's no good."

People conjectured about Owsley's bankroll, and one day I got a pretty good idea of its magnitude. Tramp pulled up to my house on his motorcycle. "Hey, George! How 'bout takin' the Chrysler on a little drive? We gotta get some money for the Man."

"Whatta ya mean?" I always had assumed that Owsley got his forty percent cut when the deal was closed.

"He asked me to put it away for him," Tramp explained.

That was my first strong indication that Tramp's ties to hipster friends were stronger than club loyalties. And Owsley's trust in Tramp also was substantial—if the size of the nest egg meant anything.

At each bank, the routine was the same. Tramp went inside, was admitted to the vault area, dipped into a safe deposit box and exited with shocks of currency that he stuffed into a suitcase on the back seat.

"How much we gonna bring him?" I inquired.

Tramp only smiled and shrugged. But after he sauntered out of a bank on East 14th Street with $80,000, I knew it was time to keep my .357 magnum ready. Gripping the pistol with one hand and steering with the other, I drove to several more banks. Along the way, we eyed every passing car and pedestrian, and monitored the rearview mirror. Matters easily could have become deadly. Many men had murdered for a small fraction as much money.

After the final pickup, we were dripping with sweat and ready to shoot anyone or anything confronting us. We killed an hour watching the car from inside a sporting goods store. Then we drove a short distance out Telegraph Avenue to the Sears parking lot. Walking briskly, Owsley approached, grabbed the suitcase, thanked us, then drove off. As the man at the top, he could afford to let others do his banking. But he wasn't above counting his money. Later that day, he telephoned Tramp to complain the suitcase was $1,000 light. There was only $326,000!

XIV—Running for Fun

"Don't think we've turned softies. It's just the really heavy exhibitionists are in the background now. Today it isn't the idea to go out and cause a scene out front. Like, I wouldn't go into a bar and shoot three people with my patch on. Like, I'd take my patch off."—"Big Don" Hollingsworth, 6-5, 225-pound vice-president, to a reporter on the 1970 Bass Lake run.[28]

Runs generally brought out the best and worst in us. Runs were times for both interclub unity and fierce individuality. Times to meet brothers from other chapters. Times to put prospects through their paces. Times to put women and outsiders in their places. Times to pour down, pop and smoke a smorgasbord of drugs in mind-burning quantities. Times for getting looser than loose and showing off just what made us Angels.

Runs weren't restrained by the clock, the speedometer,

the law or the human body's limits. The first stage was a torturously long motorcycle ride that either could freeze or dehydrate you, depending on weather. We rode in formation, with our provisions and armaments carried by a trailing convoy of cars, trucks and campers driven by women or disabled members. By whim, we'd fall into single file or fan across all lanes, piling up cars for miles. For a change of pace, we'd split the double-line highway divider, well above the speed limit, then thunder past cars, close enough to spit into the windows.

Although destinations often were kept secret, we often picked up a law enforcement escort. Sheriff's deputies followed us to their county line, then another jurisdiction picked us up. There normally wasn't much trouble on the road, but small roadside towns were another story. Whenever guys splintered off for gas or alcohol, it seemed they'd get hassled by the local heat. Taking over a one-gas-pump town was the farthest thing from our minds, although some stragglers might get attached to a barstool in one and never quite make it to our encampment.

Once the main troops arrived at popular places such as Bass Lake near Yosemite, Lake Mendocino up north or Squaw Rock on the Russian River, the authorities reserved a special campsite for us. Sometimes Sonny made prior arrangements, other times police escorts radioed ahead to announce us. But, in either case, our camp would be roped off or guarded so innocents or troublemakers wouldn't wander in. Authorities generally checked us into the camp one by one, noting our identification and bike registration and, sometimes, photographing us. One or two guys might get vehicle citations, but we let the incidents pass with no more than a curse. We had a weekend ahead of us.

As camp was made, you could see most guys traveled light with nothing more than a heavy coat or sleeping bag while others showed off their affluence by riding a motorcycle and having their old lady bring their truck or van. Tramp had a country castle—a VW bus with awnings and lawn furniture. Others, like me, had campers or vans with stereo. Some guys strung tarps and parachutes between trees as provisions were unloaded. If there wasn't enough wood on the ground, we cut some down with automatic weapons fire.

Once a ritual fire was roaring, the party was under way. Spontaneity ruled. Anything could happen, and it was a little scary. Some guys played cards over beers or dope; others scuffled or pissed playfully on each other's motorcycles. Sometimes somebody would ride his motorcycle into a tree.

A few guys would venture into the water, sometimes fully clothed. They'd have contests to see how far they could throw their women, or they'd pole makeshift rafts around.

Prospects were pitted against each other. Dogs were pushed into bloody fights to cries of, "Kill. Kill. Kill." Cisco's monkey sometimes would be stumbling around like the rest of us, loaded to the gills. And there was a din of rock music, occasional gunshots and grumbling engines.

As night came on, campfires and bodies were refueled. Guns were stowed according to club rules, and dinner was roasted on open fires or barbecues. Usually it was standard picnic fare—steaks, hotdogs, hamburgers and chicken. But sometimes a member came up with a suckling pig, and once a rustled calf. (The calf got a brief reprieve by making lots of friends while tethered to a tree, but, back in Oakland, it went the way of all beef.)

When exhaustion came on, some guys called on amphetamines then returned to the gluttony. Others just crashed in cars, under bushes, wherever they dropped. A surprising number partied twenty-four hours a day for the entire weekend.

When we partied publicly, journalists and filmmakers

flocked around, hoping to see a reenactment of *The Wild One*, to get a candid glimpse of us at play, to answer the question: What are the Hell's Angels really like? Most reporters and photographers did their work from the safety of police staging areas. Those who entered our camps often became unwilling or unwitting participants. Many were just bullshitted.

Once we were joined by a nationally known teen dance host on a Half Moon Bay outing, on the coast south of San Francisco. After cleaning out the town's liquor store and a ladies' auxiliary cake sale, we set up a camp called "Stumble Creek" for obvious reasons. Before the TV personality could put his crew in action, about 100 guys were lurching and milling, drinking, doping, mixing, dancing to car stereos, playing catch with beer cans.

It was Helen's first bona-fide run so she helped me open a "pharmacy." Back against a tree, cannisters of drugs bulging my pockets, I dispensed psychedelics to the partyers. I sold to those with cash and arranged credit for those without it. That was my idea of a great party—getting ripped with friends and making money hand over fist.

As the sun dropped below the redwoods, the picnic atmosphere was transformed into a heavy foot-stomping, broad-humping, music-thumping debacle. Mickey and Marsi, Tramp's old lady, followed the television crew around, flaunting their attributes and marijuana stogies. "Hey, man. I'll star for ya," they taunted. "Come here, baby." And when our guests politely backed away Mickey baited them, "Whatsa matter? Doncha like us?" I guess the film crew figured that a return pass might earn them a stomping. But failure to respond was worse, because it was construed as snobbery. They were out of their element and didn't know how to act.

Finally, one broad confronted the dance host: "Wanna get loaded? Try this."

151

"What's that?"

"Acid."

Refusing as gracefully as possible, he gathered his men and slipped away from Stumble Creek, leaving us without a chronicler.

During an outing to Lake Mendocino, nearly 150 miles to the north, Helen and I collapsed on a picnic table after the first exhausting day. Covered only by my military foul-weather jacket, we shivered in our sleep until we were awakened by a noisy gang bang. Out of curiosity, Helen peered into the dark but couldn't make anything out except a circle of guys and the unmistakable grunting, snickering and panting.

"Put your head down and go to sleep," I told her.

"Come on. Tell me what's happening," she begged. "I never seen one before."

I pulled the coat over her head and held her close. It was the same old story—a limited orgy became something else as more and more guys lined up for service.

By the July 4, 1968, run to Bass Lake, runs had started to seem like repetitious chores. After making the 250-mile trek without Helen and putting in one dutiful day, I putted back to Oakland in my favorite fashion—at eighty-five and ninety miles an hour through heat waves of a 105-degree afternoon, keeping the engine percolating even when gassing up.

At home, I telephoned my friend, Gordo, with a wild scheme aimed at impressing the members and making amends for my early departure. Gordo owed me a favor because I'd given him $2,000 to help get his airplane pilot's license.

In a while, Gordo was circling Bass Lake in a rented plane with Helen, Z.'s girlfriend Linda and me aboard. I leaned

152

out a window, blaring the airhorn from Z.'s boat. I was trying to get the club's attention but—though we didn't know
it then—we were drawing rifle fire from guys who thought
our plane was a challenging, if not hostile, target. "You got
the package ready?" I asked. Helen was just finishing tying
a mini-parachute, made with a silk handkerchief, to our
Angels CARE package—a shoe box sampler of my most exotic drugs.

"Hey, man, get this crate lower," I shouted to the pilot.
"We gotta get closer. Lower. Lower." As he banked over the
lake, the plane nearly went out of control because all of us
were looking out the window along one side. But I released
the CARE package. The parachute opened and floated toward the club camp. We let out hoots and blasted the airhorn—but we learned later that wind carried the package
into a towering tree. Squirrel chow.

XV—Exit an Angel, Exit the Owl, Enter an Albatross

I could excuse myself from club social functions, but jury duty was another matter. On the night of February 1, 1968, a phone call from Tramp woke me up. "Come on over," he said. "We got the asshole who ripped off Sonny's place." When we arrived at a member's house, we heard yelling so I left Helen on the front porch with Marsi.

Inside was a kangaroo court of a half-dozen members interrogating Paul A. "German" Ingalls, a twenty-one-year-old mechanic who had transferred from the Omaha chapter. Red-haired, 5-10 and 150 pounds, he was perspiring heavily and was more pale than usual. He had been charged with burglarizing Sonny's collection of coins, a valuable one. The one thing worse than stealing from a member was stealing from the president. You couldn't trust somebody like that. "Nobody rips off the chief," somebody growled.

German sensed his predicament. His blue eyes shimmered with terror. "We got direct evidence you did it, so admit it, motherfucker," one accuser screamed. German proclaimed his innocence, but his denials made everybody madder. Some guys held him by his long hair as others slapped him around and took turns zapping his face, eyes and sex organs with an electric prod. When he again denied his guilt, I yelled, "Why you dirty sonofabitch. You lying . . ." Then I stomped on his feet before the others could stop me. "Don't bruise him," Tramp warned. "Don't mark up the asshole."

At that, I was certain German faced more than a beating. Suddenly several members were hovering over him, ramming reds in his mouth. "See how you like these, you greedy shit. Take 'em, dammit." He resisted as fistfuls of reds were pushed against his mouth. Hands grabbed his shoulders and hair. Someone pinched his nostrils, forcing him to open his mouth to breathe. Some reds went in; he spit some out. Guys smeared pills between his lips, pried his jaws apart and worked his mouth. "That's it, baby. Take 'em. Take all you want." When he got weak, he swallowed whatever they fed him. His body went pliant, his eyes peaceful. "Let's get him home fast," somebody said.

I was dumbfounded. We had talked so many times about killing and the best ways to accomplish it, but it always just seemed like tough talk before. As German faded into unconsciousness, I saw my chance to exit and took Tramp aside. "It ain't cool havin' the women here. I'll get rid of 'em." I went outside and without explanation said, "Come on, girls. There's no party tonight. Lemme take you home."

German went home in a coma, was discovered by his wife at 1 A.M. and was dead on arrival at a local hospital.[29] His execution, as far as I know, was the chapter's first. It created a precedent: ripping off the president was a capital crime.

In 1968, Owsley's pending drug trial over the Orinda raid and other legal problems stemmed his chemical output, at least as far as we were concerned.[30] Nicholas Sand—a chemist first introduced to me in 1967 as Owsley's protégé—prepared to fill the vacuum.

In May, 1968, Sand showed up at Tramp's house for a meeting. "This is the man who's gonna replace Owsley," Tramp told me. I shook hands with Sand, an aloof, businesslike modish guy, then was introduced to his partner, David Leigh Mantell, a soft-spoken guy in his midtwenties. After discussing the psychedelics market in terms of new products and volume, Sand and Mantell agreed to sell us all their acid output. "Do you think you can handle 50,000 hits a week?" Sand asked.

Tramp turned to me, because I was in charge of distribution. "Do you think we can handle it?"

After figuring for a moment, I replied, "Yeah. We can handle it. No sweat."

Under the accord, Sand and Mantell would be guaranteed $40,000 a week and we would get the rest. For starters, Sand fronted me 27,000 hits of acid to see how well it turned. My customers found the strength and quality indistinguishable from Owsley's. Within a week, all the acid was sold and the money divvied up. In that first half-sized deal, my cut was about $10,000, and I gave Tramp $30,000 for Sand and Mantell.

Each week I wholesaled about 50,000 hits at a dollar each. About $40,000 went to Tramp and the chemists, and I kept about $10,000 for my people. But soon customer complaints started filtering back to me. They said the acid was bunk.

There never were complaints about Owsley's acid, so I expected the same high standards from Sand. Confronted at Tramp's house, he admitted under preliminary questioning that the bad stuff was STP, not LSD. He tried to minimize the deception, saying that the switch was an interim measure to use up a stock of STP chemicals. But the fact remained, he had allowed us to unwittingly betray our clientele—and endanger our reputation.

Sand apologized, and we agreed to peddle the STP, since he was our main psychedelics source at the time. Once STP was correctly advertised, the novelty item sold about as well as acid. Yet the temporary shift to STP permitted upstart dealers to move into the LSD market with "blue flats" and other varieties. Also, people soon tired of STP because it was crude compared to acid. Finally, we discovered Sand was selling out the back door to other dealers, at lower prices. Soon there was such bad karma between Sand and us that even accidents occurred.

In one instance, "Big Al" foolishly buried 12,000 hits of STP in his garage for safekeeping, but dampness made them a useless blob. Tramp and I threw that $12,000 lump into his XKE, then drove about 75 miles north to Sand's Cloverdale ranch. Uncertain whether the chemist would make good on the drugs, we wanted to make a heavy entrance. I tried to shoot the lock off the front gate, cowboy style, but the lock was too tough. We ended up jumping the fence and walking toward the farm house, past a small duck pond, an orchard and a stand of trees near a geodesic dome. The place had the mellowly cerebral feel you'd expect around associates of Tim Leary's Brotherhood of Eternal Love.[31]

After a tepid greeting, Mantell showed us around. It was an impressive ranch, but the people weren't. We were introduced to about a dozen men and women who reacted with some trepidation when Tramp and I took target practice on a hillside. When Sand showed up, he was a little rattled and apologized for having the gate locked. With little discussion, he agreed to replace the damaged drugs.

I thought Sand's respect for physical aggression would keep him honest. But even more than Owsley, he underestimated our business savvy and tested us.

The case of Bald Eagle—a dealer I inherited after Foo, my

fellow club distributor, went to prison[32]—was a good example. When Bald Eagle turned down a load of STP, saying he could get a better price, I decided to identify and eliminate the competing source. The Bay Area couldn't absorb more than 50,000 hits a week.

Bald Eagle met my clan and me at the Oakland Estuary yacht harbor on a dark chilly night shortly after that. No one else was around, and the only sounds were the nearby freeway and the regular, fog-muffled slapping of water against pilings. I had invited the dealer on a "bay cruise" to talk business and socialize, but he was beginning to wonder. His eyes had that tense rabbit look, and his worried brow seemed to go halfway up his hairless head. In an apparent attempt to please, he told us he was planning a trip to Mexico to buy marijuana and the ancient Indian pottery he collected. "It'll be premium weed," he said.

"I hope you get to make that trip," I replied as we boarded the cabin cruiser.

Inside, I pointed a compelling finger and said, "Sit down in the back, Baldy. We wanna discuss these low prices. Tell us everything you know."

He sat his porky body down. But he was a pretty prominent dealer so he was reluctant to reveal his sources. When we got fed up with his evasiveness, I slugged him and buried a gun muzzle in his temple. Z. and Animal shouted threats and Durt started chaining a concrete block. When somebody growled, "Fuck it. Let's dump him," Bald Eagle started regurgitating names, places and prices. Essentially, he revealed that Sand had been dealing him STP behind our backs. To further test him, I creased his head with a pistol and the death anchor was wrapped around his feet. Bald Eagle spewed more convincing details. He passed his test.

I arranged a meeting with Sand in a parked car across the street from Evergreen Cemetery. Naturally, Sand denied everything. It took a light pistol whipping to freshen his memory. "You don't wanna end up there yet," I said gesturing toward the gravestones. Cringing, he acknowledged his double-dealing and begged forgiveness. He promised to discontinue back-door sales and to abide by our agreement.

At my urging, he further confessed that he was making STP from chemicals intended for DMT production. That wouldn't have been damning except that Sand not only was receiving free DMT chemicals from me but also was charging me full price for STP made from them. I estimated that we passed him enough chemicals—stolen by my hippie trio from various university and commercial chemistry and photography labs—to manufacture about eight million hits of STP.

What really galled me was learning from Sand that Tramp was aware of the chicanery all along. Rampaging home, I pushed my way to the telephone, past Z., his girlfriend and Helen. I got Tramp on the line at Skip's house.

"You dirty piece of shit," I called him. "You back-stabbing, slimy sonofabitch. Come over here and I'll kick your ass." Tramp shot back his own invective and said he was on his way.

I had deliberately avoided any explanation, because I wanted to confront him eye to eye. Did his hippie friends and business associates mean more than his brothers? Why did he take the back seat whenever I jacked up Sand? Why didn't he ever demand free drugs or money when Sand screwed up? Why did Sand seem immune to our fines system?

I heard the rumble of Tramp's chopper a minute later. Peeking through the shades, I saw him fall down with his motorcycle. He was loaded, and had a pistol in his belt. Grabbing a shotgun, I greeted him at the front door by cracking the stock over his head. As we went down together, he drew his Walther P-38 and clubbed back. Z. and the two women dashed outside, while we tumbled across the floor, slugging and cursing each other, breaking lamps and tables.

I fought harder, knowing why I was fighting. I splattered so much of his blood that it was amazing he stayed conscious. Finally, we rolled into the kitchen and collapsed, exhausted by the flurry. Panting, I explained that I felt betrayed and accused him of counteracting the club code and business principles. Tramp, his wild mane matted with blood, copped to nothing. He claimed he'd just forgotten to tell me about the DMT chemicals.

"We gotta talk this thing out," I said leading the way out of the bloody room to the camper. After a long talk, I gave Tramp the benefit of the doubt. He blamed Sand for the "mixup."

"Well, then, piss on them crooks," I said. "We ain't goin' for this bullshit from Sand, and that's that."

"Well, shit. Let's go get him, then."

Tramp was gung-ho and eager to prove his loyalty, but this time, I showed the restraint:

"We gotta plan it out. Whenever Sand gets outa line, we gotta remind him why he's doin' business with us. I think I made my point this time. Sand was real nice with something in his ear."

My mainstay buyers remained the hippie trio and Bald Eagle, yet I enlisted at various times dozens of smaller buyers, many of them friends wanting to turn 1,000 hits or so of acid or a few kilos of marijuana on a weekly or monthly basis. I fronted drugs or money to get most of them in business. They were Angels or ex-Angels on the skids, truck drivers or factory workers supplementing their income or buddies from my construction days or other motorcycle clubs.

A few were drifters like "Tommy Teeshirt," a longhair

with the survival instincts of a cockroach. After I fronted him a small quantity of acid, his beat became the rock concert circuit and West Coast university campuses. He did well enough to fly back here now and then to restock his kit bag. I used to pay Junior $100 to pick up Tommy at the airport in a black limousine. Then I'd sell Tommy part of my personal stash in the wee morning hours, and he'd be on his nomadic, empire-building way.

My clientele reached beyond the hipsters in the Haight, Berkeley and other youth Meccas to thousands of straights in the suburban heartland. They attached neither mystical nor political importance to drug use. They used acid and weed like liquor, or they found the transition slight from uppers and downers to psychedelics.

One of my best links to the tract home set was Duke, a longtime grass and pills hustler who owned a trucking outfit. His customers generally were middle- and upper-income closet heads. The more adventuresome ones got bored with grass, reds and whites, then splurged on psychedelics. I'm sure most never guessed their drugs came from the terrible Hell's Angels.

Duke was a suave, handsome fortyish guy with a solid image as a straight. He had a nice business, a nice house and a nice wife. We were more than business associates. He and his wife dined and partied at our house, and he called on me to help with his problems, even domestic ones. One particular night, I rushed to his home and found him pacing in his shorts. "I think I overdosed my wife," he said fearfully. "Ya know what I mean? Take a bath with her or something." Old Duke had used psychedelics as an aphrodisiac—and it worked too well. He couldn't satisfy his wife and was afraid she'd lose her mind. As other saviors started to arrive, I went into the bedroom. She was reclining on the bed, wearing little more than a shit-eating grin.

161

"You're cookin', ain't you?" I said for openers.

Her smile broadened in acknowledgment, and I guessed her scam.

"I could dig it, but I ain't gonna do it," I told her. Then I returned to Duke and pushed him toward the bedroom, saying, "Just jump between the sheets and freak with your old lady. Everything will be okay. You'll see."

Friends or not, I found that Duke wasn't always trustworthy. He farmed out a shipment of bad reds to my friend J.B.—a shipment originally intended for me—and J.B.'s customer failed to show up to make the buy. Since I was indirectly responsible for the burn, I contacted the would-be buyer in San Francisco. "Listen," I snarled over the phone. "This is the insurance company. You were supposed to be there for the pickup." Then I told a little lie. "Your negligence caused a friend of mine to be interrogated by the police. You're liable. You'll take this shipment of reds now. Your fine is $5,000, which you'll pay on demand. Then you'll sell those reds and pay us a second time for them."

The guy agreed, "Sure. Anything you say. I'll stay right here. I'm really sorry, man."

After payment was arranged, Z. and I went after Duke at his house. "Them reds ain't worth a shit," I told him. "You were gonna unload that bunk on me, weren't ya?"

Gaping at the pearl-handled .38 automatic in my belt, Duke collapsed on the floor, nauseous with terror and gagging.

"You dirty, slimy asshole," I yelled. "I ain't even pulled the gun out yet. Get on your feet and get on the phone. I want your connection." Disclosing a connection was verboten, unless a dealer wanted to forfeit his livelihood or possibly his life. When Duke hesitated, I waved my pistol and redefined the choices, "Either it stops with you or it goes on. Do you want the blame? We got a 'dead body.'

162

Whatta we do with it? Them reds ain't no good. They ain't what you advertised. Now something has to be done."

Duke called his connection and explained the situation. When I took the phone, Whitey, a non-Angel bennies manufacturer from Hayward, was on the line. I once had sold him $3,000 in uncut speed, but that didn't change matters.

"There's been a slight error and some misrepresentation, Whitey. This is very bad. It will cost you." I set up a meeting that night, and made it sound like we had a whole army of pissed off Angels down the street. Whitey was no lightweight.

When we pulled up to Whitey's place, Z. said, "Lemme carry a piece." Z. wasn't the torpedo type but I slipped him a .45-caliber Colt Commander for backup. "Okay," I told him. "Stay behind me. They can't even see you behind me. But, if one of them guys pulls out a weapon, you'd better be shootin' over my shoulder. Stay ready." Z., a shaky guy, was comically cool as he loaded and rammed home a clip.

Whitey's place was a typical suburban Castro Valley tract house, except the screened door was wide open. Not a soul was in sight but the stereo blared. It seemed like a setup.

"Come on in," Whitey called from the bathroom.

"Come on out. Slow," I replied. Whitey strolled out with a gracious smile, offered us a seat, expressed his regrets, then promised, "The whole thing will be remedied."

"We need $1,000 right now as a sign of good faith," I said businesslike, and Whitey peeled the bills out of his wallet. With hardly a word spoken, I pocketed the money and we exited.

Back in the car, I split the grand with Z. and took back my Colt. When I popped out the clip, I bellowed, "You dummy!" A bullet was jammed cockeyed in the chamber. If there had been trouble, Z. would have been useless.

* * *

163

Though Z. was never very adept with bullets or knuckles, he did learn to turn a dealer's mistake into money. And he showed me up on one occasion.

On that day, I dispatched Z. and Big Al to Frisco after Juan and Mark, a couple of Berkeley-based acid dealers, called on me for help. En route, my guys were pulled over and hassled by the police. They were thinking about busting Al, an ex-felon, for having a concealed weapon—a pocket knife—but they let him go. When Z. and Al arrived in Frisco, they found they had been summoned for a very minor matter.

"You put us in jeopardy when it was unnecessary," Z. raged at the dealers. "We gotta buy off a lousy judge now. Your mistake will cost you $55,000."

After hearing a little sword-rattling, the dealers admitted. "All right. We messed up. I guess we'll pay." It apparently was worth the money to save their hides and to keep doing business with us.

A few hours later, Z. and I were peering out the windows of Sonny's house. When Juan and Mark pulled slowly up the block in their car, Z. headed for the door. I grabbed his arm, but he said, "I can handle it, man. It's my gig, this time."

"Go to it," I said, figuring that Z. was tired of being back-up man and wanted to prove himself.

About ten minutes later, Z. waltzed inside with a sly grin. "Here, man, look what I got for us." Cool-like, he tore open his field jacket, exposing bouquets of greenbacks, in his belt, his shirt, everywhere. "Forty-five fucking thousand dollars!" he exclaimed.

Unaware that the original fine was $55,000, I cuffed his back, causing a few bills to flutter to the floor.

"Half of this is yours, George," he said.

"Nah. We gotta take care of everybody, just like in a deal," I said. "Here's what we'll do. Here's $25,000. That's yours right off the get go. Now you're about even with me and what I've got saved. Now we'll divvy up the rest, with $5,000 each to me and Tramp, $2,500 each to Albert, Durt, Animal and Foo." (Tramp was supposed to put away Foo's cut even when he was in prison, but I don't know how much, if any, reached him.)

Since Christmas was approaching, I suggested, "Look, Z. You can take this dough around to everybody as presents. It'll blow their minds."

Durt just gawked at his $2,500. "What the hell's this for?"

"Merry Christmas," Z. said.

And I chimed in, "It's your Christmas bonus. Take it. It's all legal, clear, cash money." Then Santa and I made our next delivery.

XVI—Battles and Treaties

As the club acquired some hippie trappings and became less of a fraternity of old Oakland buddies, some members compromised their loyalty or lost their taste for physical confrontation except under the most favorable circumstances. Despite the "brother" rhetoric, lots of the younger guys lived by an every-man-for-himself ethic, and keeping an individual reputation, body and finances intact became more important than club unity. Many of the newcomers didn't share a sense of history with veterans like Sonny, Skip, Johnny Angel and me. Some didn't even grasp the essence of being a Angel, what it would be like when the easy money and lavish parties were gone. The importance of the code escaped them. Rather than signifying the freedom to live by your own rules, the code was viewed as an obstacle to personal pleasure and gain, like the California Penal Code.

There were degrees of discipline among the chapters. Oakland was the most businesslike and ruthless. We demanded supreme dedication and tolerated few slackers.

Man for man, we were at least as smart, crafty and tough as any other chapter—and we were better organized, thanks mainly to Sonny. By contrast, Frisco was tainted by a bohemian softness that may have been a reflection of their home turf. Frisco was like a poorly maintained motorcycle—rusty, out of tune and not as powerful as it could be. We constantly crossed the bridge to make money in their city, but the reverse never occurred. In fact, they came to us looking for drugs sometimes, and several of their top members transferred to Oakland.

When we partied together, we gave Frisco not-so-subtle hints that we were at the throttle. In one classic reminder, I squared off brain-to-brain with "Freewheeling Frank," but everyone knew it was Oakland versus Frisco. Frank was chapter secretary-treasurer, No. 1 space cadet and official diamond in the rough among hip intellectuals.

In the opening minutes at Tramp's house on High Street, we each selected from an arsenal of drugs. "Let's try a couple of these little blue babies, Frank." "George, try some of this dynamite hash." Neither of us could walk away. First man to gulp would lose. We dueled, trying to see who could push his fantasies farthest. Then we argued, all the while toking, snorting and popping—like gunfighters passing a bottle of red-eye, half-hoping the other guy would fall off his chair. We went through word games, mind games, puns and relatively normal raps, then there were signs Frank's head was softening. Other guys saw the fear in his eyes too. He was losing it. He couldn't run. His legs might as well have been broken.

Freewheeling Frank scrambled for his dignity, but he couldn't escape the constipated smell of terror. "Let's do some more dope," he said with the desperation of a poker player wanting to hock his watch for stakes. Turning away, I eased back in my chair and started rapping with somebody else. I might as well have spit in his face.

Still, when the Gypsy Jokers shot a Frisco prospect, Frisco called on us for help. They wanted us to wipe out the East Bay Jokers while they took care of the San Francisco Jokers. Although we had cordial business and social relationships with the Jokers, we agreed for the sake of brotherhood.

On the appointed night , about a dozen of us challenged and equal number of Jokers in the New Yorker Club. Somebody suggested, "Let's take it outside," presumably to avoid breaking up the joint. I was the last Angel to head for the door, and the Jokers were behind me. Suddenly, it occurred to me that it was pointless to move outside where the cops could see us.

"Bullshit! Take it back inside," I shouted, wheeling in the doorway. My charge drove the Jokers back and scattered them; our guys poured into the bar. The Jokers went down and out under a cyclone of fists, boots and gun barrels. "Why are you guys doin' this?" asked Charlie, a friendly Joker, as I broke a billy club over his head.

"Don't ask why," I said shoving his bloody face out the back door. "Just get goin'."

Angels came first, even where friends were concerned. The irony was that the Frisco Angels, the initiators of the retaliation, lacked the muscle to dispose of their Jokers. So we had to make a trip across the bay to disband the Frisco Jokers to save our club's reputation.

For me, fighting side by side with the brothers was the ultimate thrill. And, on the evening of August 10, 1968, I got more than my share. It started at the drive-in movies, where I pulled my gun on a black guy because he wouldn't back down the row to let my car through. Following the show, I tried to run down a private cop who tried to flag me over for speeding in an industrial sector. Then, as Durt and I brought our ladies into La Cueva Mexican restaurant for a late snack, we got into a bump-the-shoulder fight with a couple of drunken Brown Berets. Durt dispatched the small guy but mine seemed to just stand there absorbing punch after punch. My arms turned rubbery before I realized Durt was behind the guy propping him up. "Hey, Durt, let him go. Will ya?" I pleaded, and the Mexican slumped to the floor.

Apparently, those two guys got their revenge later by smashing up a car belonging to an Angel's girlfriend. In the parking lot, we gathered twenty-five-strong around the car. "Let's go get 'em!" Helen picked up and axe and other women got guns to guard the vehicles, then we charged whooping and cursing like Huns. Z. crashed the front door with a steel wrecking bar—and we were in.

Surging through the bar, dining room and dance floor, we sent nearly 200 patrons, mostly Mexicans, into a frenzy. I was popping everybody who was too slow to get out of the way. Scattered fistfights became a huge brawl. Tables and chairs went flying. Tacos and enchiladas were mashed underfoot. Bottles smashed into light fixtures and walls—and one, thrown by Deacon, inadvertently split open my scalp to the bone. I was so dizzy I couldn't see straight, but I managed to punch out a few more guys. I cold-cocked one guy so hard that the clip popped out of my .45.

Once the place was destroyed, we streamed out the front door, leaving behind screaming, tearful women and groaning, bloodied men. My bloody face was the last one out. The gash was deep, so I got it stitched up at a local hospital. On the way out, I ran into a half dozen of the twenty patrons treated at hospitals that night.

"What happened to you all?" the receptionist was asking them.

"These Hell's Angels, they raid the restaurant and hit everybody," said one guy with a knot on his forehead. When he saw me, he shut up. And it was just as well too. Helen had drawn a pistol and was prepared to storm the hospital. She wanted to make sure the Mexicans were there for treatment, not revenge.

When the story hit the newspapers, there were community repercussions. Spokesmen for the Brown Berets, the Mexican-American business community and the Black Panthers pledged support to restaurateur Tony Rodarte during the long months of remodeling. Again, we were cast as chopper-hopping Klansmen. Rodarte even said members were threatening him by telephone. "The messages say the Angels will pay my damages, but if we press charges, there will be physical retaliation against us. One message said they were coming back and were going to bring their women with them," Rodarte told the Oakland *Tribune*. "These threats scare me. They scare me a lot. They've been to my place and demonstrated what they can do."

On August 31, 1968, about a week and a half later, we gathered at the Sidetrack bar for a meeting. Once the entire chapter was present and all customers took their leave, the front doors were locked and a "closed" sign was hung out. The bartender didn't raise any objections, but the cops, no doubt mindful of the La Cueva incident, spotted three dozen bikes outside and raided us. They seized $7,000 in heroin and $2,500 in other drugs, all found in a back room, hidden in walls or on the floors. Thirty-three members, plus four women, were hauled downtown in what police called the largest Angels roundup there. Charges were dropped because evidence was meager. We had emptied our pockets at the first sign of trouble.

The episode underscored our growing vulnerability. Virtually every member knew he would be facing drug possession charges, at the very least, if police found an excuse to raid his home or search him. The lawmen could strike almost at will and score. The pattern was unmistakable. In 1968 alone, the arrests of "Foo Manchu" (later convicted) and two other members in separate February raids netted $18,000 in assorted drugs, plus some weapons. There also were April raids in Oakland and Alameda that trapped five members and six women. There were several smaller busts before and after the Sidetrack. It was only a matter of time before the busts would get bigger.

Even with the club's talent for beating charges and intimidating potential prosecution witnesses, drug arrests took a toll. Legal defense absorbed large amounts of time and money. Lawyers and club bail bondsmen were kept busy counting our money. Not only were some members like Sonny checking out law books and searching for legal loopholes, but some were also escalating their criminal activity to pay their legal bills. The vicious circle of crimes to pay for crimes entrapped more and more guys, shortening membership rolls and handicapping drug operations. At any given time, at least several guys were either awaiting trial or serving county jail or state prison sentences.

Just when the legal picture was looking most bleak, the Oakland-Berkeley area was rocked by a spate of twenty-eight bombings in 1968. The explosions—which would hit eighty targets over the next four years, including the Oakland Police Administration Building—were believed to be the work of the Weathermen and other leftist radicals. But I got some indications that the club might have been behind a few.

I had supplied Sonny with bomb and hand grenade components and other explosives but had no inkling about their possible deployment until we heard a radio announcer one day describe a bombing near the University of California. "That's mine," Sonny said going on to explain that he hoped leftists would get credit for the blasts. In similar conversations, he claimed responsibility for at least one other explosion.

To this day, law enforcement investigators say they have no concrete evidence linking the club to any of the bombings. Yet the bombings worked to our advantage in two ways. First, the fireworks took a little heat off us and placed it on some of our least favorite groups. Second, legal favors were granted to us by police who wanted to keep weapons and explosives away from revolutionaries.

To get contraband to trade to the police for legal favors, Sonny swapped drugs for guns and enlisted the help of other members and retired members. Among my contributions were explosives and complete makings for military gas and hand grenades. For the good of the club, I also parted reluctantly with some of my rarest automatic weapons.

All we had to do was put out word on the streets that we were on the market for contraband. People came to us because we had a reputation for silence and discretion. Some guys wanted drugs or money in return for guns and explosives. Some narcotics contacts passed us firearms just to win the club's favor. Some guns were purchased over the counter. Some were burglarized from gun shops, homes and National Guard armories—not necessarily by club members.

Some were smuggled off military bases, or came from GIs returning from Vietnam or Europe. Some new military weapons fell into our hands before general distribution to American troops. A few machine guns originally had been confiscated in the famous 1960s police raids on the mansion of eccentric millionaire William Thoreson in San Francisco's posh Pacific Heights. How they got to us is anybody's guess.

During a dozen exchanges, hundreds of weapons and hundreds of pounds of explosives went to police. In most cases, an anonymous phone call to Police Sergeant Edward Hilliard directed police to the contraband, which usually was stashed in a motel room or on public lands. Here's what police inventories itemized:

Sometime in 1968—four or five carbines and some dynamite.

January, 1969—12 machine guns, including Russian-made ones and Thompson submachine guns, plus some hand grenades.

October 20, 1970—a .50-caliber Browning machine gun, three machine guns of various foreign makes (one with a silencer), a 16-gauge sawed-off shotgun, twenty sticks of dynamite, thirty-five fire grenades, four riot grenades, three hand grenades, a signal grenade, fourteen blasting caps and fifty 9 mm. rounds.

April 22, 1971—one German water-cooled machine gun, one Thompson submachine gun, one Colt AR-15, an M-14, a Winchester 12-gauge shotgun, six loaded clips, machine gun ammunition, four grenades, two sticks of dynamite, and a tear gas bomb. (Two of the guns were reported stolen.)

July, 1971—a number of blocks of plastic explosives, rifle grenades and booby traps.

September 27, 1971—four AR-15s, three cases of dynamite plus fifty pounds of loose sticks. (The guns were stolen from Fort Benning, Georgia, and the explosives were stolen from a Nevada City, California, construction company.)

October 6, 1971—five AR-15s and two M-60 machine guns.

October 18, 1971—four cases of dynamite.

October 21, 1971—four cases of dynamite (stolen from the Nevada City construction company).

January 16, 1972—four fifty-pound boxes of dynamite and a suitcase containing 100 pounds of dynamite.

February 4, 1972—two fifty-pound boxes of plastic explosives and two thirty-pound boxes of artillery charges.

February 18, 1972—an M-14 automatic rifle, a submachine gun, a box of automatic weapons parts, three rolls of blasting fuses, one roll of primer cord, seven grenades, two smoke grenades, two antitank mines with fuses, three tear gas grenades, forty-eight sticks of dynamite, a package of blasting caps and twenty-three loose caps, plus five sections of fuse.

The cops kept their end of the deal too. Hilliard had agreed to tell proper authorities about the turnovers if either Sonny or "Sir Gay" were convicted and they had an implicit understanding that other designated club members would receive similar help. In keeping his word, Hilliard (according to his later court testimony) went with club attorney Jules Bonjour and Deputy District Attorney Charles Herbert to talk with Alameda County Superior Court Judge William Hayes about a narcotics case involving Sir Gay. Walton faced a total of twenty-three drug and weapons violations at the time. After Hilliard showed the judge a list of surrendered weapons to illustrate the club's cooperation, Walton was allowed to plead guilty to three charges, and the other twenty charges were dismissed for various reasons. Several others apparently had their bail reduced after we turned in contraband (although the cops later claimed that the judges were planning to lower the bail anyway as a routine matter).

In 1971, after three years of such dealings, Sonny met with Hilliard and another officer behind a liquor store on Golf Links Road. When Sonny climbed in the back seat, he said he'd gotten an idea from a newspaper article that noted the failure of authorities to apprehend bombers.

"I can get you bodies," Sonny said.

"Whatta ya mean?"

"Weathermen. We'll put em in a sack. Drop em on your doorstep," Sonny said. "Just give us a list of the people. All I want is one member sprung from state prison for each body."

"No way," Hilliard said.[33]

The deals affected more than those relatively few members who benefited directly through reductions in bail or charges. They provided an illusory shield for the club. Some guys foolishly believed the police had been bought off, and that somehow Sonny would rescue them from any bust. Sonny used to say it was cheaper to get weapons and trade them in than to hire lawyers. All this tended to reinforce his awesome club stature. It made him look as though he could grapple face-to-face with the cops and get them by the gonads.

I was one of the few members who openly questioned the wisdom of dealing at all with lawmen. As far as I was concerned, cops should never be trusted, and you're only playing their game by trading. It seemed like the cops were making bail higher and higher just to get more guns and explosives. Besides, on a more basic level, I figured that cops make a living putting us in jail, so handing them illegal stuff just made their job easier. For those reasons, I was down on trading, and I only helped when asked.

If the trades had been made public then, both sides would have been red-faced. Pragmatic bartering with criminals at least appears to be a perversion of law enforcement goals, although it goes on every day. But more surprising was the notion of archetypal bad guys like us bargaining with lawmen. It would discredit our ballyhoo about devotion to absolute truth and to the outlaw lifestyle. It would show that we were tough and uncompromising only when we could afford to be.

Our public image and reality were different animals. It's true that our lifestyle was raw, but it was based on the premise of indestructibility. Its foundations were rocked every time the embalmer or the jail keeper captured a guy wearing the red and white. But somehow the police and the news media bent to the propaganda that we were lovers of no one, coldly cruel brutes without fears, responsibilities or concerns. Men with the minds of children, the bodies of jungle beasts and the inclinations of satyrs.

In reality, most Angels and their women were similar to Helen and me. Many of us had natural intelligence and horse sense, although it was often hidden behind B-movie behavior and gangster jargon. Lots of us were undereducated in the three Rs and overeducated in street survival. Some were insecure and anti-intellectual; many made it through high school, but few sampled college. And, although guys came from happy and unhappy homes, rich and poor ones, there were quite a few alcoholic parents and broken marriages in their pasts. For lots of them, the club was the only family they had or cared to have.

More than a few members or their women confessed fears to Helen and me. Fears that our reckless race couldn't go on forever. Mickey told Helen that she used to sit on Elsie Barger's gravestone talking over problems, and once she spent the night in the cemetery after taking a beating. And I found some sensitivity in even big galoots like Russell and Tiny, although they normally stashed it behind whiskers, muscles, tattoos and mean eyes.

The Hell's Angels truth sessions, the ones we needed for sanity and survival, usually were camouflaged with drugs or bizarre behavior. To an outsider, it might have looked like a freakout, a pair of bull loonies beating their heads against the world, but we got down to basics. Picture Deacon and me crouched over a few tiny rocks in an open field, talking and wrestling with the mysteries of our minds and the universe. Or picture Winston and me ripping our brains with PCP, literally banging our heads together, digging the sounds, saying over and over, "I'm a dummy. I'm a dummy." Each of us was dealing with the destructive chemical and psychological forces by admitting them.

Lots of times, I think we wigged out on drugs to satisfy our subconscious need to communicate fears and nightmares. With time, all of us had experimented enough with drugs to know how much we could swallow within complete control. I think we pushed ourselves over the limit sometimes to reveal ourselves. An Angel who embraced his brother on a bum trip or shared a "profound experience" with him never again was alone. When you revealed your weaknesses and your inner self to another Angel, you both were bound by it.

Sonny was a lot like the Pope, the President and the board chairman of General Motors. He had to live up to a tremendous image. Ninety-nine percent of the time, he exposed only that hard exterior. If an Angel was right, he had to be eternally right. If an Angel was evil, he had to be Satan incarnate. He had to be the ultimate Hell's Angel, twenty-four hours a day, seven days a week. And he couldn't just take a couple of weeks' vacation when he got tired of it.

No matter how many criminal charges cluttered his head, he kept his chin thrust forward and talked with relish about jousting with the cops. But those of us close to him saw him prodded to paranoia and overreaction. He wore disguises sometimes. He made phony driver's licenses in a makeshift photo lab. He monitored police radio frequencies by the hour. He kept several telephones and, as a precaution against bugging, unscrewed the mouthpieces whenever he was conducting business in a room with phones. He hid pistols and extra clips around his bedroom—even under his pillow—and stashed heavier weapons in wall panels. A tall chain-link fence and his dogs provided his outer security ring.

To old friends like me, Sonny clearly was just a man, an extraordinary yet worried man. But to others—and maybe to himself—he was a god among bikers. Other guys could fall down stoned and bawl in terror, but he couldn't. When he learned his tolerance for a particular drug was low, he absolutely refused to use it. The last time he took PCP he was on a trip with me and Z. For hours, Sonny just lay on his couch with his hands over his eyes, unable and unwilling to handle any more. He was hurting and he couldn't afford to have his aura dimmed very often.

XVII—The Trap Shuts with a Bang

"Do you know the worst thing I hated that club for? It made George feel there was no God. He told me, 'I'm God.' He got the feeling of power from the Angels. They felt they could do anything and were in control of everything. When George told me he was my god, he didn't mean it exactly. It was a big shot role he had to play. Being an Angel was a self-preservation trip. You had to stay on top of it, make a puppet of everyone. That partially came from acid, where you had to get one step beyond. It's godlike. It's power like you've never known. That's when the trouble started with George. He got to feeling he was God himself, with power over life and death."—Helen Wethern.

The club was Helen's nemesis. She blamed it for putting the children in a secondary position, and it seemed grossly unfair to her that I would be fined $50 to $100 for staying at home rather than attending club functions. In effect, she

178

believed I was being penalized whenever I was a good husband and father.

Her worries weren't mine. In fact, I made matters worse. In late 1968, Z. needed a place to conduct a liaison with Jan, a moderately hip former topless dancer, so I invited them home. Z. left his regular old lady, Linda, in Alameda and moved into our laundry room with Jan, making the place habitable with a mattress, a few posters and candlesticks.

Helen at first welcomed the female companionship, although Jan was a dead weight in the household. When Z. and I went on business, the women glazed their brains, then went shopping or entertained each other with anecdotes. For a change, Helen felt worldly and secure in her moll's role. By way of bragging, she hauled out her Llama and showed Jan how to load it. As she was cocking the hammer, however, her finger slipped and a slug ripped through one of the walls, already perforated by about thirty bullet holes. "Wow. Do that again," Jan said excitedly, but Helen was sobered by it.

The friendship soon withered under the pressure of competition. Z. and I tried to see who could dress his lady flashiest. The women would go shopping then come back and model. Helen hated it, and she wanted to evict our houseguests—but our involvement was destined to grow more tangled.

The trouble started in December, 1968, when I went shopping for property north of San Francisco. A realtor found me a beautiful 153-acre ranch near Ukiah in Mendocino County. There were no buildings, but I easily imagined a house in the wooded terrain near one of the creeks. The $25,000 pricetag was a bargain, yet it would nearly deplete my funds. So I convinced Z. to split the cost, although he wanted to keep his name out of the transaction to avoid tax troubles.

I blew the title company clerk's mind by paying the

$25,000 in cash. When I discussed the ranch with Zorro, it was as a country retreat for the club, with shooting ranges and military-type pillboxes on the hills. When talking to Helen, I billed the property as a pastoral place for family and a few friends, somewhere we could escape city pressures and teach the kids life was more than a red and white patch.

A few nights later, on January 16, 1969, the euphoria ended abruptly. Haunted by DOA paranoias, I sweated and paced, worrying about what to tell the IRS when they would ask how an unemployed lather could buy a ranch outright. "I'm gonna be another fucking Al Capone now," I told Helen. "I'm gonna go up the river for income tax evasion."

With each hit of peace weed, I worried more and more. I agonized over how difficult it would be to cover Z.'s $12,500 share. I was angry with myself for not anticipating the problem; I was angry with Zorro for thinking only of himself, for throwing an additional burden on me. My fears choked me, like snakes coiled around my throat.

Helen told me not to smoke any more. I stopped but I refused to take any downers. All night long I padded the house. Then, early the next morning, I telephoned my father for advice but I was too stoned to make sense.

Then I shook Z. awake, but all I got was a grumpy, "Fuck it, man. Go call a lawyer." I still couldn't make sense during three calls to Ed Merrill, a well-known criminal lawyer who helped me with the Angels Inn legal fight.[34]

After the kids were sent off to school, Helen pleaded with Z., "You gotta help him. You gotta do something. George is climbing the walls." He came into the living room to try to reassure me, but the very sight of him, his shallow concern so obvious, infuriated me. How did he repay me for setting him up in business, for making him a partner? He left me holding the financial bag. A whole night of ruminating over that had rubbed my brain raw, and I had worked myself into a very close box, feeling exploited and abandoned.

While Z. was on the couch sipping his coffee, I slipped into the bedroom, walked to the dresser and hefted my .45. Then I went back to the living room, the gun at my side, my finger finding the trigger. "You fucked me," I said. Z.'s face barely had time to widen in fear. The time for speaking or running was past. The barrel leveled. The trigger eased back, almost gently. Then, with ear-shattering suddenness, seven shots pierced the air and slammed into him. He doubled up reflexively after the first few and looked to Helen with rolling, puzzled eyes while taking the rest.

The pistol thumped to the floor among the shell casings. The smoke swirled. I felt nothing. Not the recoil. Not the steel. Not the warm spatters of blood. It was as though the gun spat hatred and death on its own. As I watched Z. retching, my own numbness turned to horror. "Do something. Call a doctor," I shouted.

Dashing to the telephone, Helen started to dial then stopped short. "George! There's no time! Take him to the hospital."

Blindly obeying, I scooped up Z. and toted him to the Chrysler. Fighting traffic, the car screeched and lurched, pumping more blood onto the seats. Z. was groaning deliriously, but I told him over and over, "Hold on baby. Hold on. You're gonna make it."

Tires smoking, I stopped just outside the emergency entrance, picked up Z., kicked open the hospital door, then ran inside screaming, "Fix him. Fix him."

"How many times he been shot?" a medic asked.

"Once," I said, but the surgeons soon found seventeen entry and exit holes and four creases. Some bullets had ripped cleanly through him while others ricocheted off bones or passed through limbs first.

"They're working on him now," a nurse said. "There's nothing you can do except take it easy."

I roamed the hospital, my eyes dissolved by drugs and

shock. People skirted me. Hospital personnel called police.

Meanwhile, Helen prepared for the inevitable. She needed to destroy our drug caches before the cops came. While kilos of marijuana burned in a garbage can outside, she flushed thousands of pills down the toilet. Then she turned to Jan, who was in a panic, and said, "If you got anything, get rid of it."

"I don't have nothin'," Jan swore.

"Bullshit." Helen knew Jan had squirreled away some reds. "Listen, bitch, you go back and check. Now!"

"I don't have nothin'. Besides, Z. would . . ."

"There's no time for that. Go get it and get rid of it."

Prodding Jan into the laundry room, Helen stood by until Jan fished out the reds beneath the mattress. "You had nothin', huh?" Helen flushed the pills, then wheeled around. "You better not have anything else. If you've got one more thing hidden in this fuckin' house and I get busted, then you're dead."

Helen called Sonny and told him what happened. "Get the place clean," he snapped. "I'm on my way over." He hurried up the walkway moments later. Jan dashed out the door, sobbing, "Sonny. Oh, Sonny." But Helen managed to drag her back in by the shirt. "Shut up, bitch. Ya want the neighbors to hear everything? The cops ain't here and I don't want 'em here."

Sonny brushed past Jan and took Helen aside. "Okay. What happened? Where are they?"

"George shot Z. and drove him to the hospital."

"Which one?"

"I guess it's San Leandro Memorial."

"I'll go over and see what I can do." With a glance toward Jan, he added, "I guess I'd better take her with me."

Back at the hospital, I was pacing in the parking lot under the apprehensive eye of a policeman. He kept his distance and smiled, friendly-like. It was a good thing he didn't rile me because I would have charged him and forced him to shoot me.

When two more officers arrived, I was wandering aimlessly among cars, looking for a friend. The police huddle put me on guard. They circled me like you'd circle a wounded beast. "We're your friends, buddy. Take it easy, now," one said, as they reached for handcuffs, guns and clubs. Their cunning didn't fool me. But I waited until they touched me before exploding. Knocked away, they came at me again. And again. Each time, I scattered them like a bear flings off hounds. Then Mace stung my eyes and nostrils. Each cop dove for a limb. I could hear their clubs thumping my skull, but I couldn't feel them. Then all I could hear was my own growling; I bit, punched and kicked. When I completely lost my breath, steel locked my wrists together and clubs pinned my neck, grinding one cheek in loose gravel[35].

When I was being wrestled toward a patrol car, Helen and Sonny arrived in separate cars. "What the hell'd ya do to him?" Helen screamed, rushing forward and pushing the cops aside. Gooey blood was matting my hair; dirt and pebbles were imbedded in my face; my clothes were torn. "What's that smell?" she yelled as she grabbed a cloth from a doctor and daubed my cuts and gashes.

"We had to Mace him because he went berserk," one cop said. "We tried to handcuff him but he wasn't going for it."

"Damn! Did ya have to use clubs? Did you have to do all this to him?"

Delirious, I told her, "Everything's gonna be okay. Go get Dad. We're going up to Mendocino." I was crying but strangely calm inside. "Wipe my face, will ya?" I said, more concerned about tears than blood. "Come on, sugar. Come with me."

The cops shook their heads, so she kissed me and whispered, "It's okay. Everything's fine. You go ahead now."

Suddenly the handcuffs felt like they were locked around my neck. "Take 'em off! Take 'em off! Take 'em off or you're gonna have a fight on your hands."

For some reason, they asked Sonny if he'd take responsibility if the bracelets came off. "Hell no," Sonny shot back. "Take those things off, and it's your trip." I guess I was more than he could handle.

When the police took me away, Sonny drove Helen and Jan to his house for some strong tranquilizers. Durt picked up the kids from school, and they played with Sonny's electric typewriter while the adults pondered their next step. Moments later, the club lookout "Fat Freddy" phoned to report a police search in progress at my house. When Sonny and Helen arrived, cops halted them at the front door—just as they carted out thirty-five guns and thousands of rounds of ammunition. The cops thought they'd stumbled on a Hell's Angels armory, but they were amazed they didn't find a single marijuana seed in that house.

XVIII—Angel in a Cage

Dazed and lost beyond my worst acid trip, I crumbled when they stood me up and slumped to the floor when they sat me down. On my hands and knees, chin on my chest, I clung to the concrete praying the earth wouldn't spin me into outer space. I called for somebody to hold the pieces of my mind together. But the cops just turned their backs.

Then a tall man turned the corner and hollered, "George, do you recognize me?" He touched my shoulder, but his voice sounded as though it was coming through a bank vault door. "George, you remember me. Don't you? Don't you? Come on, George." My fragmented vision pieced together a face. I nodded. It was attorney Jules Bonjour. One look at me apparently told him that the best legal strategy, and the most humane thing, would be to call a psychiatrist. The shrink could record my mental state after the shooting and maybe allow me to plead not guilty by reason of temporary insanity or diminished capacity.

At Highland Hospital, my wounds were mended and I

was checked by a psychiatrist—all the time handcuffed to an examination cart. Later, some psychiatrists came to my cell to write observations and to toss me a few pills. All stayed outside the bars. I was a mass of dangerous contradictions, cursing at everyone yet desperately desiring company.

At Bonjour's request, jailers transferred another inmate to my cell. The guy had friends in the club, so I talked with him for a while. Then, with the deceptive swiftness of a passing cloud, the guy became evil personified. Without warning, I swarmed over him and bit off part of his ear. As he retreated to a six-inch space between the bunks and bars, I pounded him until guards beat me back with clubs. They dragged me feet first upstairs, my head thudding along the treads.

I came to in another cell, thinking I was dead and entombed. It was the ultimate isolation—the hole. On the ceiling, a single bulb dripped cold light. The rest was bare.

In there, reality was a stranger. Night and day were indistinguishable, except for the types of food they slipped me through a little door that wasn't much bigger than the hole in the floor. My mind cranked like a red-lined engine, but I refused downers, thinking they were poison. Little things threatened me. A guard opened the door and found me urinating down the hole. "That ain't gonna do you any good," he sneered, slamming the door. I don't know what he meant, but his sarcastic voice amplified in my head like an echo. I ached for a friendly word, but my keepers seemed to go out of their way to be cruel. I hated them. I hated everyone who passed in the freedom of the corridor. Sighting through the keyhole, I squeezed an imaginary trigger. Slugs tore through them. Pow. Pow. Pow. One by one, they wrenched this way and that.

In my dark mind, even my wife betrayed me. I saw her with another man, a handsomer man, taunting me, "You'll

be staying in there, but I'll be out here having a good time."
When she threw her head back to crow, I tried to reach
them but just bounced off the concrete wall.

I envisioned my children. Poised above them was a concrete slab as large as my cell floor. When it started to slide, I
rushed forward to save them. My fingernails dug into the
stone, but the kids were pinned. With my back into it, I
could keep the slab from crushing them, but I couldn't
move it away. Then an overpowering thirst attacked me.
The dripping faucet was a mountain freshet. Finally, in my
weakness, I abandoned my post and ran to the sink, followed by my kids' last screams.

Later, I rammed my head and body against the wall until
every bone and joint ached. I sensed death would be the
only way out. I lusted for someone to mutilate me, to slice
me in thin pieces, because I was afraid that even my feet or
teeth might attack someone.

From monstrous aggression, I lapsed into childish help-
lessness. I had to express my pain and outrage and to
reaffirm my own existence. Because there was nothing else,
I picked up my own feces. I patted it, molded it, looked at it.
I smelled it and ate some of it. I drew on the wall with it. In
some strange way, it was therapeutic.

Authorities viewed me as so unpredictable and dangerous
that no hospital would take me. How could a 280-pound
Hell's Angel with killer tendencies be controlled? A strait-
jacket and padded cell? Drugs or psychosurgery? Helen
wouldn't go for any of those, but the status quo was intoler-
able. She thought my mind would be permanently damaged
unless I was released. "You gotta get him outa there," she
told Sonny. "He's gotta have somebody to talk to. Those
people don't know him." She, Sonny and Bonjour decided
that my potential for violence was so great that I would re-
quire protective supervision.

"Can you keep a twenty-four-hour-a-day watch on him?"

Bonjour asked Sonny. "Have five or six of your guys with him every minute while he recovers?"

"Sure. On a rotating basis, I guess we could."

But my violent outbursts convinced Bonjour that the risk was too high. How long could the club supervise me without a slipup? What if I never improved? Those were tough questions, but Sonny assured Helen that the club would get me out somehow. And if necessary, they would keep a permanent vigil.

Meanwhile, I was transferred to the downtown county jail. Bonjour told me to start thinking of my wife and children when my nightmares hit. I seized on his words. With a pencil, I wrote "Helen and the kids," again and again, on every inch of the cell, even under the bunks and sink. Those four short words kept my mind on the three most important people on earth.

I made progress, one careful step at a time, with occasional slips. Jailers and doctors noted my improvement, and on January 30, 1969, my psychiatrist, Dr. Bancroft M. Brooks, wrote the following letter filed with court officials:

Dear Mr. Bonjour:

I first saw your client, George Wethern, on Jan. 16, 1969 at Highland General Hospital. At that time, he was in a state of drug intoxication. I saw him again on Jan. 20 at the City Hall, at which time his condition was worse. It was my impression that this was worse than a temporary state of intoxication and represented an organic psychosis that could last for several days to several weeks. Although he was able to meet bail for his offense, it was my recommendation that he be left in jail as long as his behavior was such that he represented a potential danger. While his state still had not started to clear up by Jan. 24, I instituted treatment with high doses of Thorazine. There was a considerable improvement by the following day. I have seen him twice since then, and he had maintained this improvement.

. He has been calm and rational for six consecutive days, and it is my opinion that it is safe for him to be out on bail. If he is released on bail, I will continue to treat him . . .

Unaware of the letter and my $7,500 bail payment, I was led from my cell. I had no idea whether freedom or the gas chamber was waiting for me. I was told that Z. was making a miraculous recovery, but that could have been a trick to control me.

Yet, I walked into the sunlight again. It had been two weeks since the shooting. I was shaven and shorn, about forty pounds lighter, a different man in a different world. As I was chauffeured to a bail bondsman, I asked myself whether my mind was playing yet another cruel hoax. Then I felt Helen's arms around me. We cried for joy.

Like teenagers on our first date, we drove around the city for a while. We were stalling rather than facing that house of ugly memories. Finally I said, "Let's go home, babe."

The house was like somebody else's. The guns were gone. The stereo was silent. The blood was washed away. The drug stashes and paraphernalia were conspicuously absent. And not a single stranger was crashed on the floor.

Our first step in getting reacquainted as a family was relating our ordeals. When I described my nightmares, Helen reassured me, "I've been there with you every night. Whenever I lay, half-asleep and half-awake, it was cold. I don't know whether you felt icy cold or not, but to me it was that way in your cell. There were images going through my head, and I knew what you were going through. There were dark edges in the cell with a bright light coming down the middle. I couldn't see the walls very well, but you were over in the corners . . ."

XIX—Freedom and Fading Colors

The next day, I drove to the hospital and made my way to Z.'s room. We hugged each other; tears welled in my eyes. It had seemed impossible that such a wiry guy could survive so many bullets. Seeing him with my own eyes was the only way to wipe away all the nightmares about his death and my murder trial.

"It's okay," Z. said. "It's all right. Just don't squeeze me so hard. You're hurting me."

He fell back, his face white as his pillow, his limbs spindly as his bed frame. He looked like a starving Frankenstein monster with his right leg in traction, his right arm plastered and his torso stitched up. He was glum until he noticed Bobby.

Z. winked reassuringly at the kid and ran his finger along his zigzag sutures. "Here are my railroad tracks." Then he gestured toward his groin. "And here's my train." Bobby's apple cheeks cracked in a chuckle. He only made a vague connection between Zorro's "accident" and my absence.

He told me that one leg would be left shorter than the other, uselessly stiff. "The doctor said I'll never ride a motorcycle again. And this won't be any good either." He nodded toward one of his arms.

"Don't believe everything the doctors tell ya," I replied with little conviction. "If ya wanna do it, you can. Just work at it.

"And, just call me anytime you need help," I added. "Money or anything."

Before Z.'s discharge, I paid some of his expenses and did what I could to help Linda by delivering a hospital-type bed to their place. But when Z. arrived, he steeped himself in prescription drugs and self-pity. He was plenty down. When he walked, his game leg dragged. He hated his physical therapy, so he quit. He cursed his condition—and me. He turned most of his frustration on Linda. Sometimes, when he tossed things at her or roughed her up, she'd telephone me, begging, "Please help. I can't do a thing with Z."

More than once I found Z. loaded on "scrips" and ranting. Then I'd warn him, "Z., don't take all that shit. You'll kill yourself. Do something. Exercise. Eat." A few times, I got him to eat but he'd lapse into resentful fits of depression. Out of guilt, I just stood there and took his abuse, even when he threw food in my face.

Eventually, I got tired of the visits and the insults. My insides churned whenever Linda called or dropped by to complain about Z.'s health. Helen and I listened halfheartedly, but callous as it seemed, we were struggling with our own recovery.

Rather than pick up my guns, chopper and telephone, I returned to construction and the stability of regular hours. My mental wounds would mend faster there than in drug negotiations. Instead of drumming up drug business during lunch hour, I put out feelers for building materials for the ranch.

Drugs were the least of my concerns. I quit cold turkey, even my Thorazine prescription. I wanted to avoid everything because the distinction between medication and dependency was a fine one for me. Drugs had driven me to the threshold of murder—and that was a threshold I never wanted to cross.

I blamed drugs in general and DOA in particular for the shooting, and I crusaded against them. I preached to Helen, close friends and some members—the very people I'd turned on.

At J. B.'s house, I told my side of the shooting and described my jail ordeal. Then I pleaded, "Let's quit getting loaded. Give it up."

Everybody listened politely, but nobody was about to give up a lifestyle, not even Helen. "Take my reds. Take my psychedelics. But don't take my grass away," she told me. "It makes me feel good. It makes me feel loose. It helps me laugh sometimes, even though our life's been a lot of bummers."

The shooting did turn the club against DOA, after it was widely reported at California chapter meetings that I blasted Z. while overdosed on the stuff. And just a few days after the shooting, Winston overdosed on it and stormed out of the house with a machine gun and a bucket of rusty nails, telling his old lady he was going to build a church on their property and would shoot anybody trying to stop him. That apparently was the last straw for Sonny, who'd had his own bad DOA trips. He told me he surreptitiously had a sample delivered to the police for analysis in Washington, D.C. Word came back that DOA was phencyclidine hydrochloride, or PCP, an animal tranquilizer. We'd been taking anywhere from a dozen to 100 times the proper dosage for an animal the size of a man. The club voted to ban the drug.

Forgiveness was not a club forte, but I never expected to be treated as an outcast. Lots of members seemed afraid to walk down the street in front of me. I was paying the price of violating the ultimate club law. By shooting Z., I had implicitly threatened every member's life.

At meetings, parties and chance encounters, guys kept their distance. In their black-white thinking, Z. had gotten the worst of it since he bore the physical scars. They could give blood to Z., but they couldn't give forgiveness and reacceptance to me.

The shooting blew a deep division in club ranks. Some members treated me like a maniac. Animal, a strict constructionist of club law, and Vern said things like, "He shot a brother, so he should be shot . . . I'd have killed him myself if it was me." Neither apparently had the gumption or the backing to take action.

Other members, such as Winston, argued, "If George shot Z., he musta had good reason." Sonny, loyal to me and none too fond of Z., resolved the divisive talk by backing me. In fact, for years to come his running joke with me would be, "The ambulance driver really blew it. You were in too much of a hurry with Z. I already was on my way over with a shovel." He would even make the quip in front of Z.

Sonny, Winston, Tiny, Big Don and retired members like J. B. and Paul were about the only ones who continued to come by the house after the shooting. Sonny told me right from the start, "If ya wanna talk or anything, just call me. To hell with everybody and everything. Don't worry about nobody else but you." I would call him any time of the day or night, and he would come over. He wouldn't stay long, maybe an hour or so, but he calmed me. Helen would get him a cup of coffee, then we'd start talking. Sonny cared, and he showed me he would stick by me, no matter what.

It was comforting to have the top man in my corner, because so many guys who had shared our drugs, food and good times for years quit coming over. They never called to ask if my family needed help with mounting legal or medical expenses.

The absence of Tramp hurt me most. He coldly informed

me that our partnership would have to end because Sand refused to deal with me anymore. "You understand," Tramp said. "You can't go to these people now. They're scared of you because of the thing with Z."

"Don't worry about it." I accepted the phaseout because I didn't want to tax my head with dealing anyway. However, the phony ring of Tramp's announcement disturbed me. Did Sand use the shooting incident as an excuse to rid himself of a nemesis? Did Sand really complain at all, or did Tramp just use him as an excuse to end the partnership? Did they collaborate for a bigger piece of the action? One thing was clear. Tramp sided with a nonmember at the expense of a brother. It countered the club code and wounded me.

Helen also saw the hypocrisy of members who freeloaded day and night during the good times, then deserted me in hard times. "These are your brothers?" she asked me in a rage. "The ones that you always stuck up for and put me down for? Where's the comradeship, love and concern you brothers have for each other? Stick it in your ear!"

I thought everything would blow over, but then Z. had a relapse. He was rehospitalized with pneumonia and a staph infection. A note with the single word, "Help!" brought me to his intensive care room. I had to pose as his brother to get in there. Z. was sprawled in an oxygen tent apparently waiting to die. His passivity infuriated me. He had played on my guilt and used me as a crutch long enough. I felt he was deliberately hurting himself to punish me.

"If you lie there and die, then you kill both of us," I said. "I've had it, you fucker. If you wanna die, then die. If you wanna live, then get up and let's get outa here. Get up! Don't give up!"

Z. got pissed off enough himself to rally and go home. He spent that year's Bass Lake run convalescing in the rear of a station wagon and would limp badly for more than a year.

But he proved the doctors wrong and later rode his motorcycle again. To his scars, he added a tattoo: "45's ain't shit. 17 holes, 4 creases," and displayed it with haughty defiance.

Z. begged out of the ranch investment. I obliged him, thanks to a $12,500 loan from Sonny. Settling of that score somehow let Z. and me retrieve our friendship. We even planned to track down the PCP traffickers and jack them up for a stiff fine. Neither of us was in any shape to be playing heavy roles just then, but the daydreaming narrowed the rift between us.

Helen always doubted Z.'s sincerity. She thought he was waiting for the right opportunity to kill me. When she heard Z. had been practicing with a rifle, she told me, "George, don't trust that man. Look what you done to him. He relied on his good looks, his body, his whole appearance for his hustle, and that's all he knew how to do. And if that's taken away, he's got nothing left. Who's he gonna blame? You. I don't care how palsy-walsy he is now. Don't trust that man."

I scoffed, "No way. He won't do anything. He can't do anything. It's not in his nature."

XX—A Patch for a Patch

Helen and I drew mental sketches of our ranch house by thumbing through stacks of *Better Homes and Gardens* and debating the advantages of various materials and constructions. Our house would be modeled, we decided, after a photo of a meeting lodge, with rough-sawed natural wood, a dominant high-ceilinged hall and smaller adjacent rooms.

We selected a building site at the foot of a woody hillside. We paced off its dimensions and imagined it completed. Our blueprints called for the heaviest materials, including huge exposed beams and an elaborate piling foundation. I paid a local contractor $1,000 cash to cut a road, then another contractor drilled three test holes for wells.

From the start, the ranch belonged to my family, not the club. The two-hour drive gave us weekends away from the city and brought us together. The kids moped around the camper at first, then they shed their urban conditioning and explored. Sometimes J. B.'s family came up, but often we were alone, clearing land by day and relaxing around a campfire by night.

For the first time, we communicated as four individuals. There was no telephone, no television, no procession of dealers. Every conversation was discovery. Helen and I learned our kids had developed deep feelings and active minds. We encouraged frankness, and I explained what I had done to Z. and why. What it meant to lose your mind and the struggle in getting it back.

By spring of 1969, the foundation was poured. I still wore the red and white, and faced trial for assault with a deadly weapon with intent to commit murder, plus three other felony charges of battery on police officers.

My club ties were tenuous, although I attended meetings and runs, hoping time and tenacity would bring me back in good graces. One weekend, we put down our ranch work and decided to drop by a club run at Squaw Rock on nearby Russian River. I pulled on a black leather vest with a death's head, kicked over my Harley and swung Bobby aboard. He was six years old and thrilled to be along. As we raced south, he leaned forward and yelled in his high-pitched voice, "Go faster, dad!" When I grabbed a handful of throttle, it was like grabbing a train passing at fifty miles an hour. The bike started shuddering at ninety-five so I backed off. "Go faster," Bobby complained. "How come you won't go faster?"

The question still unanswered, I downshifted and banked into the turnoff. Sheriff's deputies checked us into the camp. Most guys endured the screening and photographing with no more than a grumble, but they simmered when Bobby was subjected to the same treatment. "Whatta ya think the kid's gonna do?" somebody growled. "Shoot up the place or something?"

Rather than disappoint the deputies, one Angel handed Bobby a submachine gun, and the kid let fly, spraying lead wherever recoil pointed him. Swearing deputies and laughing Angels scrambled for cover until the clip was spent. No one was hurt, so the deputies issued a stern warning, then hung back, fielding catcalls and curses.

Again, Bobby became the center of attention. Z. gave him a .30-30 deer rifle as a gift, and Tramp, who was feeling no pain, balanced a beer can on his head. "Go on, kid," he said. "Shoot it off. You can do it."

Bobby hesitated, because this time more was at stake than a blue jay. With members egging him on, he looked to me. "Nix," I said, and he shouldered his toy.

Just then, Helen drove up with Donna. Bobby ran forward shouting, "Ma, lookit what I got from Z." Standing in the background was Z., still emaciated and hobbling. She cast a suspicious eye his way and said, "That was nice of him, but be careful with it."

Holding full cans of beer, Helen and I tried earnestly to socialize, but we mixed about as well as oil in water. We went up to folks who seemed to be having fun, and tried to ignore the coolness that tinged their hellos. Then we split up.

Helen stopped to talk to Magoo, his arms tattooed with his state and F.B.I. criminal identification numbers, his gut girded in bandages. He was propped against a tree, booze and grass scattered around him, a hippie girl fussing over him. "I hit the pavement at sixty-five and eight bikes piled into me," he explained. "The revolver in my belt did a number on my guts." He showed nine inches of stitches on his belly.

Helen also exchanged pleasantries with Marsi, Mickey and Sharon, but neither of us could get comfortable. "We gotta take the kids home," I said finally. A few people nodded good-byes, then we took off, a social obligation fulfilled.

A short time later, I went to a party at Tramp's house, hoping again for acceptance. "Hiya, George. Howya doin'?" a few guys called. But, when I passed behind a cluster of them, they stopped talking and turned to see what I was up to. After eleven years, I was an outsider again, under suspicion, a pariah. I couldn't talk my way through the wall of mistrust. The guys who wanted me out never had the guts to say it to my face. Instead, they let me carom from one person to the next. Their "let the crazy bastard alone" attitude humiliated me, so I started for the door before the first guys fell down stoned. Mickey stopped me and took my arm. "I don't feel any hostility toward you," she murmured. "And I'm not afraid of you. I just wanted you to know I don't feel the way the rest of them do."

I thanked her and rode homeward, my feelings wound as tight as my 74. When I dragged myself inside, Helen looked up from the television. "Whatsa matter, George? What happened?"

"It was almost like being alone," I said, smearing my tears. "You couldn't walk behind anybody without them looking over their shoulder at ya. How could they be that way? They don't want me around anymore. I'm gonna have to quit. That's all there is to it."

During a sparsely attended meeting at Monk's house that Friday, I turned in my colors for the last time. My resignation was accepted mutely, as though I were bowing out under disgrace. There was no pardon, and my pride ruled out any apology. No man should need to explain himself to his brothers.

There would be no reversal. I would cease to be a Hell's Angel and would enter the limbo of retirement. I would retain more status than someone who had never won his colors, but less than a current wearer.

A close friend, Durt, picked up my club flag and confiscated a pair of death's head drawings by one of our neighbors. They allowed me to keep my five-year plaque, because my name was etched in it—and no one could take away those years.

My resignation and other factors, both calculated and accidental, increased my chances for acquittal or a light sentence. The court had received my psychiatrist's letter and character references from my union and my employer. On my own, I sold my thirty-five confiscated guns.

Finally, I went to court wearing a dark suit, looking to all the world like a reformed man. The remaining question was whether Z. would testify against me. When he failed to show for the first two hearings, it appeared that the club's unwritten rule against testifying for the prosecution would save me. On August 13, 1969, he was seated in the spectator section along with J. B. and Irma. Municipal Court Judge Allen E. Broussard asked Z. if he would cooperate.

"I just wanna get outa here," came the reply. "I just want everybody to be able to turn around and go home." He refused to press charges.

The district attorney's office dropped the felony charges of assault on the ground that two officers had moved too far away for convenient testimony. In return, I pleaded guilty to misdemeanor assault, resisting arrest and miscellaneous lesser charges.

On September 18, I was handed a 180-day suspended sentence and two years' probation.

XXI—Retirement at Thirty

Technically, any reason—illness, family problems or even loss of interest—was good enough to get you out of the club. All you had to do was say, "I quit." But you could only "retire" if you could break off all communications with the club, for retirement ran counter to the club motto, "Angels forever, forever Angels." It was a cousin to desertion.

If you retired, you could ask nothing of the club unless you had something they wanted or had influential friends. Yet the club could demand almost anything of a retiree. You might be asked to provide weapons or bomb-making materials. You might be asked to conceal contraband or to put up a member on the lam. You might be visited in the middle of the night by stoned, tired or hungry bikers marooned in the neighborhood. And you never withheld hospitality for fear of being labeled a turncoat.

Discussing club business with any outsider, even a family member, was verboten, because you might be divulging information useful to a cop. News media contacts were prohibited, of course, because former members couldn't speak for the club—and putting something in the newspapers was like handing it to the cops.

Retirees had to tread softly around actives. In confrontations, the power balance usually belonged to the active member, no matter how "heavy" you once were. Allowing friendship to supersede club loyalty would directly violate the code.

If you could throw aside old club friends or get far away, you could avoid most of these problems. But you also would miss out on the fringe benefits available to a well-liked retiree. Sometimes the club or individual members would intervene on a retiree's behalf if he were injured or jailed or financially strapped. Loans would come from wealthy members or the club treasury. In effect, a popular member might enjoy a sort of health insurance, blood bank privileges, bail service and legal aid. Depending on the retiree's standing, he could be almost as well taken care of as an unpopular member. That was the residue of brotherhood.

Contrary to popular belief, members almost invariably remained "active" when sent to prison. You don't throw off the protection of the Hell's Angels name when you go into a place like San Quentin. In fact, a number of guys enhanced it by getting friendly with the Aryan Brotherhood, a white supremist, biker-dominated prison gang that included some Manson Family members and competed with black and Mexican-American gangs in the prison drug trade.

Although a long prison sentence kept a guy off his motorcycle, it didn't always keep him from making money. Nest eggs were set aside for prominent members such as Foo Manchu. I handed Tramp a cut of every sale involving Foo's old buyers, and Foo's old lady was supposed to hold it for safekeeping. We also supplied jailed Angels with narcotics for pleasure and profit.

Specifically, we used to smuggle stuff into San Quentin to Foo and other guys. We filled waterproof rubber snake-bite kits with crank or coke. Then we went to the little building outside the prison gates where they sell paintings and other things made by inmates. We bought a picture then asked to use the bathroom. A flush or two of the toilet and that dope was behind the walls in the sewage plant or someplace where the guys could get it. The club put plenty of drugs in "Big Q" using snakebite kits, or having women pass it to the guys when they kissed in the visitors' room. I only went once to San Quentin, but I delivered drugs a few times to the Alameda County jail by slipping flattened tin-foil envelopes under a door to a trusty.

There was no easy way out of the club. The Hell's Angels was more a way of death than of life. The old heavyweights, the clique of my longest and closest club buddies, were a microcosm. Jerry went to the grave after tangling with a train. Waldo went to heroin so totally that I couldn't lure him away with money, a motorcycle or a job. Junior wasted himself with speed, going from a hulking 300 pounds to a frail 160 or so. And I came close to losing my family, my mind and my life.

Yet out of weakness and circumstance, I was unable and unwilling to completely slip the club's grasp. For more than a decade, my closest bonds had been club bonds, and I couldn't sever all relationships. Even long-retired friends like J. B. and Paul maintained some nostalgic contacts with Sonny and others, and they took in occasional club dances or parties.

When deer hunting season opened in fall of 1969, Z. asked J. B. and me if we'd like to join a few of the guys on a weekend outing. I accepted because Z. had been my hunting partner in previous years and our friendship had mended somewhat with his wounds.

We drove to a hunting camp in the Sierra Nevada, east of

Fresno. Vern had rented the cabin and invited Animal, another member who'd called for my head after the shooting. At the time, I was unaware of their threats against me, but I was wary because of old grudges.

When Z. broke out psychedelics Friday night, I begged off at first, and he told me, "I know what you're thinking . . . Everything will be cool." So I went on my first LSD trip since the shooting, mainly to prove to myself and the other guys that I could handle it.

The next morning, as our jeep jounced toward a productive deer area, I was dazzled. The sun rose quickly, neutralizing the cold and warming the landscape. Everyone fanned out on foot, and swept through a likely-looking canyon hoping to flush bucks.

After hours of fruitless brush beating, I paused to drink from a creek. When I looked up, I was eye-to-eye with a buck on the opposite bank. My first shot dropped him, squealing. A second to the head put him away. The sloppy kill bothered me, but that night we laughed about my good luck.

The hunt was savored around the campfire. We were all on the same psychedelics-enhanced wavelength except Animal. He dropped reds instead and let out the worst in his nasty disposition. The rest of us took his verbal harassment for a while, then I jumped up. "Cut out the bullshit," I said. "We don't need it."

Lunging without warning, Animal seized my throat. As my breath was being wrung away, I said once through my clenched teeth, "Lemme go, dammit!" Animal relaxed his grip. "Let's talk about this," I said.

"You shoulda been shot for that thing," the little scrapper shouted. He went on a tirade about the sanctity of club rules and the need to punish violators.

I broke in, shaking my head. "Man, that's not where I'm at now. I learned the hard way that you can't shoot people to solve things. That's the difference between you and me."

Animal didn't buy that. It probably seemed the ultimate in hypocrisy coming from me, a guy who'd used a gun for years. He repeated that I should have been shot under the club's eye-for-an-eye code.

"I couldn't shoot nobody again," I said. "The shooting put me through changes. You might be able to do that to me, but I couldn't do that to you now." Then somehow I shifted the argument to Tramp, Animal's onetime mentor. "Something was totally wrong with the way Tramp treated me, nixing a brother for someone else," I said. "I got shafted."

That only made Animal madder. He bristled at the criticism and broadsided me with curses. Then he stormed away. I tingled with adrenalin. The confrontation, word by word, gesture by gesture, played over in my head. I became disgusted with myself for not fighting back. Reason told me that fighting and shooting didn't make a man. But once the opportunity to retaliate had flown, my emotions and conditioning told me something else.

J. B. picked up on my shame and anger. "I was ready to jump in there and get him," he said.

"You said the right thing," Z. added. "You were right about the shooting. It's the past. Forget it."

The confrontation haunted me even after we returned home with our deer carcasses. I moped around the house for a few days, and not even Helen could coax me to talk about what had happened in the mountains.

XXII—Altamont and Other Horrors

"Nobody has ever accused the Hell's Angels of wanton killing, at least not in court . . . but it boggles the nerves to consider what might happen if the outlaws were ever deemed responsible for even three or four human deaths, by accident or otherwise. Probably every motorcycle rider in California would be jerked off the streets and ground into hamburger . . . " —Hunter Thompson. [36]

The rest of the world learned on December 6, 1969, what the Angels and law enforcement officials had known for years. The blissful optimism that marked the hippie vision of the club was self-delusion.

From the moment Angels had rumbled through the Altamont crowd on choppers, kicking those who got in their path, they played the disdainful aggressors. The only questions were when and how they would find an excuse to butcher somebody in that flock of 300,000.

The club came to party, although their mission became
the protection of the Rolling Stones and other performers
from zonked-out freaks who might stampede the stage. The
Stones "hired" them at the suggestion of the Grateful Dead.
The pay was $500 worth of beer, which the guys collected
can by can while patrolling the stage.

Altamont was billed as West Coast Woodstock, another
free rock festival. There were no tickets or fences to restrict
the flow of people or their cars. There only was a token
force of private cops who would have been better suited to
watching for shoplifters in Macy's. Medical supplies were
short, transportation so paralyzed that performers were hel-
icoptered there.

Against this backdrop, the glass-littered raceway was
more suitable for a tragedy than a love-rock festival.

Amid bad vibes and marijuana clouds, people packed
against the stage in suffocating density. By dusk, the Angels
had waded into the crowd more than a dozen times, thumping people with boots and pool cues for violating the stage's
sanctity or the club's sensibilities. A few Angels bikes were
knocked down, either in retaliation or by accident, and that
caused more counterattacks. Whenever a person was selected for a clobbering, the throng parted like the Red Sea to
give the Angels swinging room.

From the club perspective, all their violence was in self-
defense. "The people who touched the Angels' bikes got
thumped," Sonny recounted later in an interview with San
Francisco radio station KSAN-FM. "Most people that's got
a good Harley chopper got a few grand invested in it. Ain't
nobody gonna kick my motorcycle. And they might think
that because they're a crowd of 300,000 people that they
can do it and get away with it. But when you're standing
there looking at something that's your life, and everything
you've got is invested in that thing, and you love that thing
better than . . . anything in the world, and you see a guy

kick it, you know who he is. And if you got to go through
fifty people to get him, you're gonna get him . . . "

At sunset Mick Jagger and the Stones exploded into
"Jumpin' Jack Flash. It's a gas, gas, gas!" As a sea of wor-
shipers surged forward, a young black man with a white
woman was confronted by an Angel who apparently was
offended by the pairing. The first signs of a scuffle brought
Angels pouring from the stage. A gun appeared in the
black's hand, a knife flashed behind him. With a desperate
flourish, he fled then fell. As Angels put boots to his face
and ribs, he yelled, "I wasn't gonna shoot you," and disappeared from view.

There were great waves of boos when the music stopped
mid-song. Keith Richard put down his guitar and announced, "If you don't quit it, we're not going to play."

Added Jagger, trying to rally the crowd to a sense of community, "Brothers and sisters, come on now . . . Everybody just cool out." The band resumed "Sympathy for the
Devil," then again pulled up short as death heads swirled
over a body. One more start and stop, then Jagger cried, "We
need a doctor, and an ambulance."

The young black, eighteen-year-old Meredith Hunter of
Berkeley, bled to death as some in the crowd roared for
more music. The first medics to reach him said death was
inevitable. He bore five stab wounds in the back and a gaping hole below his left ear. The rest of him was stomped and
battered.

A number of myths died along with Hunter. The myth of
the Angels as guardians of the flower children. The myth
that the countersociety required no keepers of the peace.
The myth that people who enjoy the same music and drugs
are one.

During Altamont, my family and I were at the ranch
building for the future. We really felt like we were escaping

the club's destructive influence, but we were deluding ourselves, just as the hippies had.

At 4 A.M. one Monday in early 1970, we were home in
Oakland when Sonny awakened me with a phone call. "I
gotta talk to ya," he said. "It can't wait. Can I come over?"

"Sure," I said.

When he showed up, he whispered, "I've got a body I gotta get rid of. Broad committed suicide. Blew her brains out
at a party."

"What the hell happened?"

"Your friend was up to his old games."

No elaboration was needed. He meant Tramp. I knew all
too well how Tramp's sadistic antics could get out of hand.
His Yeti-like looks were enough to scare some people, but
he also played monstrous head games, especially with
women when they were loaded. When he rapped and man-
euvered his insanely elastic face, things got so intense that
he didn't need to threaten rape to terrify a woman. But he
was insistent when he wanted some flesh, and he usually
got some, even if it meant trying to mount a writhing LSD-
powered woman as he did one night on my living room rug.

Sonny explained that the dead woman—whose name he
deliberately omitted—was stoned out during a party at a
club house off 55th Avenue when Tramp singled her out for
head games. In the middle of it, she grabbed "someone's"
pistol and pumped a slug through her brain. [37] Sonny said
there could be problems if the coroner's office found the
body and traced the bullet to an Angel gun. Then he asked,
"Are those well holes still open? She's been in a garbage can
for a couple of days and is getting pretty ripe."

"More or less."

"Well, then I need the keys to the ranch."

I agreed to accept the corpse, partly to repay an old friend
for his unflagging loyalty and partly because of his $12,500
financial interest in the property. Pressing the gate chain

keys into his hand, I said, "I need 'em back within a week. Use the hole nearest the house." That way part of the ranch could be sold safely: we could keep the house and a little surrounding land without worrying about a new owner accidentally digging up the body.

When I returned to bed and told Helen, she cried, "How could Sonny do that to a friend? That's a terrible favor to ask somebody." All I could do was point out Sonny's years of kindness and express hope that someday we could forget about the body.

Days later, Helen and I drove to the ranch. The grass was winter green, the creeks running muddy through grotesque oaks. Near the unfinished house, we came upon a mound of freshly turned earth. It was only a dozen yards from the foundation. We were heartsick and nauseated. Our dream was desecrated.

"Who was she?" I asked as we stood over the grave. "What was she like? What did she look like?"

"I wonder if her parents know about her being dead," Helen said, with a shiver. "We don't even know how old she was. We don't even know if she was a young girl in high school or one of the older ones that knew what she was doing, more or less."

(Years later, we would find out that she was Patricia McKnight, twenty-six, from Texas, who'd been hanging around the club for a while. We even had met her at some of Skip's parties.)

That body was working on my head all the time. I had just survived that shooting nightmare and developed a healthy approach to living. Then, all of a sudden, I was sitting on something a lot heavier than drugs. No one could have paid me enough money to take that body, but I did it for Sonny.

We believed Sonny because he generally told the truth— and this story was very plausible. Mamas and other club women were susceptible to overdoses, gang bangs, erratic behavior. If this were murder, Sonny likely would have said so or said nothing at all. After all, I was privy to one homicide, and had kept the secret. And around the club, sharing heavy information placed the greatest burden on the recipient.

Although he and the club had taken another piece of my life, I worried about Sonny as an old friend. It seemed he was riding into a blind alley of criminal charges and would crash sooner or later. After the burial, I took him aside and said, "Come on, man. It's time to retire. It's time to get a rocking chair and get outa this rat race." I argued that it no longer made sense for a bunch of thirtyish tough guys to be biking around with signboards on their backs, challenging the cops to bust them. "If you gotta deal, at least put on a business suit," I said. "Be Sonny Barger respectable businessman."

Sonny shrugged it off. He gave the impression he could beat police raps forever. He would fly the death's head until his luck and organizational skill failed him. He would rely on his guns, his deals with police, his expert disguises, his knowledge of the law, his phony ID cards, etc. Special circumstances took the red and white from me, but that patch came close to being part of Sonny's body, the code an embodiment of his personal principles.

In mid-February 1970, Tramp apparently left the club at about the same time he left this earthly life. Knowledgeable club friends told me that at least one member was down on him because narcotics paraphernalia was found in his house. On St. Valentine's Day, Tramp died as German had died, of an overdose of downers. The death was a strange one, simple on the surface yet highly suspicious to those of us close to the club.

The Alameda County coroner's office reported that John

Terrance Tracey, born 12-21-39, a native of Michigan, died at age 30. Last occupation: two years of self-employment. Cause of death: "suspected suicide" with Seconal, a euphemism for saying there was no certainty about who administered the overdose. "Reportedly a former member of the Hell's Angels, this man was recently expelled from the organization," said a report, lending credence to the theory that Tramp didn't do himself in. "The afternoon of 2-13-70, he called his common-law wife and told her he had gotten up enough courage to commit suicide and was going to take Nembutal. On her arrival at the home (1060 Underhill Road), she found him unconscious, and together with a friend took him to Highland Hospital where he was admitted to emergency at 20:27. There a barbiturate level of 3.1 was found. . . . "

A hint of a different scenario came a day later. The phone rang and one ranking member told me, "We've got something for you to listen to."

Another member came on the line and barked, "Now hear this." Then came a tape recording of a man gasping, coughing, choking, as though on vomit or blood or wine or something, seemingly fighting for his life. It had to be Tramp. The choking stopped abruptly and the receiver clicked, leaving me alone.

I was dumbfounded and trembling, my ears ringing. To this day, I don't know what they were doing. Maybe they were trying to scare me. Or maybe they were giving me some sort of gratification because Tramp had burned me. I just knew it was Tramp and it was real heavy, so heavy that I didn't ask for an explanation.

At the direction of his parents, Tramp was buried at St. Mary's Cemetery on an Oakland hillside overlooking the bay. His gravestone didn't carry the customary death's head etched in black marble—and there was no big funeral. In fact, only a few club women even bothered to watch him go under.

You could tell plenty by a member's final sendoff. A guy in good standing would have the death's head on his coffin, would be wearing a fresh set of colors and would have his motorcycle parked next to him, right inside the funeral parlor. More than a hundred members, representing all the chapters, would come along with emissaries from other outlaw clubs. Angels would be pallbearers.

Magoo's funeral about a year later was a glaring contrast to Tramp's. Magoo, one of the club's most popular guys and sort of the honorary club physician, died of a heart ailment in the back seat of his VW while taking a lunchtime nap on his teamsters job.[38] The funeral home was packed with dozens of club families and members, plus Magoo's own relatives, including his wife and mother. Outside, other guys got stoned and drank under the watchful eye of the police. When the prayers were over and it was time to view the body, a couple of loaded bike groupies stood over the coffin yelling, "Magoo! Get up, Magoo! Get up." They were trying to resurrect him, right there in front of his horrified family.

"I ain't goin' for this bullshit," I said. And, although I wasn't an active member, I hustled those dumb broads out of there. I didn't care who was offended. Magoo was my friend.

Magoo was laid to rest beneath a small tree at Evergreen Cemetery. His black headstone was chiseled with the club emblem. After some words were said, some people smoked parting joints and left the roaches smoldering in an ashtray—just in case he wanted one last hit.

XXIII—Living With the Dead

"The dream was ended. It was like living a nightmare. When I first knew the girl was there, I didn't want to go up to the place. When George showed me where she was, I didn't want to go near it. We lived in hell for a long time. You just knew the police were going to find it, because you can't ever get away with anything. On the other hand, Sonny was smart, and we thought he'd get away with it if anybody could. It took about a year before I could go to the ranch and forget about the body. You gotta go on, because it was done. So we kept building and planning."—Helen Wethern.

During 1970, we developed a family routine. We were like thousands of middle-class city families. I put in my eight hours a day. Helen tended to domestic duties. The kids got good grades in school. And on weekends we fled to the country.

In preparation for each weekend, I hustled building materials and help. An estimated $15,000 worth of stolen and donated appliances, lumber and other material eventually would reach the ranch. And nearly all the labor would be free. When I needed a plumber, an electrician or a brick mason, I'd call, "Hey, whatta ya doin' Saturday?" As professional courtesy they'd come up to the ranch, and they'd usually go home with some dope or a case of liquor.

Each weekend as many as fifteen guys—Angels and former Angels, construction workers and old friends—converged on the ranch with wives, old ladies and children. There was as much merrymaking as working, but the house took shape. My construction buddy Ben and I did most of the framing, but J.B. and a number of active members, including Winston and Z., hung floor joists and raised walls.

When the women weren't passing us cool drinks and food, they were hauling lumber in trucks or driving into town for hardware or supplies. Helen and the kids lugged enough stones by hand to build a huge fireplace. And to surprise Helen, I had the mason inset a big jade-colored rock—her favorite—as the centerpiece.

Our neighbors befriended us, but law enforcement officers apparently were convinced the place was a Hell's Angels clubhouse, a launching pad for vice. After some area burglaries, a plainclothesman drove through the ranch gate, backed up by squad cars hidden in nearby trees. He questioned me about the burglaries and implied we would encounter resistance if we tried to establish a biker colony.

"Look, this is my house," I said. "It's for my family . . . I ain't gonna risk it by burglarizing somebody down the road. He's got nothin' I want. I got more than he does anyway."

That harassment made me bitter. The house was outfitted with a $400 intercom and we planned a front gate speaker. We also acquired a magnetic eye alarm but never installed it for fear deer would touch it off at night. Instead, we commissioned a gate sign that carried the skull and crossbones and read: "No trespassing. Survivors will be prosecuted."

There were festive times too, such as Tommy's wedding. It was a small, simple affair that started with a party the night before. In addition to my family, Tommy and his bride-to-be, Marilyn, the guest list consisted of the window washer Kooie, the former Frisco Angel Napa Bob, his lady Carol, J.B. and Irma with their brood, Duke the dealer and his red-bearded friend whose name I quickly forgot, although he smoked more dope and snorted more coke than the rest of us put together.

The following morning the wedding party gathered under giant oaks on a grassy hillside. Tommy, elegant in new bell-bottoms, fingered a gold band as his betrothed smiled beatifically and smoothed leather skirts over her hips.

Duke was supposed to supply the minister. With a grandiose wave and a grin, he gestured toward the camper. And out stepped the red-bearded guy, his long hair gone, his bald pate catching the sun. He cut a satanic figure in purple robes—and it took everyone a moment to realize that today's minister was yesterday's doper, minus his wig. "Who is this guy?" someone asked.

"Wow. We've been partying with him," I chuckled. "That's our minister."

By that definition, J.B. was a Doctor of Divinity and Sonny was a bishop. The red-bearded Mr. Q. was a mail-order minister with a mail-order marriage ceremony, but he did a creditable wedding with Tommy and Marilyn joyously loaded and reading their vows from a parchment scroll scrawled with their hopes and dreams.

XXIV—Angel Without Colors

In city or country, I still looked the part of a Hell's Angel, minus the patch. With my 280 pounds, black beard and battered face, people couldn't help gawking whether I was astride a bar stool, grocery shopping or attending church and school events with my family.

My appearance and my past locked me into a biker's identity, yet I was as proud of my kids as any father. Unlike the George Wethern who missed his son's birthday a few years before, I was always on hand. Good report cards were rewarded, bad ones punished. There were family breakfasts following First Holy Communions.

In fact, Bobby's communion benefited my family in more than one way. Among the parents milling outside before Mass, we bumped into my assault trial judge, Allen Broussard, and his wife. There we were, a former Hell's Angel and a black judge exchanging pleasantries and chatting about our children. When the ceremony commenced, we sat behind the Broussards, excited for our son and glowing over the good fortune of running into the judge at church. After the Mass, I strode into the sunlight under the aura of respectability.

In the view of the court and my probation officer, I was moving relentlessly along the road to rehabilitation. Part of my new image was genuine, part my natural acting ability. I cast off the club. I was employed. I took an interest in my children. I was building a family home far from my criminal homeland. And my court-mandated urine tests indicated I was abstaining from drugs. (Before the tests, I always allowed sufficient time for my body to dispose of drug residues.)

So, on August 28, 1970, at the request of my probation officer, Judge Broussard modified my probation from two years to one and terminated it, commending me for my rapid rehabilitation. On the way home, Helen and I celebrated by getting loaded out of our noggins.

We were back in the drug scene again. Starting with grass and a few reds, we gradually worked our way into speed. We liked crank for the bedroom, but when we'd been going all night long, we'd take some reds then sleep for a few hours. As Helen used to say, "You can't have any get up and go without a little rest." It became a regular cycle. After a few days of speed tripping, we'd take some tranks to even out our heads. We usually were cleaned up and ready to rip by the next weekend.

Though substantial, our drug consumption was moderated by our stash. There no longer were thousands of free hits skimmed from deals. Instead, we relied on the largess of dealer friends and our own spending power to keep an ice chest of drugs in the hills.

One drug remained conspicuously absent—PCP. As soon as my head could take the strain of gunplay, I prowled for PCP sources, hoping to stop the flow. Sometimes Z. went along as I followed up information gleaned during small dealings and social contacts, but mostly it was my own crusade.

Winston put me on a trail leading to Eddie, a curly-haired shyster who came to my house with a 6-foot-6 torpedo. "That stuff you're peddlin's no good," I told him, launching an account of my own disastrous experiences. At the conclusion of my story, Eddie was steady, but his bodyguard's eyes were filled with tears. He admitted that his own brains were festering and ready to pop after two weeks on the crap.

"Kick back, buddy," I said, taking him by the shoulder. "We'll take some reds, and there's some Jack Daniels over there. You'll be all right, but you gotta let time take its course. Lie down on the couch and let time pass."

With the big guy defanged, I got down to business with Eddie. I originally planned to give him a .45-caliber noseplug and a $50,000 fine, under the threat of bodily harm. But on second thought, it seemed likely that he would just redouble his efforts to make up for the fine.

"Okay, Ed," I declared. "No more PCP. Nix on it. Stop dealing it and you'll be saving yourself $50,000. That's how much I was gonna fine ya."

Ed acquiesced and dragged his bodyguard out of there. I didn't have any future problems with Ed, but one day his bodyguard—who hung out with club acquaintances in Hayward—showed up at my house with Z.'s former old lady, Linda.

Sonny came over to join the party, and the next thing I knew he was forcing the big guy into my bathroom. I burst through the door. The guy was cowering in the bathtub and Sonny was climbing all over him, pistol-whipping him. When I demanded an explanation, Sonny yelled, "There are two hundred people depending on me, and this bastard's got a loose mouth. I'm gonna shut it." It seemed the guy had opened his mouth about some of Sonny's dealings in front of the wrong people—and word got back to Sonny. To avoid serious gunplay, I pushed Sonny aside and put in a few licks of my own. The bodyguard apologized, begged for mercy then promised it never would happen again.

I continued my quest for PCP sources. It was doomed to failure because stopping stuff that could be produced easily and that made bunk weed into a potent psychedelic was like strangling the wind. But I tried to enlist some unlikely allies.

When the Intelligence Division of the IRS calledd me to its Oakland office on St. Patrick's Day, 1971, the last thing on my mind was PCP. The IRS wanted to inspect my returns for 1968 to 1970 and all my canceled checks to determine whether I could have purchased the ranch with legal income.

A co-worker suggested that I take my problem to a union official. The official in turn gave me the names of an Oakland bar owner and a retired cop who owned a construction outfit. The notion of soliciting a crime from an ex-cop was hard to digest, so the union official and I met with the proprietor of a bar near the gun store where I had unloaded my collection. The union official explained what I needed. "It'll be no problem," the barman said.

At a later meeting, the bar owner signed a paper saying he had lent me $15,000. The price of the cover was $1,650, which we referred to as "interest." The barman said our mutual friend would get a cut, but the union official denied that so I slipped a case of booze into his car.

At my next IRS interview I submitted enough documentation to escape tax charges. My W-2 forms didn't account for much money, but a number of "personal loans" covered the balance.

"Whatta ya care about this little bit of money for?" I said to sidetrack the agents. "There are more important things to work on."

"Like what?"

"PCP."

"What's that?"

"A drug we call DOA, or Dust of Angels. I don't know what it is exactly. I just know what it does. You feds supposedly sent a sample to Washington for testing. You tell me what it is."

Their interest really was aroused when I told them the club banned it after I shot Z. on the stuff. The shooting rang a bell, so they started questioning me about club backers, apparently looking for legitimate businessmen and lawyers who secretly dealt with the club. When they got no answers, they asked me why a retired Angel would associate with the club if he weren't dealing. I told them my main bonds were old friends and a shared loathing for PCP.

During two visits, I convinced those IRS guys that someone on PCP could come down and gobble up their kids at the schoolbus stop. They thought they really were into something big. I got them more concerned about that drug than money and income. They asked me whether PCP had political implications, and even wanted to know if the Communists introduced it as a plot to overthrow the government. They asked me if it might be part of a plot by a foreign government to introduce drugs into the water supplies.

"I don't know, but it could be," I said. "When I find out, I'll let you know. As far as this drug is concerned, I'm working the same way you are. I'm trying to do away with it. And if I get to the source before you do, I hope you guys have the guts to testify on my behalf at my murder trial."

XXV—Big Tom and Charlie

"A Hell's Angel is in an honor society, man. We live by some of the strongest rules going—and if you break one, you might not have the chance to break another—that's how strict we are. But they are our rules—not something somebody lays on us."—"Rotten Richard" Barker[39]

On a crisp springtime Friday in 1971, my ranch-bound family highballed north on Interstate Highway 80, oblivious to a series of nearby events that would irretrievably alter our lives.[40] The fifteen-member Richmond Angels chapter was meeting in a clubhouse at 1530 Hillcrest Road, a San Pablo tract house near the bay. The garage was filling with Harleys. A couple of women loitered on the porch. Members sprawled around the living room watching TV and awaiting new arrivals.

The guys who straggled inside were as nasty looking and husky as any chapter's members, but they lacked the prestige and business sense of the Oakland clan. Richmond reflected the provincial character of industry-fed one-horse towns such as Port Costa, Crockett and Hercules. The members were mainly small-town locals who dealt drugs on a limited basis, with less volume and less finesse than Oakland. They were the equivalent of a AAA baseball team—marginally profitable, close to the big leagues yet easier to break into.

That night the unlikely pair of "Big Tom" Shull, twenty-four, and diminutive Charlie Baker, thirty, were introduced as hot prospects by "Festus," a 250-pound convicted second-story man. Shull—a red-bearded six-footer with a 250-pound weightlifter's body—could bench-press 350 pounds and already looked like an Angel in his stereotypical biker's regalia. He had cultivated that image since he and Baker drove west from Georgia about a year before.

A hefty combat knife usually hung from Big Tom's motorcycle chain belt with a buckle that said "God be with us" in German. He wore a swastika earring and Highway Patrol-type motorcycle boots laced nearly to the knees. A brassy style fit his Georgia twang. Big Tom worked hard at being an outlaw, wheeling and dealing on a dime scale, boosting cycle parts, making as many enemies as friends—and frequently dreaming aloud about someday wearing the "red and white."

Easygoing Charlie tagged along in ever-present contrast. A short, pigeon-toed former Augusta police motorcycle mechanic, he looked puckish with his dark curly hair and mustache, wire-rimmed glasses and railroad engineer's cap. Fun—the 100-mile-an-hour streaks to the mountains, the parties and the women—lured him to the California cycling havens. Once there, he followed his ambitious buddy to the Bay Area, then found a girlfriend and a motorcycle mechanic's job in Rodeo.

* * *

"They're friends of mine. Treat 'em right," "Festus" said to introduce the pair, but they were asked according to custom to wait outside during the business meeting. Like everyone else, Tom and Charlie would have to go through a long apprenticeship before the club would consider allowing them to come up for a membership vote.

Although "Festus" took off after the meeting, Big Tom and Charlie elected to stay and socialize. The two Georgians and another prospect, 300-pound Edward "Junior" Carter, were sent out for whiskey, rum and a few cases of beer. After a few belts, the party moved to the You and I bar in Crockett. The group stayed about three hours, drinking and shooting pool until they were warm enough for the ride back.

The drinking bout reconvened at the clubhouse. Mescaline and LSD were passed. Barker plowed rows of cocaine, and people horned it through a rolled up $100 bill. There were only a few women, all more or less spoken for, so the entertainment took a different course.

"Whispering Bill" Pifer—a tall, gaunt Angel who got his nickname after losing his larynx to cancer—went to the kitchen to fetch coffee for Tom and beer for Charlie. "Tom's been wanting to come around the club," he told a few members. "Ya wanna check him out?"

"Let's put some acid in his coffee," suggested Rolland Crane, twenty-nine.

"Sure. That's a good idea," added Barker. Eight or ten tabs of green LSD were stirred into Shull's coffee, then Crane plopped some acid in Charlie's beer too.

When hallucinations crawled into their heads, the two guinea pigs were put into a "trick bag." Big Tom was shown a photo of Dr. Martin Luther King Jr. and was told that the black leader might be the next President. Shull started yelling epithets and stomping the picture.

The president soon initiated another round of tricks.

"Gimme your wallet," he said, and Shull obeyed, not wanting to irritate the honcho. Then Barker went to Charlie and pretended to pull a sheriff's office courtesy card from the wallet. "Did you know your friend was a cop?" he asked, grimly.

The little guy's eyes bugged out. "No. I don't believe it. No," he cried.

Barker used Charlie's wallet to pull the same trick on Tom. "That little guy's a narc," Barker said. The heavy implication was that Big Tom either would have to disown his buddy or take on everybody else.

"I'll kill him. I'll kill him," Tom roared, leaping to his feet and swinging wildly.

"Grab the sonofabitch," Barker shouted and half a dozen men—Crane, "Big Boy," Paul F. "Badger" Mumm, William J. Moran, Whispering Bill and his sixteen-year-old son—tried to hold Tom down. The women hung back, and Charlie tried to calm his buddy. But Big Tom kept hollering, "The devil's after me. The devil's after me." He thrashed with the muscle of an insane man. He was so beyond control that Barker telephoned onetime Angel "Big Red," and told him, "Bring some seconal over here, and fast."

The men couldn't throttle Big Tom's body or his rocketing brain. For forty-five bloody minutes, grunting, straining guys were locked on his limbs, taking turns grabbing his long hair and smashing his head on the floor, trying to batter him unconscious. His blood was splattered everywhere. At last "Big Red" and another biker arrived with reds. Handfuls were jammed into Tom's mouth. In a few minutes, he relaxed sufficiently to be pinned and hogtied with hands roped behind his back and another rope taut between his neck and bound feet. "I'll kill you sons of bitches," he hollered.

"Take him into the back bedroom so nobody will hear him scream," Barker ordered. Virtually everybody was

225

needed to move him. Screaming madly, he was left alone.

The party went on for about ten minutes, then Pifer was sent back to see if Big Tom was quiet. Tom was quiet all right. His mouth was wide open, his tongue swollen, his eyes rolled back in his head. Pifer put an ear to his mouth. Nothing.

Pifer ran into the living room. "I hope you're happy," he gasped weakly at Barker. "You killed the sonofabitch."

Barker, Crane and Moran rushed to see for themselves. When they emerged from the bedroom, Rotten Richard ordered the women out. Then he pointed at Charlie and told Pifer, sergeant at arms for the night, "You kill that sonofabitch. We don't want no witnesses."

"Screw you," Whispering Bill rasped back. "Do it yourself." When the order was repeated, he punctuated his refusal with his middle finger.

At a new order, Moran jumped Charlie, knocked him to the floor and wrung his neck. Charlie stopped his uncontrollable bawling and went strangely calm. Each thump of his heart seemed to jack his eyes open a fraction wider. Several members held him down while Moran sat alongside him, squeezing his neck and repeating, "This guy don't wanna die. This guy don't wanna die."

Moran used his own belt as a garrote. When that failed, he called for a rope and a stick. Knotting the rope around Charlie's neck, he inserted a piece of broken chair, then cranked it tight. For five minutes or more, the rope chewed deeper—until Charlie's heart stopped. The rope was cinched to make sure he stayed dead, then his body was dumped in the bedroom closet, a few feet from Big Tom's. There was some talk of killing one or more of the female witnesses, but everyone figured they were too scared to squeal. Pifer assured everyone that his son would be tight-lipped too.

Still, much needed to be done. By 6 A.M. Saturday morning, some members were using Barker's truck to haul bloody furnishings to the dumps for burning, while Pifer and Badger scrubbed the house. Later, Pifer and Barker stripped the bodies of wallets and other personal articles, flushing some and burning others in the sink.

When the cleanup was finished, Rotten Richard called Sonny on the kitchen pay phone, saying he wanted to come over and discuss a "problem." As Richard was leaving, he told "Festus" to dump the dead men's motorcycles in the bay.

On Sunday, Pifer was summoned to Barker's house for further orders. The stench of death hit him as he walked past the trunk of a Cadillac parked out front. Inside, Barker told him that he would be driving the car Monday because he was the straightest-looking member.

"Where are we goin'?" Bill asked.

"You'll find out."

Meanwhile, Zorro showed up at the ranch with Mickey. In private, he told me, "Sonny wants to talk to you right away. It's important." We took Z.'s pickup to the phone booth in front of the Blue Bonnet Cafe, then dialed Sonny.

"I got a couple more bodies," he said.

My heart froze in my chest. I was stuck. Not only was Sonny asking another heavy favor, but also Zorro, a creditor by virtue of the shooting, was playing messenger. The pressure was staggering.

Once I granted reluctant permission, Sonny said, "Okay. Tell Z. the best spot or pick the spot, then you give him the gate key and get outa there. I don't want you involved."

Back at the ranch, I made up an excuse to return immediately to the city. J.B.'s family was compelled to pack up too because, ever since the first burial, we insisted that no one use the ranch out of our presence. We were afraid that someone might plant other bodies without our knowledge.

As the two families prepared to leave, Z. and I drove around the hills looking for a suitable spot. I settled on a well test hole about fifty yards from the highway. "I'm holding you responsible," I said handing Z. the key. "Make sure the guys do a good job. And take the clothes off the bodies before you bury 'em." I had recalled hearing in movies that stripped bodies decay faster.

At about 4 P.M. the next day, Pifer was instructed to drive the Cadillac over the Richmond-San Rafael Bridge and head north on U.S. Highway 101. He was to watch his rearview mirror and obey the directional signals of a trailing Ford station wagon full of Angels, guns, picks and shovels. If the Highway Patrol or sheriff's office stopped his low-hanging car, he was to get out, reach into his wallet for identification then hit the pavement. The club escort would cut down the lawmen with automatic weapons fire.

"Where we goin'?" Pifer asked.

"Don't ask questions," Barker snapped. "We have a choice of four different places to go, but this one's the closest."[41]

Before taking the wheel, Pifer splashed three bottles of Hexol on the bodies, which had their rigor mortis-stiffened arms broken to fit into the trunk. Then he cruised up U.S. 101 until the trailing car flashed its right turn signal. After they took the Boonville Road turnoff a few miles south of Ukiah, Z. met them near the freeway and guided them to the ranch.

"Get the goddam bodies outa the car," Rotten Richard barked. "We don't have all night." He and Z. cradled submachine guns; Carter, Crane, "Festus" and Pifer got to work. While tools were unloaded, the bodies were stripped and the clothes kicked into the hole. A moment later, there were two large splashes in the well and two white forms floated to the surface. The burial crew submerged the bodies with two bags of lime, a crisscross of boards and other construction material, then filled the hole with dirt.

XXVI—An Unfillable Pit

There was a big difference between the first body and the second two. The first wasn't quite legal, but it wasn't murder as far as I was concerned. The second two also bothered me because Z. was involved, and he was one cat I didn't trust. Afterward even Sonny apologized for sending Z., well knowing that I was having my own troubles with him.

The apology meant nothing when I found a dead man's sock at the grave. My suspicions went rampant as I mulled it over. Was it a setup or just a careless burial? Getting madder and madder, I raced back to Oakland and brought the sock to Sonny. "Look what I found at the hole."

Sonny crushed the thing angrily. "Shit, man, I'm sorry. I'll take care of it."

The next weekend, I was reinspecting the grave when the sun glinted off a man's necklace chain. Furious and frightened, I drove home to Oakland, then called Zorro over. "How did this thing get there?" I demanded.

Z. clammed up, so I whacked him a few times with a

pistol then dragged him to Sonny's house. "Sonny, I'm gettin' fed up with this crap," I said. "Z. was responsible for handling that burial trip. He either fucked up or somebody's framing me."

Sonny took the chain and said again, "I'll take care of it, George."

Still steamed up, I berated Z. "My kid has more guts than you. I oughta take you over my place and let him punch ya out on the front porch." Z. took the humiliation without a word in his own defense, but he was understandably worried about clearing himself.

He showed up at my place a few days later with Rotten Richard. Until then, I only knew that two nameless men were killed by Angels. The chapter and the individuals involved were mysteries to me.

"If anything was dropped, it was Richard's fault," Z. blurted, to absolve himself in the botchup.

Richard nodded assent, thanked me for helping out, then quickly changed the subject. Neither he nor I wanted Z. to entangle us any further. We were uneasy because we realized the murderer had been introduced to the gravekeeper.

"Just let it all go," I said. "Forget about it. It's over with." Then I brought out some dope and we got stoned. I itched to thump Z. again for his stupidity and selfishness.

After Barker was gone, I screamed at Z., "Why do you do this?" He tried to run but I cornered him in the living room and lashed his head with a gun barrel.

Of all times, Durt and Sir Gay dropped in. They were outraged that a nonmember was belting an active. "Hey, George. You're not supposed to hit a member and you know it," Sir Gay protested, advancing. But Helen halted him and Durt with a shotgun while I pounded away. Z. pleaded for help; Durt shouted, "George, please just stop hitting him until we check something. Okay?" I let up, then he turned to Sir Gay. "You go talk to Sonny and find out what we're supposed to do. I'll stay here."

A minute later, Sir Gay returned to report, "Sonny said whatever George said is all right." That dismayed Z. and amazed everyone, including me. Sonny had granted a non-member permission to violate a cardinal club rule. But after a few more licks, I let Z. up.

Z.'s brooding silence worried me, and I thought he might try to take revenge. Feeling very alone and vulnerable, I sought out a new club ally, someone who also would have a stake in keeping the bodies buried. I started inviting "Deacon" Proudfoot—who became president of the Oakland chapter in 1974—up to the ranch. He helped me dam a creek with a bulldozer, then I instructed him to smooth the ground above the two bodies.

"Ya know why there was a mound there?" I said later. "Because two dead guys were pushin' it up.

"Z. handled the burial, but I don't trust him," I went on. "Watch him close. Keep me informed. Watch Z." Deacon, as an emerging leader, was in an ideal position to observe Z. and to feel any heat generated by those bodies.

No matter how smooth the ground, no matter how high the grass, there was no forgetting the bodies. Being stoned and working on the ranch helped a little, but there was a shortage of funds for both.

For the second time, my panacea was drug dealing. My new partner was "Napa Bob" Holmes, a former Frisco Angel and forklift operator. He wasn't called "Napa" because he hailed from that wine country town: he claimed he did time in the state mental hospital there. The way Bob told it, he was sixteen when he pulled a gun on an old man in an alley and demanded money. The man supposedly laughed and said, "Gimme the gun, kid." Then Bob repeated, "Gimme the money, mister." When the man again said, "Gimme the gun," young Bob gave it to him. Shot him dead.

Napa Bob remained a Billy the Kid character. Even in his

early thirties, he loved shoot-em-up tactics and toted a silenced .22-caliber pistol. The 6-3, 215-pounder wore wooden shinguards to protect his accident-scarred legs, and he constantly was dreaming aloud about someday making big money in a drug business. Lacking experience and connections, he pestered me to give him pointers.

One day I agreed to work with him. Tiny and Durt fronted me crank to distribute through my old and new contacts. Speed sold about as well as LSD once did, mainly on its merits as a party drug, and that was the direction the club was taking.

My best customers were Frisco president Lawrence "Moose" Chesher and his sidekick, "Crow." Numerous non-Angels also were ripe for my return, since the Oakland chapter had lapsed into slovenly business practices, with too many members getting stoned instead of tending the store. (The first signs surfaced shortly after my resignation: my hippie trio became heroin hypes, and Tramp crawled back to me and asked for help in disposing of some STP.) Old connections such as Duke welcomed the opportunity to deal with someone other than active Angels with long criminal records and high visibility.

So my new partnership flourished, though with more restraint and less muscle than in the old days. I was careful not to impinge on the territory of active members, especially my suppliers.

The amphetamines were apparently trafficked through Los Angeles. I accidentally encountered the club's connection making a drop of a suitcase full of meth at Tiny's house. And the guy's old lady turned out to be Tina, a tall raven-haired groupie who did her thing with Magoo then resettled in the Los Angeles area.

This second time around, my biggest transaction was only six pounds of speed, which would wholesale by the kilo or ounce for about $15,000.

As the partnership originally was conceived, my job was getting the drugs and lining up customers while Napa's was sales and delivery. Unfortunately, Napa showed more aptitude for playing hoodlum with his .22-caliber convincer. After he came on heavy with some good customers, I took him aside. "Hey, man, that's no way to do business. You can't go around sticking up these people. The idea is to get them to like ya. Treat 'em right so they keep coming back." It was no use. Charm was not in his repertoire, so customers bypassed him and came directly to me. Napa was left with few duties.

For about six months, the volume of crank, cocaine and other drugs stabilized into a substantial supplementary income. Then Moose transferred to the Oakland chapter and dealt directly with Tiny. Though that cut me out of one middleman's position, I continued dealing whatever was abundant, picking up enough speed to stay stoned and enough money to finance ranch improvements.

Napa and his old lady Carol were fun to have around the ranch. They were avid readers, health food freaks and dabblers in palmistry and astrology. Carol was a stout-boned, brassy woman who came across like a bull dyke, but speed slimmed her to more feminine proportions—and she and Helen became friendly, if not friends.

When Napa wasn't bantering with his old lady, he was fantasizing with me, mostly crazy schemes. We even talked about buying a "helicopter kit" to build a chopper to cut down on driving time to the ranch. I was one of the few people who took Napa seriously and would listen to all the dreams.

Napa's mother stole him from a nineteenth-century time capsule. He often said he would have preferred living in the Old West, pulling off stage robberies like the one on our ranch a hundred years ago. And one night in our camper, he stroked his dark, neatly trimmed beard and mused, "When I go, I wanna take somebody with me. The more the better."

"Why?" Helen objected. "I just can't see it. What good would it do?"

"Everybody oughta carry a gun like in the Old West," he said. "That'd be great. You could have an argument with somebody and just say, 'Fastest gun wins. Let's go.' If ya wanted something, you could take it."

"Nah. That Jesse James thing don't work."

I debated on Napa's side that night until we badgered Helen to tears. But on another night, I gave Napa a good gulp of his own philosophy. He arrived loaded on reds, joining Helen and me, my brother and some girl he was alternately mounting and stuffing with peyote, plus Sam, a family friend who dealt a bit.

Napa made the mistake of playing the hardass and fiddling around with his .22 like a silent gunslinger. It burned me up. An argument ensued and I jumped him, bashing his head and face with a shotgun. My brother Michael, though I'd broken his leg in a recent family dispute, jumped in on my side. We hammered old Napa into a bloody heap, busting his false teeth and kicking him out to his car.

Napa and I remained bosom friends, just as I remained friends with J.B. despite tiffs with him. In our circles, drugs or club conditioning could twist an insignificant gripe into a punishable offense. Our capacity for forgiveness matched our capacity for punishment where longtime friendships were involved.

Even Z., after all our clashes, was welcome at the ranch. More than once Helen and I had discussed severing our relationship with him, but I valued his friendship. Z., the inveterate hustler, could be genial and generous and fun to have around.

In 1972, Z. frequently came with a young, outdoorsy woman named Shirley, a college coed with a five-year-old son by an invalid husband. Sometimes we'd meet at the McDonald's hamburger joint in Novato, then make plans to get together later at the ranch. Z. and his lady set up a base camp at Telephone Pole No. 144 near the Russian River headwaters, then they drove to the ranch for socializing.

We were impressed by Z.'s sterling behavior around Shirley—until she dragged in one night, sobbing and confused, with her son. "Z. winged out on downers," she said. "He was going crazy with the gun. I can't go back. I had to wait until he fell asleep to leave." She said Z. blew up when a foundling Australian Shepherd disobeyed him. He chased the dog up a hillside with rifle fire and, when Shirley objected, he threatened to do the same to her son.

We put her up for the night, then drove to the telephone pole in the morning. Z. was stomping around with his rifle, so I shielded Helen. There was no telling how he'd react to the man who crippled him. "What's happening?"

"I knew what I was doing," he said lucidly. "If I really wanted to shoot the dog, I could have. I was just tryin' to scare it."

I nodded. There were times when I too felt the need to put fear into humans and other animals.[42]

XXVII—"The Filthy Few"

"The Filthy Few is a status earned when an Oakland chapter member kills someone for the good of the club in front of a member of the Filthy Few . . ."—A confidential report by the Organized Crime Branch of the California Department of Justice in 1973.

"The Filthy Few's maybe 10 or 11 guys in the Oakland club who do all the heavy stuff. It's bullshit about them having to kill in front of other members. Things more or less worked like this: If someone was doing business and burned the club, the president tells you to get the people necessary to do it. You call two other guys and arrange a meeting with no one else to be there. The three of you go out and kill him. If you don't get caught in the act, you'll never get caught." — A local investigator.

Although authorities generally agree the Filthy Few is a trusted inner circle of club members, there is some dis-

agreement about the intraclub group's membership require-
ments and about the sorts of killings done in the club's
name. Still, the uncertainty is understandable since the
Filthy Few's activities are the most closely guarded secrets
in an extremely secretive organization.

In spite of the fact that very few Angels have been successfully prosecuted in homicides, the state's ninety-one-
page report in April, 1973, said that Filthy Few membership
was won by murder and that there were thirteen known
members in the Oakland chapter. The figure was based
upon the number of Angels wearing the Few's red and
white patch with a double lightning bolt that resembled the
Nazi SS symbol. However, it should be noted that only one
of the thirteen had been convicted of homicide.

The state report also said it was "suspected" that contract hits were accepted from nonmembers who knew the
club's reputation and sought out Angels for murder for hire.
The price supposedly ranged from $4,000 to $10,000, and
the hit mechanism worked like this, according to the report:

A member first contacted about the hit took the money
to a meeting of the Filthy Few. The name of the intended
victim or victims and their addresses were written on a
piece of paper, then hit assignments were drawn at random.
The money was held by the club until the assassination
was accomplished. Sometimes a time limit was imposed,
other times the killing was at the member's convenience.

However, some local investigators said killings were carried out more informally by close friends within the Filthy
Few. They said that only members directly involved would
be privy to incriminating details. That way any snitch
would incriminate himself and would finger himself for
club retribution. "I don't believe they ever would take an
outside contract," said one officer who worked Angels cases
for a decade. "To protect themselves, they would have to
kill the guy paying them to make the hit."

I knew the Filthy Few as carousers who named themselves at a wild bash in Yosemite National Park after one
Bass Lake run. I never knew the Few as anything more than
a gung-ho intrafraternal group. Maybe they got heavier after
I resigned in 1969, but, knowing each of the thirteen members and remaining close to the club, I doubt seriously that
each one had killed though some seemed capable of it.

Socially, the Filthy Few was no different than other inner
club groups such as the Federales, the Dirty 30 and the
Wrecking Crew. There was good-natured competition
among the groups, and each would try to have the best at-
tendance at club functions. In fact, you'd hear guys shouting when they arrived at a party, "The 30's are here," or
"The Federales are here."

The Wrecking Crew, said by some investigators to be a
demolition team, was formed by guys who ripped apart a
man's house and threw all his belongings in a swimming
pool for some now forgotten offense. State investigators
said the Crew became the club's explosives division, peddling explosives as well as deploying them to handle contract jobs and internal club business. The state listed five
Oakland members in 1973.

The Federales mainly were members of Mexican-American descent and were said by state investigators to be dealing in explosives, prostitution and narcotics with Latino
crime groups, particularly in the San Jose area.

Members frequently changed groups or belonged to more
than one group at a time. Some guys formed their own
groups, based on social and business ties.

Even after my retirement, the club was on the market for
guns for trading and guns for their personal use, and I supplied some in return for speed from Tiny and Durt and coke
from Sonny. I also sat on stolen or otherwise illegal weapons for the club, including a Maxim silencer belonging to

Sonny. Not only was the president interested in powerful automatic weapons for police trades, but he also sought out untraceable pistols of small caliber, mainly compact and easily silenced .22 and .32 automatics, the kinds of guns commonly used in professional killings.

Although it's debatable whether the club offered extermination services, I was twice approached by people seeking hired killers.

In late 1968, the Berkeley dealers Juan and Mark wanted me to snuff an upstart competitor in exchange for a thirty-eight-foot ketch docked in Sausalito. They said a young dealer named Jose robbed them of $25,000. He supposedly set up the heist by having his old lady shack up with Juan and Mark. Supposedly when the dealers came home with the money, Jose and his old lady were waiting with guns.

I was more amused by the yarn than interested in a second boat, so I turned down the offer. However, Jose heard the club was on his case, so he split anyway.

The second time I was approached by one of my dealers, a speed freak named Dave, who said his ex-old lady was threatening to blackmail him into renewing the relationship. "I wanna get rid of her," he said. "Can you take care of it, George? How much will it cost?"

"How much can you spend?"

After hemming and hawing, he said, "About $2,500."

"I'll see what I can do," I said, as a favor to him.

I found Sonny home in bed, watching television and horning cocaine. When I outlined Dave's proposition, he laughed uproariously. "Is he crazy? Tell him it'll cost more money. At least $5,000." He shrugged it off and changed the channel.

Dave said he'd think about it, but never made another offer.

XXVIII—The Screw Turns

While I kept a low profile, the club frequently hit the headlines. The publicity made me uneasy because my continuing association with the club made me vulnerable to police action. I wanted be forgotten, just as I wanted the bodies to be forgotten. Yet each story implied that the club and its associates entered the 1970s as more than white society's rebels and ruffians.

The pattern was clear from what we read in the San Francisco *Chronicle* :

—April 11, 1970—Sonny was arrested on drug charges when Donald Howarth, thirty-six, a movie industry property master and by his own description "a former Mr. America from Studio City," was caught walking toward Barger's house with $350,000 worth of heroin and cocaine in a suitcase.

—Mid-June, 1970—Sonny temporarily stepped down to fight the charges, not knowing that they later would be dropped because Howarth was arrested before he could get the narcotics inside. However, Howarth would be sentenced to five years to life in prison.

—June 25, 1970—The home of figurehead president Johnny Angel was raided by narcotics squadders. When Johnny answered the door, he stuck a 9 mm. automatic in one cop's gut until a search warrant was produced. Small quantities of narcotics and a small arsenal led to his booking. Charges later would be dismissed, but he would be convicted of assaulting a bartender on January 26, 1971.

—July 15, 1970—A multijurisdictional raiding party arrested Winston at home on federal weapons charges. As a federal agent started to scale the backyard fence, a local officer warned, "Don't do that. There's an African lion in there." The fed laughed until his head cleared the top of the fence. Winston was held on $50,000 bail, and Kitty Kitty was released to Sonny's custody. Winston later would be sentenced to two years in prison on a gun possession conviction, which would run concurrently with a five-year term for selling drugs to a federal undercover agent.

—July 29, 1970—Winston's neighbors appeared before the City Council demanding an ordinance against the keeping of dangerous pets.

—December 21, 1971—Law officials testified at the trial of Alan Passaro, the Angel accused of the Altamont slaying, that the club is prone to Mafia-like reprisals against snitches. William Bennett, head of the special intelligence detail for the state attorney general, said, "We consider them to be one of the more violent outlaw groups in the state. . . . Witnesses have refused to testify. They were scared." And an Oakland officer concurred: "They are taking care of people who snitch on them, [with] severe beatings and threats of actually being done away with. . . . One person told me he would rather go to the state penitentiary for twenty years than be involved with the Angels and get caught at it. . . . Informants have related to me that they flatly refuse to do any work involving the Hell's Angels." Despite such testimony, Passaro was found not guilty after pleading self-defense.

—March 21, 1971—Sonny and my old paramour, Mickey, were arrested in an industrial area in a car with three pistols, a teargas grenade, a telephone tapping device, burglar tools, two black masks and twenty-five feet of cord. Intentions unknown, Sonny was booked on charges of possessing weapons and burglary tools. The case later would be dismissed.

—July 13, 1971—Sonny was sentenced to a year in prison for gun possession charges stemming from the 1970 raid on his house, plus three months for bail jumping. "I don't go hunting," he had claimed. "I don't like to kill. That shotgun isn't mine."

—July 19, 1971—Forty-five persons, including twenty-six Angels, were arrested after Orlando Zuluetta, forty-three, a top-ranking lightweight boxing contender in the 1950s, was stabbed to death at a party for a retired Angel at a San Francisco bar.

—December 18, 1971—Fifteen officers raided Sir Gay's home, seizing six automatic rifles, one semiautomatic, six handguns, one hand grenade, three ounces of plastic explosives, a mortar shell, a flare gun and a rocket launcher, plus $500 in drugs, $17,000 in cash and a couple of tons of motorcycle parts. After pleading guilty to possession of cocaine and dangerous drugs, he would be sentenced to two to ten years in prison.

—January 22, 1972—Sonny and four members were booked for investigation of kidnaping after some Angels were found badly beaten in the trunk of a car stopped in a high-speed chase through Redwood Regional park. Durt and Bert were flushed out of some nearby bushes, and the trunk yielded Dan Jarman, twenty-seven, with cuts and bruises, and William D. Hood, twenty-nine, alias "Willie the Hood," and Russell Huddleston—with his throat slit but still breathing. Both Hood and Huddleston were bound and gagged, their fate fairly obvious. The occupants of a second car tossed out four handguns and a shotgun, along with an ammunition pouch and a wide leather belt with a silver buckle that read "Sonny Barger Jr., 1957-67, president Oakland Hell's Angels." Sonny Russell Beyea and Gary Popkin, twenty-seven, were apprehended. Bail ranged from $200,000 for Sonny down to $125,000 for Bert. The charges included attempted murder, kidnaping and assault with a deadly weapon. But all five would wind up pleading guilty to a lesser charge of unlawful imprisonment.

The case dragged me even deeper into club affairs. Sonny asked me to put up the ranch as bail bond collateral. I had trusted him enough to use the ranch to bail him out on some earlier charges, including bail jumping, but the car trunk caper brought four other members into the picture. I agreed only after Sonny guaranteed no one would jump bail and jeopardize the property.

After a Ukiah realtor appraised the ranch at $160,000, Gary Popkin, Sir Gay and I went to the office of Sonny's bondsman, John Ballastrase.[43] I became leery of the arrangement when I heard that Sonny's own sister, Shirley, wouldn't put up her home as collateral. I finalized the deal only after Tiny brought the bondsman's brother, Tony, to the house to reassure me that the property wouldn't be lost.

There was a hint of a threat. After the bondsman was gone, Tiny told Helen, smilingly, "Your weakness is the kids. I could always get to you through the kids."

"Touch my kids and I'll blow you away," she flared.

Once bail was made, disillusionment set in. I had traded my family's dream for a wrinkled $160,000 piece of paper. If any of the five defendants skipped town, I might as well have lit a cigar with that paper.

My biggest concern was Beyea, convicted in 1971 of manslaughter charges after several guys were killed in a motorcycle gang fight at a Cleveland, Ohio, car show. Beyea—along with "Mouldy Marvin" Gilbert—recently had been charged with fatally stomping a twenty-four-year-old longshoreman who made the mistake of using the thumb-clasping "nigger's handshake" when he came to inspect a motorcycle. Russell already had missed one court appearance.

Matters got worse on May 28, 1972, just three days after Sonny and two other guys asked the state Supreme Court to quash the kidnaping charges because of "irreparable damage to their personal reputations." Sonny, "Whitey" Smith, Gary Popkin, Sir Gay and his wife Anita were arrested in four murders linked to interstate dope trafficking and a quest for $90,000 in cocaine. During the busts, twenty-five guns were nabbed, nine at Sonny's home, along with film negatives of bogus driver's licenses, an unidentified human skull and thirty-one photos of exotic weapons including one of the alleged murder weapon, a silenced .32-caliber automatic like those used by Allied spies during World War II. (Charges against Anita Walton later would be dropped, but the others would be tried and acquitted on charges of murdering reputed Texas drug dealer Servio W. Agero—the only murder to come to trial.)

Amid all this, I met urgently with Durt and Bert to try to find out whether Russell was planning to hit the road. "If he's gonna jump bail, I got things I gotta dig up," I said.

With a quick shift of his eyes, Durt hushed me. Bert apparently was in the dark about the bodies, and it would be better to keep him there.

"Yeah," I added to cover my slipup. "I gotta dig up them damn marijuana fields at the ranch."

Unable to get any assurances from them, I went to Tiny, the highest-ranking member not in jail or on the lam.

Tiny—a smart, forceful heavy who came close to the Angels ideal—was handling business while Sonny stared at the bars. He gave me his word that Russell wouldn't skip out. "But, man, we still gotta do somethin'," I pressed him. "I gotta get them bodies outa there. They're drivin' me nuts." "All right, I'll go with ya," Tiny offered. "Just tell me what to do."

I backed off when I did some serious thinking about digging up three bodies and finding another place to dispose of them safely.

A chain reaction was touched off by Tiny's guarantee that no one would jump bail. As a condition for Russell's surrender, Tiny was supposed to eliminate the key prosecution witnesses. One vanished; a second fled to Washington state. And, authorities said, a third, supposedly a doper, was held captive by the club and supplied with all the drugs he wanted. All were threatened with death if they testified, authorities said.

After Tiny told Russell the coast was clear, he turned himself in May 22. However, Tiny had miscalculated. Prosecutors used preliminary hearing testimony by one witness, and a second witness was returned from Washington under armed guard.

The testimony showed, according to a formal statement by District Attorney D. Lowell Jensen, that:

On Feb. 24, 1972, Bradley Parkhurst, the victim, went to the residence of Connie P. with a friend of his, Clyde B. . . . They entered the basement which was occupied by Connie P. and defendant Marvin Gilbert, who was working on a motorcycle. Words were exchanged between Gilbert and Parkhurst, and when Parkhurst offered to shake hands, Gilbert claimed that was a nigger's handshake. . . . A fight commenced and it is unclear who struck the first blow. Nevertheless, Gilbert, who outweighed Parkhurst by almost 40 pounds, was knocked to the ground and Connie P. ran upstairs to get assistance for Gilbert.

It took approximately one minute for Russell Beyea, Frank H. and Dennis S. to reach the basement. . . . It appeared that Parkhurst was still winning and was either on top of Gilbert, or Gilbert was staggering in the corner. Beyea grabbed Clyde B. and shoved him with his face to the wall and told him to stay there. Beyea then grabbed Parkhurst and delivered two vicious blows to the victim's face. Beyea weighed 265 pounds, some 98 pounds more than Parkhurst. Gilbert then struck Parkhurst in the chest, knocking him to the ground, and the defendants proceeded to beat and kick Parkhurst for approximately 10 to 15 minutes, notwithstanding the victim's repeated pleas for them to stop. . . .

When Beyea and Gilbert left, the victim was laying on the floor covered in his own blood, moaning, choking and coughing. . . . The victim was a mass of cuts, abrasions and lacerations, and his tooth which had been knocked from his mouth was removed from his stomach. . . .

It is believed that Russell Beyea is the heavyweight in the Hell's Angels and for that reason, the organization pressured Marvin Gilbert to take the stand during the trial to exculpate [him]. . . . Against the advice of his lawyer, and because his life and the life of his girlfriend were threatened, Gilbert did in fact agree to take the stand. However, during a recess at which Gilbert, Beyea and their two attorneys caucused, it was agreed that tactically Beyea stood a better chance for acquittal if Gilbert was not subject to an extensive and thorough cross-examination. At the time the jury indicated they had reached a verdict, Gilbert was again told that he was to jump to his feet and claim that he did the killing alone so as to free Beyea. However, Gilbert did not do this and both men were convicted [of second-degree murder August 17, 1972].

After the jury's verdict and in the presence of a deputy sheriff, a Hell's Angel approached Gilbert and told him there was nowhere he could hide and in effect that he was a dead man. Within a week or two after conviction, and presumably due to threats on his life, Marvin Gilbert wrote a statement which attempted to exculpate Beyea and which was to provide grounds for a motion for a new trial. Said motion was denied. . . .

The day of the conviction Tiny became extremely paranoid. Being the highest-ranking member out of jail, he figured he was next in line for a bust. And, more importantly, his failure was indirectly responsible for putting brothers in the joint. The possibility of discipline loomed. "Who is it that's got the contract on me?" he asked another member, hoping to get it out in the open. "Is it you? Is it . . . Who?"

That same day Tiny gave his wife power of attorney and disappeared, leaving behind all belongings, including his motorcycle and custom Corvette with a HAMCO-1 license plate that stood for Hell's Angels Motorcycle Club Oakland. While several members were making claims on his property, his wife, Benita, filed a police missing persons report September 22. She said she feared he "met with foul play" because he was behaving strangely and disappeared "under mysterious circumstances."

In the ensuing months police received intelligence reports that Tiny went to a watery grave. One, purportedly overheard when Sonny and some other guys were in jail, said Tiny was taken aboard a cabin cruiser and shot repeatedly with a 9 mm. pistol. There was another that he came to rest on the bottom of a High Sierra lake. But later there were supposed sightings in Mexico and Southern California and other Western states.

My view was that Tiny split before being crushed between the club and the cops. It was just like him to leave with nothing but a shirt on his back, because that's the way he arrived from back East. He didn't care much about cars and bikes and houses. He'd be happy with just a pocket full of dope and money.

Tiny was the complete Hell's Angel—gunsel, dealer, high roller, officer. He worked for Sonny and did his own thing too. When I was out of the club the first time, he came into power. He was big, 260 to 280 pounds. He could be just as sadistic as anybody. He was smart enough. He liked to get loaded, and he was well liked. What else do you need when you've got all that going for you?

XXIX—Winter's Coming

In the fall of 1972, while the club was hounded by legal problems, my family set a January, 1973, target date for moving to the ranch. I planned to get a construction job in nearby Santa Rosa. Helen wanted to plant a vegetable garden, raise some chickens and get a milk cow. Bobby looked forward to zipping over the hills on his off-road motorcycle. And Donna's imagination put her astride a horse, galloping the green fields. That was our dream.

But the storm of our life had been gathering. Around June, 1971, Richmond member "Whispering Bill" Pifer heard from friends that the Oakland chapter wanted to eliminate him as a murder and burial witness. To check it out, he called Angelo Barberi and said he was planning to transfer to the Oakland chapter.[44]

"Don't do it," the veteran member told Pifer. "You're crazy if you do it."

"Whatta ya mean?"

"Take my word for it. Don't do it."

A short time later, Pifer transferred to Oakland anyway, mainly so he could keep close tabs on those who might try to kill him. The chapter accepted him, apparently so they could watch him closely and pick their time. On a number of occasions when Pifer got loaded with Sonny and Sir Gay, he was asked if he ever talked to anyone about the bodies at the ranch. And Sonny intimated that Pifer had a loose tongue.

On the Labor Day weekend of 1971, Pifer, his son and fifteen members were on a desert run to Southern California. During a stop near Banning in Riverside County, Pifer noticed that some members seemed to be unobtrusively encircling him.

Repeatedly cocking and uncocking his pistol, Sonny talked remotely about Angels and dying. Matters were getting too intense, so Whispering Bill left his bike behind and walked away. "Okay, let him go," he heard an Angel say. "There's a truck waiting for him."

At the edge of the road, Pifer told his son to split on his own bike. "Don't ask any questions and don't come back," he said, then started hitchhiking. He was picked up by two young men in a 1950 Chevrolet, but became suspicious when the driver blinked his lights at a truck following them near Banning. Pulling a gun, Pifer ordered him to keep his hands on the wheel and turn into a drive-in restaurant up ahead.

Once the car stopped, Pifer jumped out and, when one of the men appeared to go for a gun, he fired a few shots to guard his retreat. Escaping into a crowd, he took a cab to a bus depot and returned to the Bay Area.

Finally, Pifer went to the Antioch Police Department in 1972, hoping to tell his story and get protection for his family and himself. Two sergeants took the information but didn't seem to believe him. Six to eight weeks passed without a return call from the police, then Pifer bumped into

Pittsburg Police Sergeant Frank Tiscareno, the brother of one of his biker friends. As they talked, Pifer divulged that he had terminal cancer but didn't mention the club.

A week later, he sent his daughter to bring Tiscareno to his house. As they sipped coffee, Pifer dropped bits of information about the club. Then he told the whole story.

Tiscareno took action. After a preliminary investigation by local and state authorities, Pifer was driven to the Ukiah area and identified our ranch as the burial ground. A search warrant referring to Pifer by the code name SFT-1 was issued. And October 30, 1972, the day Sonny and three other Angels were scheduled for trial on murder charges, the warrant was served.

XXX—The Family in Captivity

UKIAH—The Sheriff's Department here reported finding three bodies in what was called a Hell's Angels burying ground and the gruesome search will continue today. The bodies of two men and a woman were dug up on a 153-acre ranch six miles southwest of here by a trenching machine which probed well holes. The owners of the ranch, George Wethern, 33, a 260-pound lather, and his wife, Helen, 29, were arrested on narcotics charges and held in the county jail on $100,000 bail each . . ."—The San Francisco *Chronicle,* November 1, 1972.

UKIAH—George Wethern, the renegade Hell's Angel, nearly blinded himself Tuesday night by jabbing pointed pencils in his eyes, Sheriff Reno Bartolomie reported yesterday. He said Wethern 'just went off his rocker . . . Wethern told me he was unnerved and under such pressure that he didn't know what he was doing . . . He said he dearly loved his wife and had no intention of harming her . . .'"—The San Francisco *Chronicle,* November 10, 1972.

* * *

The day after my murder-suicide try, I was feeling help-less and lonely. My eye injuries left me in almost total darkness. I was confused. I wasn't even sure Helen was alive until she and my sister were led to my cell.

As they approached, I tilted my head far back and peeked under one swollen eyelid to get a fuzzy half-view. My hands and feet were manacled, no slack in the chains. My eyes were puffed twice normal size, ringed in black and dotted by burn marks, with a pencil hole through one eyelid. When I hobbled close to the bars, my sister—though she dealt with mangled accident victims as a nurse—was jolted visibly, and Helen fainted. Although my wife was carried back to her cell, the momentary meeting at least allayed her fears that I was dead, and my fears that I had seriously injured her.

The meeting filled me with hope. I wanted desperately to survive, so I explored my confinement, learning to maneuver without tripping or bumping the furnishings. My only company was the sound of my chains until two friendly trusties came. They administered my eyedrops and helped me work my pants past the chains so I could go to the bathroom. I felt like an infant, yet their jokes eased my humiliation.

Whenever alone, I was overcome by claustrophobia. The chains, bars and blackness crushed me. But it was itches that finally made me fight my chains. One day to get at an itchy eye, I successfully manipulated my trussing a fraction of an inch at a time like Houdini. Then I summoned the sheriff to show him I could reach my eyes—yet hadn't gouged them out. "Reno, these chains ain't doin' me no good," I pleaded. "I want out of 'em. Can ya do something?"

"We'll see," he said noncommittally, but the irons were gradually removed.

In the absence of personal contact, Helen and I discovered what the chaplain called "the miracle of paper." We wrote virtually nonstop, pausing only to eat, exercise, sleep, receive visitors and testify. We generally wrote five to ten letters a day—with more than 500 eventually delivered by a priest, trusties, deputies, matrons and attorneys. Her first letter, dated November 10, was read to me because I couldn't see:

"Honey, I forgot to tell you something. When they turn out the lights after you say your rosary, think about me, 'cause I'll be thinking about you hot and heavy. . . . But if you get tired before then, just think about me as you're falling asleep. Love ya."

My response was dictated to a trusty:

"Every time I lay down to go to sleep I think about you. I can hear you whispering in my ear. Just being able to see you through the bars is okay for now, but we'll be together again real soon. I hope we can be together on the outside soon with the kids. . . . Love, George."

"Babe," I wrote November 11. "I hope they let us back together so that we can make whoopee and so I can plan on getting us out. You look beautiful even through one blurry eye. . . . I hope they can take my chains off today or soon because it's a pain in the butt, and my buddy Jim is getting tired of wiping my ass. Ha. Ha. Love, George."

"Good morning," she wrote November 12. "Well, it's been two weeks—wow, it seems like two years. . . . It's raining again. Can you see outside? How are your eyes feeling? Are you still in a lot of pain? . . . I had a hard time convincing them to let me have a pencil. LaVonne (the matron) told me if I was going to try to hurt my eyes to use the eraser end (ha ha)."

I messaged on the 15th: "Sugarchest, So how's things with you, you delectable dish you? Sure hope they let me visit with you again tonight. . . . Drop me a line and rap with me. . . . Love, Cyclops."

On November 17, she told me, "Dear George, when I

heard you whistle, I couldn't believe my ears. I had to answer it. I thought you were coming in here, and when you
didn't, I was so disappointed. The matron Joyce said, 'So
close yet so far away.' How I hated to agree with her. . . ."

On Saturday night, November 18, I reported triumphantly, "I got that damn fly in my cell finally—with two swings
of a sandal. I had a big wanted poster of the fly that this old
wino name of Doc Holiday drew for me. I had it hanging
with a reward of three days' worth of cigarettes. Now I got
to collect my own reward. . . .

"P.S.—Something keeps happening with my bad eye, so
maybe. . . . I think my eye is coming back. Thank God."

"You're not going to believe this," she scrawled back,
"but my eye has been twitching and I've been gently rubbing it—and while I do it, I think of you and say to myself,
'Please let his eye go back. Please.' I've been doing it about
five days. . . ."

I wrote November 20, "Days like today are going to be re-
membered for the rest of our lives. . . . It was so good to
touch you and hold your hand. I sure miss being able to
hold you when I want to. It sure would be nice to hold you
in my arms without bars between us. The next time you see
Father Roger or anybody, have them ask old Reno [the
sheriff] for permission to get together, even for an hour. I
better send this over before I collapse from the
hornies. . . ."

She responded, "I'll send in another request to the sheriff
for permission to share a cell for our anniversary. I think
he'll understand. He seems like a real good family man. The
last time I seen him, he was wearing a pink tie that his
nine-year-old daughter gave him. She was afraid that he
wouldn't wear it, so he was wearing it for her. I told him,
'You're a very good father.' That was a very hot pink."

I wrote later that day: "Next to you and the kids, I think
my greatest love is beautiful music, and just about all music is beautiful in one way or another. After thirteen years

of marriage, I think I've finally learned to see the best in music and people. I love everybody, but I've also learned you can't help everybody.

"In fact, there's a guy here that's so confused he's calling everybody killers and wants to kill. I offered him rosary beads, and he said, 'No thanks.' When I said I was only trying to help, he said he wanted to stick a shank in me. I said I was sorry, then I said a prayer for him. Poor guy, I know he's going through hell. I been there."

I messaged the next day: "There was a shrink here from Contra Costa County to talk to me about testifying there. Everything went beautiful. The shrink was outa sight. I think he answered more of my questions than I did his. We got into Greek mythology because of my eyes. He thought I got the idea from King Oedipus because he put his eyes out with two brooches. But I set the shrink straight and told him why I thought I had to die. . . .

"But enough of that. . . . I just thank God for you, you little vixen you. You got more class and gear than a semi truck. I'm proud of you. You're beautiful, you're sexy, logical, soft, well mannered, intelligent, and most important, you're mine. Now the only question is how I get to you. Got any hack saw blades? Maybe a small cutting torch? Even a good fingernail file. . . ."

Thanksgiving Day she wrote, "Well, here's the All-American Turkey Day. Everything looks crisp outside. The sunrise started out with oranges and pinks and started fading into greys and blues and purples. . . ."

And I replied, "I've been thinking about a lot of things in the past, and I want to say I'm sorry for ever hurting you physically and mentally. I'm sure as hell going to make it up to you and the kids. Maybe we can help other people from getting involved in drugs, so they won't have to go through hells too. I know quite a bit about drugs through my own stupidity, but I think I can turn it around to help other people. If some of the damn drugs can be stopped through my efforts, maybe some of the killings will stop. If what I'm going to tell saves one life, it'll be worth it. . . . Well, enough maybes. I'm going to listen to the football game and wait for the turkey."

The following day, a letter from the children:

"Dear Mom and Dad, How are you? We hope you are fine. We are doing fine and we're having fun staying with a lady whose husband is a deputy sheriff. We love you very, very much and we hope God will let Daddy's eyes be better, and we all will get together soon. . . ."

And Helen wrote, "Huey, I just got the letter from the kids. You told me not to worry about them, and you were right. . . .

"Did you hear the music outside? Santa Claus is here. A pickup truck was pulling a platform with horn players, and Santa on his sled. . . . It was nothing fancy, but it was real. When a bunch of kids ran up to Santa, I started crying, feeling sorry for myself. . . ."

On November 27, after getting a haircut, I was led from the jail by about a dozen shotgun-toting deputies, then flown by small plane to Contra Costa County. I was to testify at preliminary hearings for four Angels, including Z., in the slayings of "Big Tom" and Charlie. Waiting to be called to court, I stretched out on a bunk then looked up. There on the wall was a death's head drawing with the name of Bill Moran, a Richmond member accused in the murders. It irritated me so I erased it. Shouts of "snitch" filtered down from another cellblock. In that hostile place, I wanted to write my wife, but jailers refused me a pencil. Improvising with a red ink of spittle and match heads, I wrote painstakingly with a matchstick:

"Thank God for matches. Sugar, I love you and the kids. I can't wait until we're together outside of jail, like it is supposed to be. . . . Love, George the Matchhead."

The next day, I was in the communal shower when

another inmate whispered, "By all rights, I should try to kill you right now."

I had expected my life to be threatened, if not taken, in any jail, so I briefly explained my predicament, how I was trapped between the cops and the club, then said casually, "Do what turns ya on, man."

"Hey man, I didn't know that's what was happenin'," the guy said. He showed some sympathy, then later smuggled me a pencil to write my letters.

"Dear Honey," I scrawled when the guards weren't looking. "I was supposed to go to court today, but I got there and found the D.A. had laryngitis. I hope and pray he gets better so I can go to court and get back to you. . . ."

The D.A. still was sick the next day, so I was driven back to Ukiah for the weekend. On Monday, December 4, I wrote from the courthouse after testifying:[45]

"Hi, babe. It's easy telling the truth. We're on our way. I feel good. I was a little bit nervous in the beginning, but I learned to be a little patient and played their lawyer's damn little game. I knew I was going to tell the truth, and what else is there to it? You just have to take your time in answering, just make sure you don't make a mistake. My part of the preliminary only lasted two hours. For lunch, I made Rich [attorney Richard Petersen] get me two cheeseburgers, fries and a small Coke. I bet I'm one of the first guys who's ever had a cheeseburger in the back of a police car with handcuffs on. . . .

"In court, I found out something for you. You're the only one for me. Your enemy Judy was there, the only friendly face in the audience. I found out that first loves are neat, but last loves (you) are always. I love you with my whole body and soul. . . ."

After a brief domestic crisis over Judy's appearance, Helen wrote December 7:

"George, Remember the Mexican restaurant La Cueva on Foothill? Ronnie the matron said she knew the owners and that the Angels wrecked the place. My face turned red and I couldn't help but smile. She said, 'You guys weren't there, were you?' I told her what I thought had happened. It blew my mind. It's a small world. . . . "

"Hi, Sugar Plum," I wrote December 9. "I was just talking to a couple of guys and they mentioned the kids. Why don't you write them a note telling them to write? Or I'll order them to write. The little poop butts. We're softies, but heck, mom, we got to lay on them once in a while. Love, G. . . .

"P.S.—When my sister comes, ask her if she would buy the kids Xmas presents with the money she gets from selling the car."

"I'm mad," I wrote the next day. "Rich [the lawyer] told me about somebody saying I was a gunsel for Sonny. And the other night, Deputy Tuso asked me about Z.'s old boat and said that supposedly 'Tiny went for his last boat ride.' . . . It seems like somebody is trying to set me up for a murder rap. But, hell, I didn't kill nobody. . . ."

"To hell with them people," she agreed. "You didn't kill nobody. If they try to pin anything on you, it would be a lie and we got two good lawyers who would fight it."

My message the morning of December 12: "I just seen the eye doctor. My eyesight in my good one is better than his. But the other one, well, it don't look too good. Whether it's permanent or not only time will tell. If it's permanent, I got only one good eye. By losing one eye, I gained faith. I got a hell of a deal. . . . I can see the snow outside. Yipeee. I love you baby. Signed, Eyeball."

She wrote back immediately, "We can't give up hope. Whenever there's the slimmest chance, we'll cling to it. Father Roger just told me the newspaper said, 'The Wethern family should be together for Christmas.'"

A day later, I sent her a poem written by trusty friend Ken:

"The Family. . . . To them new life is living and giving.

They have found themselves. Take all the bad things and put them on the shelf. They have found life from a separate place from much thinking and God's good grace. They have found that all the pills and lids mean nothing compared to the kids. I've talked to George for hours on end and found myself an everlasting friend. When he came here, he was a spaced out cat, but now he's found life and where it's really at. He has changed from days of grief to a solid belief. His wife I've never gotten to know, she must be a wonderful person because George says so. She has a winning smile and a wonderful look, she's number one in anybody's book. The days that we've spent have really been a pleasure and it has been something I'll treasure. I hope to see you in years to come if you can put up with someone so dumb. We'll meet again. But, until then, have confidence and a constant grin. Ken."

"Boy, did my heart just jump," I wrote December 22. "Whitey the trusty said, 'Feds.' I was praying they were here for you and me, but they were here for a Mexican fellow. . . . I seen the sheriff later. He wanted to know the name of the girl buried on the ranch, so he could give her a decent burial. But I didn't know it."

"Merry Christmas," I scrawled on the 25th. "How are you? Them carolers were up here last night. I shook hands with one. They didn't sing all that well, but it was better than nothing. . . .

"It's evening now. This has been one of the most enlightening days of my life. I won't fail you. I promise. I want my wife to trust me like the Good Book says. I realize now the two things I did wrong in my life were shooting Zorro, and trying to kill myself and almost killing you in the process. If I had killed you, I might as well have killed myself every day until the year 2001. . . ."

To cheer me, she replied, "You're fantastic. I love you. Get it on, dummy (ha ha). Ain't we all! Your biggest fan, your wife."

The day after Christmas, I told her, "They may not let me out tonight because there's a guy here that used to be a Daly City prospect. I had met him two or three times. But, don't worry. If he or his partner want to try to kill me, let them. . . ."

"I ain't worried," she wrote back. "You can take care of yourself. Besides, I don't think anybody would try anything. You just got caught in the middle. You just told the truth after somebody finked on you. Nobody could expect you to take the rap for something you didn't do, especially not with your family. . . ."

Nonetheless, I reported the next day, "I almost messed up. I tried to get through the bars after a guy threatening me. They badgered me, saying a couple of things like they seen a picture of me with a knife stuck in it. And one guy told my friend Bob that he seen a picture of me all mangled up on a chopper. . . ."

"Are you all right?" I began my next frantic letter. "I exploded again, mom. This time they went too far. They started talking about you, and I won't ever let a bunch of assholes talk in that filthy, lewd way about my wife. I was scared, then it passed the point of fear and I blew it. At least I wanted to use my bare hands this time. The deputies had to use Mace to stop me."

She replied, "Thank you for sticking up for me, but I don't want you to get all upset over it. Lt. Friend told me you were okay, then they searched my cell because they thought I was hiding tranks and that I might try to do myself in, in a suicide pact. I told them I had the kids to think about. . . ."

On December 29, I wrote: "FLASH. I just heard that they cleared Sonny and those other guys on their murder beef. I took a trank after the shock. I wonder how they beat their case. Well, it still don't affect me. I may just have to testify in more trials. . . ."

She replied: "I was really upset about Sonny too. They

said he got off because he was home in bed asleep with his old lady at the time of the murder. And they said the key witness against him was a liar and had no credibility. On the six o'clock news, they said he was still being held on narcotics charges, and they set a $100,000 bail. Plus he has a federal gun beef and income tax evasion.

"At first, I felt relieved like you did that he didn't get a murder rap. But that feeling went away and, God forgive me, I wished he had been convicted because of how it might affect us. At least there's that man dying of cancer [Pifer] so you're not the only one left to testify."

Then we saw the following wire service story:

OAKLAND(AP)—A jury deliberated 9½ hours over three days, then returned a verdict Friday acquitting four Hell's Angels members of murder and arson in the May 21 killing of reputed Texas narcotics dealer Servio W. Agero.

A yelp of joy came from Sharon Gruhlke, girlfriend of Ralph "Sonny" Barger, Hell's Angels leader, after the court clerk read the verdict in Alameda County Superior Court.

Defense attorney James Crew commented "Super!" after the verdict. But his clients made no immediate comment after they were cleared. Observers said the aftermath of the two-month trial seemed "lackluster."

Judge William J. Hayes thanked the jury of six men and six women for their dedication, then threatened the panel, which had been sequestered, with contempt of court if they discuss their deliberations with the public or the media.

The jury decided that Barger, 34; Sir Gay Walton, 28; Gary Popkin, 28; and Donald Duane Smith, 28, were innocent of murder. All but Smith were charged with arson, and they were cleared of that.

Agero was discovered shot to death, lying in a bathtub in a burning Oakland house. The prosecution contended Barger was the triggerman and that the other three helped in the killing.

The jury did not believe the story of the state's star witness, Richard Ivaldi, who testified Barger shot the sleeping Agero with a "weird bazooka-like handgun" to get a suitcase with up to $100,000 worth of cocaine.

On the last day of 1972, I wrote: "The place just got crazy again. Them guys in C tank are flooding the place and making noise again. The guards had the water off for a while and are just turning it back on. I had one guy hollering 'rat' at me from over there and making jokes about me, but I just ignore it. It don't do no good hollering back; I stay calm and let the wind blow. . . ."

"Dear Honey," she said January 3. "The waiting isn't so bad because it seems they're trying to find out what's happening in Washington. At least we're seeing how our bureaucratic government works—SLOW. I wish they'd tear up all the red tape and make confetti of it and wish us a Happy New Year."

I wrote later, "I'm locked up tight right now. There was a big bust in Willits and they brought in twelve young kids. I feel like an old man, an old pro among all these big dope dealers (ha). They ain't even dry behind the ears. Now all I got to do is convince them dope isn't where it's at. . . ."

Helen wrote January 5: "Mrs. Jean S. of the Welfare Dept. was just here, because of what Donna said in her latest letters about fainting. Mrs. S. assured me she was okay but weak from the flu. She said our daughter's feeling blue and has been crying. I guess she was disappointed like us about the family not being together for Christmas. I'm writing her a comforting letter. . . ."

I wrote back: "I'm sending a letter to the kids. Read it first, and if you don't like it, tell me. I mentioned a time for our release but left it vague. And if that time doesn't turn out to be right, I'm going to straddle someone's back. If they keep farting around in Washington, I'm going to take my chances on the streets. I ain't going to see my kids get sick over this, and that's it. . . ."

That night I was knocked flat by the flu. As I sprawled on my bunk in a feverish sweat, the undersheriff entered. "Come on, George. Leave everything here. We'll take care of it."

As we approached the women's cell block, he whispered, "Your wife doesn't know we're coming." Then he called loudly, "Hey Helen, you want some company?"

"Company? Yeah. Yeah," she cried bolting upright.

"If we let George visit, do you think you could do some kind of a job on his whiskers?" the officer asked. "Can you clean him up a little?"

XXXI—A Family Reborn

An hour or so before dawn, U.S. Marshal Arthur Van Court arrived with his deputy, Cobb Vaughn. My beard and long hair were in the trash can, and our possessions were stuffed in paper sacks. When we said good-bye to the jail staff, they made sure I had my eye medication, then sent us off like family members, wishing us good luck.

Weakened by the short walk to a waiting Lincoln Continental, I collapsed on Helen's lap in the back seat. The marshals looked like affluent deer hunters in sheepskin and wool, with heavy weapons in blankets on the front seat. Van Court was friendly yet businesslike. He alternately chatted with us and kept up radio communications with escort cars from the Mendocino County Sheriff's office.

I was incapacitated, but the marshals were wary anyway. Vaughn sat sideways, scanning the road and side streets for trouble, keeping one eye on me.

When my fever seemed to rise, Van Court radioed ahead to a doctor who gave them pointers on treating a viral infection. At the county line, the marshal waved off the sheriff's escort, made some evasive moves to make sure we weren't being followed, then picked up a new escort of two Marshals Service cars, each with two deputies fully armed. At Van Court's order, one car pulled ahead and the other dropped behind.

During a day-long drive, I rippled with chills and sweated while Helen carried the conversation. The marshal told us the children would join us at a "safe place" before relocation in a permanent home. And he helped us select new first and surnames, comfortable ones that would help us avert slipups that could lead to discovery. From that moment forward, our true identities were revealed to deputy marshals solely on a need-to-know basis.

That night I was so nauseated and tired that I turned down a steak dinner at a roadside restaurant. Then, with a new sheriff's office escort, the cars threaded a mountainous one-lane road, the headlights catching the contours of snowbanks and timber against the starry sky. The tires jounced over a poorly maintained road, past some cheery cabin lights, to a secluded house in a pine grove.

Too ill or tired to appreciate our surroundings, Helen and I dragged into our bedroom. At least three deputies would be guarding us around the clock. "Just think of us as a few extra husbands," joked one deputy. "We'll be just one big happy family here." Our children were in a foster home and would join us later, he said.

A few marshals were posted in and around the house, with several more in reserve nearby. They worked twelve-hour shifts, keeping rifles, shotguns and handguns ready. To supplement sentry dogs, a mixed bag of anti-intrusion devices was planted. There was an invisible electronic eye security beam around the house. Seismic alarms detected approaching footsteps, and standard burglar alarms prevented break-ins at doors and windows. The equipment was so

sensitive that raccoons and deer tripped it, sending marshals to the windows with darkness-penetrating "Star
Light" scopes to see whether the intruder was human. Our
mail and Christmas gifts from relatives and friends were
forwarded to us but always inspected to guard against
booby traps.

The marshals couldn't afford to take chances with the
lives of any sensitive witness, but Van Court—security
chief for Barry Goldwater's 1964 presidential campaign and
previously a twenty-year veteran of the Los Angeles Police
Department—said protecting us was one of his most poten-
tially dangerous tasks. The threat of retaliation was real.

There was no way to be absolutely certain that a death
contract was out, since such agreements seldom are written
or advertised. However, after our arrest, there were law enforcement intelligence reports of a "hit meeting" during
which an assassin was designated, and known Angels later
were sighted snooping around the Ukiah area. Besides, killings have been motivated by far less than my offense—
being the first person to openly break the club's code of silence.

"I would safely assume there's a contract put out on the
Wetherns, just based on the Angels' reputation," Jack Nehr,
special agent with the state Department of Justice, once
said. "Anyone who turns and goes toward law enforcement
automatically is in disfavor of the club. Here was a guy who
was entrusted with responsibility and information, and he
turned against the club."

It also would be safe to assume that my collaboration on
a book that exposes the club's criminal activities and internal structure wouldn't sit too well with the club. As one
knowledgeable Oakland officer said, "If the Angels found
out that a guy sat down with you and told you the inner
workings of the club, his life wouldn't be worth a plugged
nickel." And another longtime investigator thought it un-

wise to be quoted directly. "You know, there are still lots of nutty members out there, and there's no telling what they'll do," he explained. "I don't want to go out some morning for the newspaper and not come back."

During the next month, Helen and I normalized our relationship to an extent and prepared for a fresh start. We set up a temporary household and established a good rapport with our protectors by playing cards, watching television and chatting about mundane stuff such as sports, pets and politics. With our bodyguards in tow, we even went grocery shopping with money provided by the government. (Our monthly subsistence payments eventually reached $750.) [46]

In consultation with the marshals, we narrowed down prospective occupations, taking into account my skills and education. Meanwhile, other marshals looked for a place where we could realize our dream of small-town living. Each likely site was checked for outlaw types and evidence of organized crime, although not many gangs roamed that region with the exception of the Omaha Hell's Angels.

Then I underwent plastic surgery to render me unrecognizable to former associates. I crash-dieted and dropped my biker vernacular. These changes, along with adjustments in grooming habits, transformed me into a nondescript man in his thirties. Helen, a pert and youthful thirty, required only minor changes in hairstyling, makeup and mannerisms.

Later, the children joined us in a belated, emotional Christmas celebration with snowman-making, a feast and presents. The most important gift was togetherness. We laughed together over our new names and identities, and rehearsed new life stories. And we looked to the future, anxious to again be a family, under one name, one past and one roof.

The marshals assembled a "paper past" for us—new birth

certificates, baptismal certificates, school records, Social Security cards, driver's licenses and other identification. Then they took us to a town and showed us a house where the neighbors and the neighborhood had been screened.

"We'll take it," I said. The land unfolded freely in all directions, and there were real people in those unfamiliar rows of tidy homes and compact stores. A few churches, the Grange Hall and the high school stood out against the icy blue sky. It could have been any one of thousands of communities across the country, distinguishable to the passing motorist only by its name.

Before we moved in, all our belongings that bore even a hint of our past were destroyed, sold, altered or carted to the dumps. We were warned not only against taking drugs and associating with criminals but also not to send the children to parochial schools, because that might help would-be assassins narrow their search. We were given telephone numbers to call at the first sign of anyone suspicious and were assured that help would arrive quickly. Calling former friends and associates was prohibited, and calls to relatives were restricted to special federal lines that make tracing impossible. Any mail was routed through a number of federal facilities to protect our location and our identities.

Once we were settled in our modestly conventional home, we were apprehensive about the masquerade ahead. Overnight our task shifted from concealment to assimilation. Almost immediately a neighbor invited us over to play cards. Walking toward their door, we wondered whether we could pull it off. "Honey, you just gotta play it by ear," I told Helen. It was a real heavy experience just playing canasta. We survived by acting like wallflowers, thinking that they wouldn't invite us again if we didn't talk much.

We gradually loosened up around other people, although we were paranoid about not having a twenty-four-hour guard anymore. We wondered if the club could find us by some chance and even considered whether to place the children someplace safer. But we decided we were a family and there was no point in going on without the kids.

Like any uprooted family, we had to decide where to shop and work, what sort of friends to find and how to entertain ourselves. We looked for jobs and we built up credit, although it was difficult with a limited past and no credit history.

We missed our old friends a great deal, but we made new ones, cautiously. They were people whom we could trust with our lives, but we never tested that trust by confiding anything about our true past. That was a horrible temptation and it kept us from really getting close to anybody. I remember Helen told me once, "It's tough not being able to tell friends or co-workers the specifics about your past experiences. Ya know, there's only four people in our world now. That's us."

Family outings became a regular thing. We talked openly about problems and plans, picking up where the good times ended at the ranch. We operated as a team, with Helen and I working and the kids going to school. And Helen, whose inner strength and loyalty surfaced again and again in jail, became a liberated woman in her own way. For a change, she really stood up to me—and got away with it.

Of course, all of us had a residue of fear that we'd be located by the club or found out by our friends. On the streets, I'd sometimes see a suspicious person and get a flash of recollection. I'd turn around and go the other way, then check out the person from afar. I'd have plenty of nightmares in which I was shot, and Helen was haunted by news stories or movies in which people were blown up starting their car.

Blown cover was a more immediate family concern. Keeping life stories straight became a serious game, and the children played as adeptly as Helen and I. More than once, they covered for us or corrected us when details from our past inadvertently slipped out.

Because he was a few years younger, Bobby stayed closer to home than Donna, who was entering her mid-teens. Helen and I hosted a party for her, and we chaperoned her first high school dance. I was doing my best to become a decent husband and father.

Brawling and intimidation were erased from my behavior. And I even checked my temper once when one of Helen's co-workers made a pass at her. There was a time when that guy would have been bounced into a hospital, but I was working on my self-control, learning to function the way other people function. I still need to make myself meeker, but it's difficult when guns have been part of your repertoire for so many years. When I first returned to society, I was worried about not having a gun, but now I don't like guns. They make me nervous.

And we also have stayed clear of all narcotics, believing that one drug experience could drag us back into daily use. Of course, we occasionally run into marijuana in social settings, but we always turn it down and do our best to avoid such situations. One of the big frustrations is not being able to tell people, particularly young people, just how destructive drugs can be, to tell them about our jarring "acid flashbacks."

Within a year of our lifestyle change, we were re-established and in no need of government financial assistance. Through my own initiative, I was making better than average money in a new career with independence. Helen was working hard, and the children were getting good grades. We all took considerable pride in having carved a secure place in a strange community. We were living a satisfying present and saving for the future—dreaming again of 150 acres in the country.

271

EPILOGUE

"This is the beginning of the end of the Hell's Angels. . . ."—Mendocino County District Attorney Duncan James, in 1972.[47]

"We're getting bigger and better. . . ."—Ralph "Sonny" Barger, in 1977 from Folsom Prison.[48]

The year 1972 could well have heralded the decline of the Hell's Angels. In the quarter-century since some excitement-hungry ex-World War II fliers formed the club in Fontana, California, the Angels survived periods of relative obscurity, public indignation, countless law enforcement investigations, prosecutions, bad press and some outright harassment. But in 1972, an unprecedented barrage of criminal cases battered key leaders into prison cells.

In Oakland alone, Barger was sentenced to ten years to life in state prison after pleading guilty to four felony drug

272

counts, federal income tax evasion and gun charges. Sir Gay, Barger's second in command in the early 1970s, received a two-to-ten-year term in February, 1973, for cocaine possession for sale and dangerous drug possession, to run concurrently with a six-month to fifteen-year sentence for drug possession in Sacramento County. Gary Popkin, Sir Gay's partner, served a county jail term in 1973 for possession of dangerous drugs, and Bert Stefanson, secretary-treasurer at the time, was sentenced to state prison for five years to life for possession and transportation of cocaine and explosives. The Richmond chapter also was decimated by convictions of several members and former members, including ex-president Richard Barker, in the slayings and burial of the two Georgia bikers.

These convictions along with several others wounded the entire organization and left a leadership vacuum outside prison walls. Authorities felt the club never had been more vulnerable, and they expected the Angels to crumble in chaos and disorganization. They also believed they could move aggressively against the club members because public outrage was at its highest level since the so-called "Monterey Rape" in the mid-1960s and because most law jurisdictions were finally aware of the club's mainstay activities and basic structure. The state, which assigned full-time agents to the Angels, led the way in compiling information for intelligence files and prosecutions. But federal agencies and virtually every local jurisdiction with an Angels chapter developed specialists on the club.

The most telling blow against the club obviously was the imprisonment of Barger, so law enforcement officers wanted to keep him there long enough to administer a coup de grace to the Angels. In fact, Alameda County Assistant District Attorney Donald P. Whyte wrote in a formal court statement filed August 2, 1973:

" . . . Barger at large poses such a significant threat to

society as a whole that the Adult Authority should seriously consider incarcerating him for life. . . . Barger in no
sense should be considered a small-time local hood: his
influence is extremely widespread. . . . All chapters apparently owe allegiance to one another, and in particular to
Ralph Barger and the Oakland chapter."

Part of that allegiance was attributable to Barger's dura-
bility. His leadership, dating from the late 1950s, was a
stabilizing force in a group with an extremely high turnover. For example, so many Oakland members were killed,
crippled, jailed and retired that by 1973 only a handful of
old-timers remained active, including Cisco, Johnny Angel,
who reportedly invested in a motorcycle shop and catering
service, and Skip, who later retired to Maine.

The attrition rate from the late 1960s was nearly as high.
A large chunk of the membership was behind bars for vary-
ing periods—Sonny, Sir Gay, Popkin, Stefanson, "Fat
Albert," "Foo Manchu," Winston, Russell, "Mouldy Marvin" and others. Zorro served a 180-day county jail term after pleading guilty to accessory-after-the-fact charges in the
slaying of the two Georgia bikers, then he reportedly went
straight, returning to school and his girlfriend. Donald D.
"Whitey" Smith was a fugitive after escaping from county
jail but he later reportedly linked up with the New York
chapter. Tiny was a missing person, and the possibility of
foul play remained under investigation. Tramp overdosed
under questionable circumstances. German's overdose
death remained an open case. Stork was executed by bullet,
and investigators believed it to be an internal killing related
to his drug dealing aspirations. Napa Bob was shot to death
by his former employer in self-defense. Monk was missing
and authorities were investigating reports from several
sources that he and his old lady, "Little Bonnie," were murdered and buried beneath a concrete driveway slab. Fat
Freddy was murdered. Magoo died of a heart attack. Hi Ho

Steve was reported ordered out of the club for his flighty behavior. Junkie George and Waldo were bounced out for shooting heroin. L'il Al and Jimmy Hewitt drifted away. (Hewitt and an active Angel, Bobby England, were arrested in May, 1977, in a raid on an Oakland speed lab.)

The Oakland leadership was inherited, at least nominally, by Edward "Deacon" Proudfoot, president, and Raymond "Boomer" Baker, vice-president. Neither had ever been regarded as a heavyweight in the organization, but they seemed to hold it together with help from several senior members—such as onetime figurehead president "Big Don," Animal, Johnny Angel, Durt, Norton Bob and Cisco.

Even more important, Sonny Barger remained an active member behind the granite walls of Folsom Prison, the state's lone maximum security penitentiary. He surely had little trouble communicating with the club either through the prison grapevine or direct visits. Sharon, who became Mrs. Barger during the term, came to see him regularly, and club members came to pay their respects. Barger could no longer make day-to-day decisions, but investigators believed he was serving as a venerable jurist of last resort and quite obviously as an advisor.

By the same token, the club showed the world occasionally that their untitled leader was not forgotten. They marketed "Free Sonny Barger" bumper stickers and T-shirts. And on his birthday in 1974, a small plane buzzed Folsom and dropped leaflets wishing him, "Happy Birthday Sonny Barger." Prison officials said the club planned to have a skywriter swirl the same message on a subsequent birthday, but the stunt didn't come off for some reason.

During the mid-1970s, the Oakland chapter responded to stepped up pressure by winding down some activities. Arrests trailed off. "Sonny might have passed on his drug connections, but the Angels are so quiet that I don't think many big decisions are going on," one Alameda County investigator said after a year or so of relative inactivity by the club. "They're not dealing wholesale amounts of drugs like they used to. I don't even think anyone in Oakland has served a search warrant on the Angels since Sonny went in. The big stuff went to San Jose."

Intelligence reports said that Barger had designated San Jose president Fillmore Cross as his international successor during a Bass Lake run before his imprisonment. If so, that was a clever maneuver, because authorities were concentrating their attention on Oakland. Also, San Jose—population 495,000 and one of the fastest-growing cities in the country—provided an ideal base and breeding ground for club endeavors, especially drug dealing. It was a cruising town with many minor league motorcycle clubs, a city surrendering orchard after orchard to Southern California-type suburban sprawl and industry which employed blue-collar workers, a group that traditionally had supplied most of the organization's members and outlets. The chapter also had some Mexican-American members and had established excellent drug contacts in the Southwest and Mexico.

In 1974, when investigators started zeroing in on San Jose, Angels there and in rapidly growing Southern California chapters mounted an antidrug campaign, of all things. They bought billboard space and passed out bumper stickers with the slogan "No Hope With Dope." Led by Los Angeles president Bob Lawrence and San Jose's "Crazy" Cross, club members warned high school and college students about the evil of "hard drugs" and in the process attracted considerable news media attention.

Angels also gave Christmas toys to underprivileged children in L.A.; they gave blood in San Jose. The premise behind the drive was valid but unstated: Drug busts had eroded membership, undermined brotherhood and financially burdened the club. And as Cross told reporters, "The guys couldn't function properly, couldn't be dependable members, didn't show up for meetings, forgot to pay dues. You couldn't rely on them for nothin'. They weren't outlaws anymore. They were dope addicts."

Despite the rhetoric, the club's main "hope" was not to squelch dope use, but to alter their image so they could deal it in greater safety. There were few signs, beyond their rented billboards, that the Angels had gone straight. In fact, about a year and a half later, Cross was sentenced to four years in prison after pleading guilty to amphetamine possession charges relating to a Santa Clara County speed and coke ring run by bikers.

The hypocrisy aside, the concurrent antidrug campaigns were significant because they demonstrated that club communications and coordination remained intact. And they indicated that leadership would not be a fatal problem. Maybe no one would emerge with Sonny's charisma, organizational talents and worldwide reputation, but he had left behind a complex yet easily maintained machine.

This machine had been analyzed extensively in law enforcement reports yet no one was able to dismantle it. The primary reason was that few informants emerged, and none in a position to destroy the club. As one Oakland narcotics agent said, "There was a time when George could have busted the entire chapter, but he wasn't willing to talk then."

Perhaps the closest anyone came to infiltration was an innovative attempt by the Treasury Department's Bureau of Alcohol, Tobacco and Firearms. Under the Omega Program operating from 1973 until early 1975, two dozen agents, about half in California, formed their own outlaw clubs and associated with the Angels and some other renegades. Law enforcement sources said Don M., a photographer and Oakland Angel facing possible criminal prosecution, introduced a few agents to the chapter, hoping for leniency. After the agents rode with the Angels for a

while, the club somehow got wise to them. Before any action could be taken, the bureau learned of the discovery
through a post office delivery error. A photograph intended
for a Hell's Angels post office box in Los Angeles ended up
in an adjacent box and the renter turned it over to authorities. On a group photo of bikers, someone had circled Don
M., labeling him "snitch" and had circled one agent labeling him "the Man." The agents involved were jerked off the
streets, and Don M. was shipped out for a new identity under the federal witness protection program. The agents had
made a number of coke purchases and other buys that re-
sulted in several arrests, but the program's main accom-
plishment was gathering of intelligence information.

The mid-1970s were decision years for the Hell's Angels.
They could have pruned back their illegal activity and become largely a social club. They could have gone underground, putting their motorcycles and colors in mothballs
and buying business suits. Or they could have stayed as un-
changed as their Harleys.

Unwilling to surrender their motorcycles and the style
that went with them, the Angels compromised by operating much as before, with some power shifts and a lower profile. Since 1975, investigators reported, the organization has
expanded geographically and numerically while continuing
to deal drugs on a large scale, especially amphetamines and
cocaine. Like more conventional organized crime families,
the club has avoided publicity and has made new forays
into legitimate businesses, though certainly not on a Mafia
scale. There also have been further indications the club was
killing its own to handle internal disputes.

By 1977, the club had established chapters in Oakland,
San Jose, Daly City, Sonoma County, Marin County, Richmond, San Francisco, Vallejo, Sacramento, Los Angeles,
San Bernadino and San Diego in California. There also were
chapters in Omaha; Cleveland; New York City and Buffalo;

Bridgeport, Connecticut; Durham, North Carolina; Lowell, Massachusetts; and Alaska. The Angels claimed international chapters in Switzerland, Austria, England, West Germany, Australia and New Zealand. The total membership was a closely kept club secret, but law enforcement estimates generally ranged from 350 to 500 in California and from about 750 to 1,000 worldwide, excluding the numerous prospects and even more numerous hangers-on.

The Hell's Angels was still regarded as the largest and most powerful outlaw club in the world. With the release of several veterans from prison, and the addition of several new members, the Oakland membership swelled to nearly forty again. San Jose maintained its solid position, and there was a flurry of activity in the centrally located chapters between the San Francisco Bay area and Sacramento. The Richmond-Vallejo area appeared to be the center of activity in late 1976 and early 1977, as indicated by the arrests there of four Angels fugitives, one sought in a Connecticut murder.

When pressured in one area, the highly mobile organization concentrated its activities in other locales and maintained unusually low visibility. There were long periods during which members seldom were seen in full regalia except when riding en masse to runs, funerals or other special outings. But even these infrequent public appearances seemed to shout: The Angels still are finding drug money the easiest money, and the members are hanging on to their patches long enough to push the average age to thirty or more.

An example: A contingent of about twenty-five Oakland members rode toward Folsom Prison on August 6, 1976 to pick up Foo Manchu, who had served eight years on a narcotics conviction and was paroled to study for his anthropology degree at the University of California. En route, one Angel and his female passenger sustained broken legs in a collision with a car driven by wrestling promoter Roy Shires. The famous blond wrestler Pat Patterson was a passenger, but the Angels went ahead and allegedly stomped the promoter and took away his .38-caliber revolver and championship wrestling belt. Deacon and two other members were arrested for investigation of grand theft, assault with a deadly weapon and robbery, but the rest of the group picked up their thirty-six-year-old convict brother. And they brought him a gleaming motorcycle to ride home.

Another example: In early January, 1977, San Francisco president "Harry the Horse" Flamburis and his twenty-year-old roommate, Dannette Barrett, were murdered in their Daly City house, both bound and gagged, then shot with a .22-caliber automatic pistol muffled with a pillow. Flamburis, a longshoreman never regarded as a heavyweight, owned a bike and a van; his house was furnished with expensive antiques; at least half a dozen guns were stowed, and a hidden safe contained an estimated $1,500 in gold and silver coins and about three-quarters of a pound of speed. Police theorized Harry was killed by an acquaintance for trying to force his way into some heavier speed action. Flamburis' funeral indicated, however, that he apparently remained in high club esteem. An estimated 200 to 300 Angels and other bikers from all over the nation joined him for the ride to the cemetery. A month or so after the burial, his motorcycle was interred with him. And the next day, an arsonist torched his house, destroying the beautiful furnishings and damaging his van.

A third example: In January 1977, a San Francisco County grand jury indicted Flamburis' successor, "Flash" Gordon Grow, another Angel named Odis "Buck" Garrett and three other persons on pimping and pandering charges relating to the operation of a "nude encounter parlor." One key witness was Margo E. Compton, twenty-five, a former parlor employee. But on August 7, 1977, Compton, her twin six-year-old daughters and a nineteen-year-old friend in the Coast Guard were found murdered in a Gaston, Oregon home. Authorities said she had feared for her life and had moved to Oregon as a safety precaution. All four victims were shot execution style—once each in the head. There were no signs of a struggle, although a loaded .357 magnum revolver was a few feet from the body of Compton, who was reported to be a good shot. The murders remained unsolved. But Garrett was sentenced to one to ten years in prison for pandering, and Grow was sentenced to six months in county jail, fined $2,000 and placed on five years probation.

These events and others like them have proved wrong those who predicted the club's demise in the mid-1970s. The Angels showed again they were more than a little like their Harleys—crude, mighty and capable of running on one cylinder when necessary. Amazingly, the club survived and grew although Barger's imprisonment left it with less than full power. But that power may have been restored on November 3, 1977 when Barger was paroled.

There is no telling how big the club will become. Yet one thing appears certain: As long as the motorcycle is around, there will be some men willing to ride the life-death edge of the Hell's Angels.

Notes

1. Sadilek, a strong, well-liked leader with a flair for humor and theatrics, retired after heading the Frisco chapter from about 1958 to 1962.
2. The "Snake Pit" was named after the 1948 movie about mistreatment in a mental institution, starring Olivia de Havilland and Celeste Holm.
3. Described by police close to the club.
4. The Alameda County Coroner's office found a blood-alcohol content of .18 per cent.
5. A California Department of Justice estimate.
6. That year a fifteen-page report by Attorney General Thomas C. Lynch catalogued a series of atrocities supposedly perpetrated by Angels. Example: "On April 24, 1964, a group of eight Hell's Angels invaded the home of an Oakland woman, forcing her male friend out of the house at gunpoint and raping the woman in the presence of her three children. Later, that same morning, female companions of the Hell's Angels threatened the victim that if she cooper-

ated with the police, she would be cut on the face with a razor." The report said there were 463 Angels (apparently a gross overestimate) who were convicted of a total of 1,023 misdemeanors and 151 felonies.

7. Author of *One Flew Over the Cuckoo's Nest* and other novels, as well as a dabbler in antiwar politics.

8. From a police witness.

9. San Francisco *Chronicle*, October 6, 1965.

10. American Taxpayers Union was a right-wing group of homeowners who were fed up with the taxation system. It operated in the mid-1960s, then went inactive. A former member denied the group had any gun policy.

11. San Francisco *Chronicle*, November 4, 1965.

12. San Francisco *Chronicle*, November 13, 1965.

13. San Francisco *Chronicle*, November 19, 1965.

14. Police said Tramp avoided felony convictions although he had been arrested for narcotics offenses, battery and public cunnilingus.

15. On December 17, 1966, more than 250 hippies surrounded Park Police Station singing Christmas carols and chanting for the release of two popular Frisco Angels— "Chocolate George" Hendricks, thirty-four, and "Hairy Henry" Kot, thirty-seven—who were arrested during a candlelight parade "to celebrate the death and rebirth of the Haight-Ashbury District, and the death of money." The San Francisco *Chronicle*, December 18, 1966.

16. Police figures showed that reported crimes more than doubled in the Haight in 1967, with seventeen murders and 100 rapes.

17. DMT is short for diemethyltriptamine, a very strong hallucinogen that is usually taken in tablet form.

18. Thompson's *Hell's Angels*, copyright 1966, 1967, p. 271, Ballantine Books.

19. Secretary of State Frank M. Jordan reported the Angels became a corporation with a stated purpose of "promo-

tion and advancement of motorcycle driving, motorcycle clubs, motorcycle highway safety and all phases of motorcycles and motorcycle driving."

20. California Department of Justice confidential report from the Organized Crime and Criminal Intelligence and Investigation Branch, April, 1973.

21. In a December 14, 1968 Associated Press dispatch from London, a spokesman for the Beatles' Apple record company declined to say whether the music group supported the aims of the Angels, but he confirmed at least two Angels were given space at Apple.

22. California Department of Justice confidential report from the Organized Crime and Criminal Intelligence and Investigation Branch, April, 1973.

23. On the 1970 Bass Lake run, Barger told a Los Angeles *Times* reporter about the same incident: "You know when I got mad? When they threw it [his bike] into the estuary. . . . They should have either parked it on the street or given it back. They're all in the hospital now. They gave me their motorcycles, their clothes, everything they owned . . . because they took everything I owned. And everybody who was in their club either gave me their patch and hung up their colors or they were guilty too. We disbanded the club."

24. San Francisco *Chronicle*, August 14, 1967.

25. Several years later, police reported an incident on February 12, 1973: Albert, who'd recently completed a narcotics sentence at Washington State Prison, was celebrating his fifth anniversary of club membership at home when a young black man walked by with his wife and cousin. The black, nineteen-year-old John Nellums, got into an argument with the Angels and, according to his companions, was dragged inside. When police arrived, Albert told them he just threw a rock at Nellums and told him not to come back. The next day Nellums' beaten and stabbed body was

found in some shrubbery a mile and a half away. The murder remains unsolved.

26. Los Angeles *Times*, October 5, 1966.

27. San Francisco *Chronicle*, June 12 and June 28, 1968.

28. *Times-Post* Service, July 5, 1970.

29. The Alameda County Coroner's office said Ingalls, a Minnesota native, died of "barbiturate poisoning" and noted, "The mucous membranes of the mouth were slightly orange. . . . Postmortem blood-barbiturate level 2.7 mg per cent. . . . Undetermined whether accident or suicide." Police didn't simply close the case, because, as one investigator noted, "It was one of the strangest suicides we ever had. Apparently he walked . . . miles and got into bed after he was dead."

30. In 1969, Owsley was convicted of conspiracy to make LSD in his Orinda home laboratory, and he served about thirty months of a three-year prison sentence. Melissa never was prosecuted. In 1974, the Owl pleaded no contest to a federal charge of willfully failing to file tax returns on $239,000 for 1967-68. The chemist told U.S. District Court Judge Lloyd Burke he lost nearly all the money on bad stock market investments.

31. Actually, it was no coincidence the place reflected the Brotherhood's blending of drugs and hip philosophies. Sand, according to an April 26, 1973, grand jury indictment in San Francisco, distributed acid in July, 1968, to Tim Leary, John Murl Griggs (now deceased) and Brotherhood members at the group's ranch at Idlewild in Southern California. In a resulting "Acid Trial," believed to be the largest of its kind, there was testimony about an international drug and money-laundering operation orchestrated by some of the country's most prominent drug figures. With George Wethern among the prosecution witnesses, Sand and science whiz Robert Timothy Scully were found guilty of manufacturing LSD and conspiracy to evade federal income taxes.

Sand received a fifteen-year sentence and a $10,000 fine, Scully twenty years and a $10,000 fine. Mantell subsequently pleaded guilty to drug charges in the case and was sentenced to two years in prison. Authorities say Sand, free on bail, vanished the day after a federal Court of Appeals affirmed his conviction.

32. On February 13, 1968, police reports said, James "Foo Manchu" Griffin, then twenty-eight, was dropped by five shots from narcotics officers as he whirled with a Luger. Griffin, paroled from a narcotics term at San Quentin the previous March, was hit in the arm. Raiders confiscated $8,000 in drugs, plus a weapons cache like one discovered a few days earlier at another nearby Angel's home.

33. Based largely on testimony in the fall, 1972, trial of Barger and three other members in the murder of an alleged Texas drug dealer whose body was found in a bathtub in a burning Oakland home. Barger testified, "Over the years I traded with various police department members for the release of people from jail." He said, for example, that he left a cache of weapons, explosives and narcotics at a 55th Avenue motel in exchange for the release of one member. Hilliard confirmed that a trading arrangement had existed and brought up Barger's alleged offer to deliver Weathermen members, an accusation the Angels leader flatly denied. The four Angels eventually were acquitted.

34. Merrill, a highly regarded lawyer who took some Angels cases, was part of the defense team for Symbionese Liberation Army "soldiers" Joseph Remiro and Russell Little in their spring, 1975, trial and conviction in the murder of Oakland schools Superintendent Marcus Foster.

35. The Oakland Police Department report said in part: "The arresting officer assisted the police from San Leandro in subduing the suspect, who was extremely violent and at times incoherent. . . . The suspect struck both the San Leandro policemen, and he also struck the arresting officer with his foot."

36. Thompson's *Hell's Angels*, copyright 1966, 1967, p. 91.

37. Police investigators said later that on the basis of inside reports they believed she was sexually abused by a number of members before shooting herself.

38. The Alameda County Coroner's office concluded Magoo died January 6, 1971, of arteriosclerosis.

39. *Times-Post* Service July 15, 1970.

40. The following largely is based on the November, 1972, municipal and superior court testimony of now deceased William "Whispering Bill" Pifer, who was dying of cancer at the time. Because his voice box had been surgically removed, Pifer used a professional lip reader to testify. His testimony was videotaped and replayed for juries. It was believed to be the first time such testimony was admitted in a California court.

41. Though it is not certain what Barker meant, state intelligence reports said that various Angels owned real estate in several locales within driving range, including the Lake Tahoe area and the Reno-Sparks, Nevada, area.

42. Zorro pleaded guilty August 5, 1974 to charges of accessory after the fact in connection with the Richmond slayings and was sentenced to 180 days in county jail. His probation report later said he was living with Shirley, had severed ties with the club and was attending a community college and doing counseling work with juvenile delinquents.

43. John Ballastrasse was convicted October 21, 1975, by a federal court jury in San Francisco on two counts of perjury. He was acquitted of two other counts, also based on testimony before a federal grand jury investigating police corruption in the area. He specifically was found guilty of testifying falsely on March 19 and April 10 when he told the grand jury he had not talked with certain persons about fixing a case and had not received $9,000 in 1968 to help a man facing narcotics charges. He was planning an appeal.

44. The following is based on the November, 1972, testimony of William "Whispering Bill" Pifer.

45. Moran later was convicted of first-degree murder in the death of Baker but acquitted in Shull's death. Carter pleaded guilty to being an accessory in the murder of both bikers. Mumm pleaded guilty to being an accessory to the murders. Barker was convicted of murder in Baker's death and involuntary manslaughter in Shull's death. Crane was convicted of involuntary manslaughter in Shull's death and voluntary manslaughter in Baker's death. Zorro pleaded guilty to being an accessory to murder after the fact. Festus turned state's evidence and was not prosecuted, but his parole from a burglary conviction was revoked. Charges against Big Boy and Big Red were dismissed because of insufficient evidence.

46. The U.S. Justice Department, under the Organized Crime Control Act of 1970, was authorized to protect witnesses from reprisals during testimony. In cases where the threat was expected for longer duration, the government was permitted to make subsistence payments until the family was safely relocated. The payments ranged to about $1,000 a month at the time, depending on family size. The witnesses protected under the program ranged from East Coast Mafia figures to Hawaiian gangsters.

47. San Francisco *Chronicle*, November 6, 1972.

48. Portland *Oregonian*, Associated Press dispatch, March 20, 1977.

49. Barger spent about 3 1/2 years in prison, then was released following two favorable judicial rulings and state adoption of a fixed sentencing law. He was assigned to a special parole unit with extra close supervision.